Susanna Németh

Education studies:
issues and critical perspectives

Education studies: issues and critical perspectives

Edited by Derek Kassem, Emmanuel Mufti and John Robinson

Open University Press

Open University Press
McGraw-Hill Education
McGraw-Hill House
Shoppenhangers Road
Maidenhead
Berkshire
England
SL6 2QL

email: enquiries@openup.co.uk
world wide web: www.openup.co.uk

and Two Penn Plaza, New York, NY 10121-2289, USA

First published 2006

A catalogue record of this book is available from the British Library

ISBN-10: 0 335 21972 1 (pb) 0 335 21973 X (hb)
ISBN-13: 978 0 335 21972 8 (pb 978 0 335 21973 5 (hb)

Library of Congress Cataloguing-in-Publication Data
CIP data applied for

Typeset by BookEns Ltd, Royston, Herts.
Printed in Poland by OZ Graf. S.A. www.polskabook.pl

Contents

Contributors   **ix**
Acknowledgments   **xiii**
Foreword   **xv**

SECTION 1
Inside the school   1
Section introduction

1 **ANGELA ANNING**
   Early years education: mixed messages and conflicts   5

2 **CAROL TAYLOR FITZ-GIBBON**
   Evidence-based education: finding out what works and what hurts   18

3 **LISA MURPHY, DEREK KASSEM AND GEOFF FENWICK**
   The politics of the National Literacy and Numeracy Strategies   32

4 **DIANA BURTON AND STEVE BARTLETT**
   Shaping pedagogy from psychological ideas   43

5 **MICHAEL NEWMAN**
   When evidence is not enough: freedom to choose versus prescribed
   choice: the case of Summerhill School   56

SECTION 2
Policy, politics and education
Section introduction   69

6 **DAVE HILL**
   New Labour's education policy   73

7 **KATE MACDONALD**
   England: educating for the twenty-first century   87

8 ROBERT COE
   What do we really know from school improvement and
   effectiveness research?   99

9 MICHAEL APPLE
   Away with all teachers: the cultural politics of home learning   110

10 EMMANUEL MUFTI
    New students: same old structures   122

SECTION 3
Education at the margins
   Section introduction   133

11 IRENE ROBINSON AND JOHN ROBINSON
    Stephen and Anthony: the continuing implications of the
    Macpherson Report for teacher education   137

12 JILL RUTTER
    Meeting the educational needs of forced migrants   149

13 DEREK KASSEM
    Education of looked-after children: who cares?   162

14 JANE MARTIN
    Women and state schools: Britain 1870 to present day   174

15 DIANE GRANT
    Lifelong learning: just a slogan? The reality for working-class
    women   185

SECTION 4
Global education: global issues
   Section introduction   197

16 MIKE COLE
    New Labour, globalisation and social justice: the role of
    teacher education   201

17 ANIL KHAMIS
    Pakistan: whither educational reforms?   211

18 SUSAN ROBERTSON AND ROGER DALE
Changing geographies of power in education: the politics of
rescaling and its contradictions   221

19 JOHN ROBINSON AND TONY SHALLCROSS
Education for sustainable development   233

Index   249

Contributors

Professor Angela Anning is Emeritus Professor of Early Childhood Education at the University of Leeds. Her professional background is in urban early years services. Her research interests include Art and Design Education, early childhood, family intervention programmes, professional knowledge and multi-agency teamwork. She has written widely on services for young children.

Professor Michael Apple is the John Bascom Professor of Curriculum and Instruction and Educational Policy Studies at the University of Wisconsin, Madison. Among his recent books are the 25th anniversary third edition of *Ideology and Curriculum, The State and the Politics of Knowledge:* and *Educating the 'Right' Way: Markets, Standards, God, and Inequality.*

Professor Steve Bartlett is reader in education at the University of Wolverhampton. Steve has co-authored two recent books on Education Studies and a book for teachers on practitioner research. He has published a number of research articles on teacher appraisal, teacher professionalism, practitioner research projects and the nature and evolution of education studies as a discipline.

Professor Diana Burton is Dean of the Faculty of Education, Community and Leisure at Liverpool John Moores University. Diana has co-authored two recent books on Education Studies and a book for teachers on practitioner research. She has published a number of papers on aspects of learning and teaching and contributed chapters to several texts on initial and continuing teacher education.

Dr Robert Coe is a senior lecturer in Education at Durham University and Director of Secondary Projects (ALIS, Yellis and MidYIS) in the Curriculum, Evaluation and Management Centre. He was previously a secondary mathematics teacher with experience in a range of schools and colleges.

Professor Mike Cole is Research Professor in Education and Equality and Head of Research at Bishop Grosseteste College, Lincoln, UK. He has published widely on equality and equal opportunity issues. His latest books include *Education, Equality and Human Rights* and *Marxism, Postmodernism, and Transmodernism in Educational Theory: Origins, Issues and Futures*, both to be published by Routledge in 2006.

Professor Roger Dale has been a senior research fellow at the University of Bristol since he took early partial retirement from his position as Professor of Education at the University of Auckland in 2002. Together with Susan Robertson he co-founded the journal *Globalisation, Societies and Education* whose first volume was published in 2003.

Geoff Fenwick has worked in primary and higher education in Africa and England for 50 years, specialising in the teaching of children's literature and English. Recent work includes contributions to Pru Goodwin's *The Literate Classroom* (2005) and *The Oxford Encyclopaedia of Children's Literature* (2006).

Professor Carol Fitz-Gibbon is now Professor Emeritus, University of Durham. Her early career included teaching science and mathematics in both privileged and underprivileged schools and having two children. As an educational researcher, she started indicator systems including 'value added' in 1982 and was Director of the CEM Centre. Her books include the prize-winning *Monitoring Education*.

Dr Diane Grant is a senior lecturer and researcher at Liverpool John Moores University in the area of applied community studies. She has undertaken research into poverty in the UK, homelessness and resettlement, community interventions and lone parenthood. She is currently directing a major research project that is investigating gender discrimination and ageist perceptions, funded through the European Union.

Dave Hill is Professor of Education Policy at the University of Northampton, Chief Editor of the *Journal for Critical Education Policy Studies* (www.jceps.com), Founder Director of the independent Left e-Institute for Education Policy Studies (www.ieps.org.uk), and, with Mike Cole, co-founded the Hillcole Group of Radical Left Educators.

Derek Kassem is Programme Leader for Education Studies at Liverpool John Moores University. Before joining JMU to teach on ITT courses he taught for fifteen years in Inner London both in primary and secondary schools. Derek is a founder member of the British Education Studies Association.

Dr Anil Khamis is a Canadian national who has worked for the past decade in East Africa, and South and Central Asia in the area of education and international development. He is presently the MA Course Leader and Lecturer in Education and International Development at the Institute of Education University of London.

Dr Kate MacDonald is Course Leader for Education Studies at the University of Worcester. She taught in schools in London and abroad before working in higher education.

Dr Jane Martin is Senior Lecturer in the History of Education at the University of London Institute of Education. Her earlier published work includes *Women and the Politics of Schooling in Victorian and Edwardian England* and *Women and Education 1800–1980*. She is currently co-editor of *History of Education* and the Brian Simon Educational Research Fellow.

Emmanuel Mufti has worked in community education in Liverpool before embarking on an academic career initially at Liverpool Hope University and now Liverpool John Moores University. Emmanuel has researched in areas such as parental involvement in children's education and is currently researching student retention within higher education. Emmanuel is a founder member of the British Education Studies Association.

Lisa Murphy lectures at Liverpool John Moores University in Education Studies, specialising in Language and Literature. Having read English at the University of Oxford, she gained an MA in Linguistics from Manchester University. Prior to working at John Moores she taught English and English as a Second Language.

Michael Newman is a project education worker for a development education centre in East London, Humanities Education Centre. He worked at Summerhill School for nine and a half years, in various roles including science, English and primary teacher and curriculum adviser. He is secretary of the Children's Rights Alliance for England.

Professor Susan Robertson is Professor of Sociology of Education at the University of Bristol. Her area of expertise is in the area of globalisation and education. She is founding co-editor of *Globalisation, Societies and Education* and Director of the Centre for Globalisation, Education and Societies.

Irene Robinson is a teacher at St Stephen's Primary School, Blackburn. She has previously worked at St Martin's College, Lancaster, as a research assistant at Manchester Metropolitan University, focusing on student mentoring practices, and as a research assistant for Lancashire Education Authority developing the authority's response to the Swann Report.

Dr John Robinson is Director of Research Development in the Centre for Urban Education at Manchester Metropolitan University. He has taught in Manchester, Glasgow and Salford. At MMU he has been involved in research experiences focusing on environmental education and sustainability education. He has published numerous articles and book chapters.

Dr Jill Rutter lectures in education at London Metropolitan University. From 1988–2001 she was a policy advisor at the Refugee Council. She has also taught in London schools and worked with displaced people in south Asia. Her publications include *Refugee Children in the UK* (Open University Press 2006). She is presently researching educational responses to changing migration patterns.

Dr Tony Shallcross is Leader for International Education and designated researcher at the Institute of Education at Manchester Metropolitan University. He has undertaken evaluative research projects for Scottish Natural Heritage and the World Wildlife Fund for Nature, been Project Director for the EC-funded Sustainability Education in European Primary Schools Project (SEEPS), has edited books and published several journal papers and chapters in books in the broad field of education for sustainable development.

Acknowledgments

The authors wish to thank Clara Kassem and Elizabeth Westgaph for their valuable assistance with the manuscript.

This book is dedicated to Jackie, Clara, Sarah, Rashida, Samuel, Amy and to our students at Liverpool John Moores and Manchester Metropolitan Universities.

All royalties from this book are being donated to Médecins sans Frontières.

Foreword

Education Studies has long been regarded as the disciplinary arm of education understood as a 'subject' or field of enquiry. It provides a location for serious thought about issues in education that extend beyond the immediacy of current policy and practice. Regrettably, it sometimes too readily gets parodied as mere 'theory'. This caricature has at times threatened to de-intellectualise the study of education and result in a lack of conceptual finesse in understanding what is going on in the wider world of educational debate, policy formation and reform.

It is essential that informed professionals learn how to engage with education in a serious-minded way and come to appreciate its ideational contours and specific characteristics. They need to grapple with its underlying principles, fundamental concepts, contextual factors and global dimensions. Areas of public concern, key issues of public debate and policy developments in education all need to be approached thoughtfully and in dialogue with experts who have made these matters their life's work. Proposals that impact on education need to be carefully evaluated against defensible criteria, and the positions of powerful political proponents need to be interrogated to see whether or not they advance social justice and a proper ecology of economic and cultural experience.

This is a book that invites engagement. It will repay serious consideration and doubtless touch a nerve if you believe education matters. Its radical style forces a critical approach and cultivates honest wrestling with profound issues. Of course the book is a starting point for raising awareness, stimulating thought and informing debate – it is not a finishing point. However, it will equip its readers to begin to think through the political, social and educational realities that impinge on the local contexts and particular practices of educational communities. It will alert them to the fundamental differences in the way education *per se* is perceived and understood by politicians, education professionals and the wider society. Polarised views inevitably emerge but the authors appreciate that these need to be couched in a language of convictional civility if the dialectic of democracy is to be sustained.

The editors have substantial experience and considerable expertise in their field. They have pulled together an excellent team of academics and leading scholar–practitioners from a range of institutions. The book also has a strong international element that should help its readers become aware of global perspectives beyond the UK and contrasting political climates. The text is accessible and covers a wide range of topics while retaining a coherent framework and having a strong link with the day-to-day world of professional educators as they seek to enhance and extend learning for all.

I commend *Education Studies: Issues and Critical Perspectives* because it will not only orientate students but add to the debate. Its authors are to be congratulated on a fresh account that teases out some underpinning principles of just education and responsible schooling, recognises the pivotal role that education plays in our society, confronts the climate of central control, conformity and compliance, and yet holds on to a vision of shared futures. I hope it will be widely read and influence a mindset.

Professor Michael S. Totterdell
Director, Institute of Education
Manchester Metropolitan University

SECTION 1

Inside the school

Section introduction

When considering education our immediate thoughts often turn towards the school system. This is a natural process for a number of reasons, most notably that the majority of us have first-hand experience of the system. Therefore, it is a system that unites us, and one from which we, as former pupils of the system, have the capacity to draw comparisons between our experiences and those of colleagues, friends and fellow students. Another crucial reason why the school system automatically springs to mind when education is discussed is that it is compulsory and that it is concerned with perhaps the most vulnerable group in our society, children.

Within England and Wales there is much to be thankful for when considering our education system. It is available for all children of both sexes, and all ethnic and socio-economic groups. Effectively, no child in England or Wales is denied a place within the state-funded education system. This is not the case in every country and worldwide over 100 million children are not enrolled within primary education (DFID 2005). Whilst one of the millennium goals is to ensure primary education for all children by 2015 the main discussions within this section centre on the school education system in England and Wales and demonstrate that access to primary education does not always equate to an eradication of inequality, mainly because of a lack of critical engagement with the fundamental issues affecting the system.

Some of the issues, which have long been the cause of anxiety within the English and Welsh system, are not new. In 2005, 57.1% of pupils achieved five or more GCSE passes at grades A–C. This means that nearly 43% of children, following 11 years of statutory education left with few or no qualifications (DfES 2005). The numbers of children not achieving at the agreed expected level of 5 A–C GCSE passes does not tell the full story. There is a clear correlation between who you are and your likelihood of success. For example, boys, as an overall group, tend to do less well than girls, with 46% of boys achieving 5 A–C GCSE passes compared with 56% of girls. Secondly, the ethnic group that you belong to affects your likelihood of success, with only 25% of Black Caribbean boys achieving those qualifications. A similar picture emerges with Gypsy/Roma, Bangladeshi and Pakistani pupils who all achieve at far lower rates than the national average. However, the issue is not solely concerned with the ethnicity of pupils as evidenced by the fact that those pupils of Chinese and Indian descent are the highest achieving ethnic groups in English and Welsh society. In examining the figures further a more telling division emerges, that of the socio-economic group or class of the child. There is a strong correlation between achievement figures at GCSE level and the socio-economic group of the child. The most widely used indicator of socio-economic status within schools is whether the child is eligible for free school meals. Those children of Indian and Chinese heritage are the groups least likely to be eligible, with approximately 11% receiving free school meals, compared with the figure of approximately 50% of Bangladeshi children being eligible (DfES 2005).

Myriad reasons behind these figures are well documented in volumes such as *Introduction to Education Studies* by Bartlett *et al.* (2001) and *Sociology of Educating* by Meighan and Siraj-Blatchford (2004) and are not the main focus for the chapters within this section. The following chapters are primarily concerned with the strategies for combating such inequalities and ensuring that every child does indeed matter by seeking to work towards success for all children regardless of sex, ethnicity or socio-economic status.

However, the chapters demonstrate that much of our educational policy and practice is based on fashionable responses to problems, responses which have little or no evidence base to support them. For example, Murphy, Kassem and Fenwick in their chapter argue that the national strategies for numeracy and literacy impose a state-sanctioned pedagogic approach on teachers, and therefore pupils, with no clear rationale to support the approach. The chapter highlights the ban on the use of calculators for under-8s and demonstrates that there is no clear evidence base to suggest that this strategy contributes towards improved skills or knowledge for children.

Burton and Bartlett in their chapter demonstrate how political fashion, the rise of media-friendly initiatives and charismatic champions have led to a widespread acceptance of various educational strategies concerned with learning styles and multiple intelligences. Again the range of evidence supporting these approaches is questionable and not without its critics, yet certain schools have gone as far as producing labels for children to wear which identify them as having a preferred learning style. The chapter shows how government policy including setting and personalised learning is widely promoted as a solution to underachievement without a clear, unbiased examination of the available evidence.

Anning in her examination of early childhood education demonstrates how policy related to early childhood education is often pushed through with little consultation and an unclear evaluation strategy. A discussion also takes place regarding the types of knowledge valued by staff within centres; this knowledge is primarily what Anning describes as 'P', or personal, knowledge. 'P' knowledge is that gained via experience and reflection and is seen by staff as more relevant and important to them than 'C', or codified, knowledge. 'C' knowledge is mainly gained through academic and vocational courses which appear to be failing in their attempts to provide a valid insight into the skills and knowledge necessary to effectively work within early childhood education. Again this can be seen as further evidence of an ill-focused and inadequately researched approach to training.

Fitz-Gibbon further illustrates the ill-focused approach to school-based pedagogy in bemoaning the lack of evidence to support many of the 'taken for granted' assumptions inherent within the system. She cites medicine as a profession where only through extensive clinical trials (RCTs) have we been able to demonstrate 'what works' and 'what hurts' and calls for a similar approach to education. Fitz-Gibbon uses the example of 'Learning by Tutoring' as an extensively and critically researched approach which has substantive evidence supporting its effectiveness as opposed to many practices in schools today which are less able to stand up to similar scrutiny. The issue of randomised controlled trials is not without debate and criticisms of this approach have focused on the problematic nature of causality.

It seems incongruous that in this time of formalised inspections, league tables and a standard-driven agenda much of what takes place within our schools in England and Wales is based on strategies with little or no fully considered evidence, research or evaluation. That is not to say that all strategies are accepted without scrutiny and in fact those that challenge current practice or seek to provide genuine choice, as in the case of Summerhill School, often find themselves needing to justify their approaches with a strong and critical research base. In the final chapter in this section Michael Newman gives a personal account of the inspection regime and threat of closure that Summerhill School faced in 1999. Summerhill school achieved above average results in GCSE passes within that year yet an educational system, which appears willing to adopt politically and media-friendly initiatives extremely readily, appears less willing to support a school which outperforms national averages and was founded on principles developed by A.S. Neill, whom the *Times Educational Supplement* described as one of the twelve most influential UK educational thinkers of our time.

This section demonstrates that much of our 'taken for granted' educational strategies within England and Wales are based on limited evidence and insufficient evaluation processes. One of the main criticisms of the approach taken within schools is that they suggest that children are a homogeneous group; that is what will work for some children will work for all children. This leads our teachers to be uncritical accepters of government policies and initiatives, leaving them vulnerable when techniques do not have the desired effect and lacking in knowledge of alternative strategies to ensure that all children under their care achieve. The language of the Training and Development Agency (TDA) who oversee the training of new teachers is one of standards which 'formally set out what a trainee teacher is expected to know, understand and be able do in order to be awarded qualified teacher status (QTS) and ultimately work as an effective teacher' (TDA Website: http://www.tda.gov.uk/)

The standards are based under three headings:

Professional values and practice   Outline the attitudes and commitment expected of anyone qualifying to be a teacher: for example, treating pupils and students consistently; communicating sensitively and effectively with parents and carers.

Knowledge and understanding   Require newly qualified teachers to be confident and authoritative in the subjects they teach, and to have a clear understanding of how all pupils should progress and what teachers should expect them to achieve.

Teaching   Relate to the skills involved in actually delivering lessons, for example, planning, monitoring, assessment and class management. They are underpinned by the values and knowledge covered in the first two sections.

The chapters in the following section highlight the problems inherent in a system which seeks to provide a set of standards which make an effective teacher. That is, it is not solely an issue with standards *per se*, more the theoretical and evidence basis of those standards. In short, if information is not available to determine exactly what works with *all* children, then why, through teacher training and what occurs within schools, is current practice and policy suggesting that we do and presenting standards as unequivocal and proven when in fact they are anything but?

References

Bartlett, S., Burton, D. and Peim, N. (2001) *Introduction to Education Studies.* London: Sage.

Department for Education and Skills (DfES) (2005) *Ethnicity and Education: The Evidence on Minority Ethnic Pupils.* London: HMSO. http://www.standards. dfes.gov.uk/ethnicminorities/links_and_publications/EandE_RTP01_05/EandE_ RTP01_05.pdf (accessed 19 Jan. 2006).

DFID (2005) *Education Factsheet Millennium Development Goal 2.* Policy Division Info Series ref: PD Info 048. http://www.dfid.gov.uk/pubs/files/mdg-factsheets/ educationfactsheet.pdf (accessed 19 Jan. 2006).

Meighan, R. and Siraj-Blatchford, I. (2004) *Sociology of Educating.* London: Continuum.

Training and Development Agency (TDA) *Achieving QTS.* http://www.tda.gov.uk/ Recruit/thetrainingprocess/achievingqts.aspx (accessed 19 Jan. 2006).

1

ANGELA ANNING
Early years education: mixed messages and conflicts

Introduction

Pugh (2001: 9) described services for young children in England as 'a patchwork of fragmented and uncoordinated services'. Social services have had the responsibility for daycare, childminding and child protection, though increasingly childcare has been expanded by the private sector. Education has held responsibility for the education of 3- to 7-year-olds in nursery classes, nursery schools and primary schools, though increasingly they have colonised the education of newborns to 3-year-olds. The voluntary sector has managed playgroups and many family support services. Health authorities have had responsibility for all newborns and toddler checks through health visitors and clinics. Responsibility for play opportunities has sat uneasily between education, recreational/leisure and entertainment systems. Professionals within each of these agencies espouse different beliefs about the causes of 'problems' presented by families and prescribe different 'treatments' for their resolutions.

In a genuine attempt to improve this legacy of disparate services for children, the Labour Government has introduced a raft of reforms since 1996. The reforms include a National Childcare Strategy (DfEE 1998) and the Ten-year Strategy for Childcare (DfES 2005); universal part-time pre-school entitlement for all 3- and 4-year-olds whose parents wish to take it up, with a statutory Foundation Stage curriculum (Qualifications and Curriculum Authority (QCA) 2000), a unified inspection system delivered by the Office for Standards in Education (Ofsted), and a roll out of 1,700 Children's Centres, offering integrated services for young children and their parents by 2008 in the most deprived areas of the country.

A seminal Children Bill and Children Act 2004 enacted the principles outlined in the Green Papers *Every Child Matters* (DfES 2003) and *Every Child Matters: the Next Steps* (DfES 2004). Five key principles are embedded in outcomes central to the Children Act: being healthy, protection from harm and neglect, enjoying and achieving, making a positive contribution and economic wellbeing (www.dfes.gov.uk). Every local authority is required to appoint an officer responsible for coordinating services and records for children and young people.

The focus is on multi-agency delivery of services requiring all agencies to share information and assessment frameworks and plan together funding streams and early intervention strategies. Their coordination is to be managed by Children's Trusts. The five Children Act principles have become the new mantra of Government policy speak. The principles underpin the Ofsted revised framework for the inspection of schools. Inspections will be the lever by which an Extended School agenda will be imposed on all nursery, primary and secondary schools. Extended Schools will be required to offer a range of before and after school care for children up to the age of fourteen as well as leisure activities and family support services. These political imperatives imply radical changes for the field of educating young children in England.

Under a Labour Government early childhood education and care have benefitted from an unprecedented flow of money and attention. Dealing with the pace of change has been taxing for early childhood professionals. For them the last ten years have been both the best and worst of times! Policies have been mainstreamed by Government in advance of publication of evaluations of their effectiveness. In this chapter I will explore conflicts inherent in these radical changes with reference to recent evaluations of the Foundation Stage Curriculum, Centres of Excellence and Sure Start Local Programmes. In particular I will critique assumptions underpinning policies on *integrated services* and *curriculum reform*.

However, we need to contextualise a critique of policy within a conceptual framework. A major change in our construct of childhood is that the welfare and attainments of children are nested within the wider social context of the family and community. One of the most influential models of the reciprocal relationships between child, family and community characteristics has been Bronfenbrenner's (1979) seminal ecological model of human development. He conceptualises a young child's experience of the relationships between national *macro level* political, cultural and historical changes, the *exo-system level* of local authority policies and practices, the *meso-system level* of settings (for example the features of local community pre-school education and childcare provision) in which the child is an active participant and the *micro-level* of the particular playgroup, childminder or home setting they experience.

The conceptualisation of the ambitious and costly Sure Start anti-poverty intervention was based on the principle that for children to escape the poverty trap, interventions must target concurrently child, family and community levels. Its aim was to improve outcomes for children and families in health, education and employment in 500 of the most deprived areas of England. Sure Start local programmes were required to actively involve local communities in decisions about changing services, so that the implementation of each programme is unique. Results published so far by the National Evaluation of Sure Start (NESS) at Birkbeck College (www.ness.bbk.ac.uk) indicate the complexity of measuring outcomes in such diverse programmes. Early indications are that the impact on children and parents after three years of intervention is disappointing. There are limited findings on parental behaviours – mothers are more accepting of their babies and toddlers, and there is less home chaos for those with 9-month-old babies. We would expect that over time parental improvements would filter through to the children's developmental outcomes. The benefits for parents tend to be detected in the 'better off' families in Sure Start areas, that is not for lone parents, teenage mothers or workless households – the very populations Sure Start was designed to influence. Child development outcomes are disappointing, but it is still early days for the treatment to impact on the language, cognitive, and social and emotional development of young children living in areas of multiple deprivation. Moreover, the evaluation is assessing impact on the whole Sure Start population of under-3s, all of whom have received wide variations in services and treatments. It is much easier to detect and measure impact on prescribed manual-based interventions focused on specific outcomes such as the Webster-Stratton approach to involving parents in improving young children's behaviours (Hutchins and Webster-Stratton 2004); or a language development intervention such as PEEPs in Oxfordshire (Sylva and Evangelou 2003).

Whilst socio-cultural theory has informed models of reform for the structures and systems of children's services, there have also been changes in the field of psychology. Stage theories embedded in the 'received wisdom' of developmental psychology, which have dominated the field of early childhood education and care for so long, have been challenged. For example, Dahlberg *et al.* (1999) argued that governments and their agencies, in order to 'control' the behaviours of young children and their parents, use narrow interpretations of child development based on constructs of developmental 'milestones'. They argued that constructs of state prescribed attainment targets, often based on standards in literacy and numeracy, and the monitoring of state services designed to deliver them, constrain the way professionals deliver services and shape expectations for parents of their roles. It will be argued later in this chapter that the current political enthusiasm for promoting 'parenting' classes is based on the government imperative to prepare young children for 'school' and 'citizenship', a form of social control of young children, mediated through their parents. Such political control threatens the rights of young children to be who they are now, rather than to become what is convenient for the state in the future.

As education has been integrated with childcare and family support services, professionals have extended their expertise to the development of birth to 3-year-olds. Conceptual shifts in our understanding of how very young children learn are that:

- Babies are active learners from birth (Murray and Andrews 2000).
- The socio-cultural context in which learning episodes are situated shapes children's learning behaviours and identities as learners (Anning and Edwards 2006).
- Significant others (parents, carers, siblings and peers) play central roles in sustaining reciprocal learning relationships with young children (Schaffer 1992).

How do these theoretical and conceptual frameworks inform practice in early childhood settings?

Improvements in childcare, family support and early education

Controversial research findings in the USA indicate that children who have attended poor-quality daycare settings for full days where care has not been nurturing and warm manifest poorer outcomes in managing their social and emotional relationships when they transfer to schools (Belsky 1999). These messages, unwelcome to the DfES, also worry providers and parents. Melhuish was commissioned by the Daycare Trust in 2004 to review the effects of childcare. Key messages from research about the characteristics of good-quality daycare were:

- well-trained staff committed to their work with children
- facilities that are safe, sanitary and accessible for parents
- ratios and group sizes that enable staff to interact appropriately with children
- supervision of children that maintains consistency
- staff development that ensures continuity, stability and improving quality
- provision of appropriate learning opportunities for children (2004).

Anyone who has managed budgets in the field of early childhood services knows that these imperatives come at a cost. Our childcare services have been notoriously under-funded. Employees have had low status and poor pay. The Labour Force Survey of 2003 showed that only 12% of childcare and early years workers were qualified to Level 4 (graduate status) and almost 40% were not qualified even to Level 2. In integrated service settings graduate teachers are often more highly paid than their line managers trained in social work or childcare. As childcare and education are combined, the issue of differential funding, including salaries, must be addressed. Evidence from the influential Effective Provision of Pre-School Education Project (EPPE) (Sylva *et al.* 2003) is that children's attainments in both cognitive and social/emotional measures are enhanced when a teacher is employed in these settings. We know that community involvement in reconfiguring services, as in the Sure Start Local Programmes, is important for the empowerment of users, but Naomi Eisenstadt (in a recent article in the *Guardian Special on Children's Services*) acknowledged that:

> We know from research that parents engaging with services and having a say does deliver better outcomes for children. But we have learned much about the importance of staff qualifications and a clear curriculum for young children. Sure Start was weak on these issues to begin with, and we must learn as we gain more evidence of what works. Community development on its own will not deliver for children if it is not accompanied by high quality early education services.
>
> (Eisenstadt 2005)

The Ten Year Strategy commits the Government to an increase in the hours of funded nursery education for 3- and 4-year-olds. Parents want pre-school education, but the current half-day provision does not suit the needs of many working households. The Government is pledging wrap-around care and extended pre-school hours (to be paid for by parents). But how do we know that money spent on pre-school education is cost-effective in terms of outcomes? Research for the Effective Provision of Pre-school Education (EPPE) Project and parallel The Early Years Transition and Special Needs (EYTSEN) Project demonstrated positive effects of high-quality pre-school provision on children's intellectual and social development (Sylva *et al.* 2003), particularly for children from disadvantaged families and with additional needs (Sammons *et al.* 2003). High-quality provision pre-school education, again with cost implications, was characterised by:

- adult child interactions involving 'sustained shared thinking' and open-ended questioning
- practitioners with a clear grasp of child development and a good curriculum knowledge
- educational aims shared with parents
- formative feedback to children involved in learning episodes
- transparency in behaviour policy and practices.

EPPE research indicated that equally important for the children's attainments was the learning environment of the home. Where parents actively engaged in activities with their children, regardless of social class and levels of education, children's intellectual and social developments were enhanced. What parents do appears to be more important than who they are. A clearer understanding of the role of parents and carers in promoting young children's learning has led to increasing policy interest in parenting 'programmes'. Studies of parenting used to focus on characteristics that promoted 'competent', 'cooperative' and 'well-behaved' children, based on predominantly white middle-class perceptions of good parenting. Good parents were defined as those who offered clear models of 'good behaviour', 'firm control' and appropriate 'warmth'. But parenting 'classes' based on these patronising assumptions about good parenting are bound to fail.

The last 25 years of research has shown parenting to be far more complex and conditional. Parenting is learned within specific cultures and contexts, can change over time, can vary from one child to another and is shaped by children's behaviours. Challenging or changing circumstances in family lives such as socio-economic problems, mental or physical health crises and marital break-ups can quickly destabilise family dynamics. Constructs of family are also in a state of flux (Smart and Neale 1999) as are constructs of the ethics of care (Williams 2001). Some of the most interesting approaches to working positively with parents have been modelled within Sure Start local programmes. Hopefully such exemplars will inform practice in supporting, rather than teaching, parenting from children's centres.

In the second half of this chapter I want to draw on recent research evidence to critique:

- the impact of integrated services on professional knowledge and practice
- curriculum change and related pedagogy in early childhood settings.

Policies into practice: what works?

Integrated services: sharing professional knowledge

Early Excellence Centres were set up in the late 1990s as One Stop Shops to model integrated services. I was involved in the evaluation of three of them. They all experienced difficulties with the merging of professional activities under one roof. Professionals had to negotiate transformations from specialist (sometimes of high status) ways of working determined by their training and work experience in single agency settings, to identities as generic workers with team responsibilities for activities. It took a long time for professionals to tune into each other's ways of working with and talking to and about clients. Teams had to acknowledge the distress of their professional identities being destabilised. Where conflicts were not well managed, confronted and resolved, professionals were unable to move beyond the phase of destabilisation, to an enhanced sense of who they were as professionals. The same findings emerged from research for the MATCH project on multi-agency teamwork in services for children (Anning *et al.* 2004; Anning *et al.* 2006) and from a National Foundation for Educational Research report on multi-agency working (Atkinson *et al.* 2002).

One of the Early Excellence Centres was on the outskirts of a town in an area of high levels of unemployment, families on benefits and a transient population of incomers, often with several children, moving into larger empty council house properties. The new centre was developed from a well-established nursery/infant school. Traditionally 4-year-olds had been offered a place in a reception class in the main school building and 3-year-olds a half-day nursery class place in a small separate building.

When the DfES committed to funding an Early Excellence Centre on the site, 4- and 5-year-olds were offered half-day leading to full-day places in a foundation stage unit in a refurbished wing of the school. Upgrades included creating separate outdoor areas for the children. A children's centre was created in the vacated nursery class building offering crèche facilities for under-3s, family support and training opportunities and holiday play schemes for school-aged children. The building was extended to offer adult training/workshop spaces and facilities for designated social services and health staff. Social services and health staff were seconded from mainstream services to work there part time.

Despite being next door to each other and serving the same families, priorities within the two buildings remained radically different. Educational staff in the foundation stage unit were inevitably drawn into the 'school' agenda of standards in literacy and numeracy and baseline assessments. Their main focus was on the *children's* cognitive, social, emotional and physical gains (in that order). Social services, further education and crèche worker staff in the children's centre focused on the needs of *families* in the community, in particular, with parents and their under-3s perceived to be at risk.

These priorities were represented by different ways of working. Children's centre staff operated in informal, almost domestic, modes. Staff in the foundation stage unit remained anchored in the more formal and authoritarian world of nursery education. The reification of their distinct, but complementary, versions of knowledge was exemplified in contrasting activities and associated equipment and resources. One metaphor for differences was the purchase of furniture. Increasingly in the children's centre a social services furniture model of settees, coffee tables, kitchens and bathrooms was installed. Though the furniture in the foundation stage unit was modified – for example 'softer' seating as settees and floor cushions were bought for both adults and children – the overall impression remained of traditional child-sized furniture geared for the learning needs of under-5s. The adults (even those of considerable girth!) had to perch on those small chairs to engage in interactions with the children.

The managers were acutely aware of the conflict created by different contracts, conditions of work and professional opportunities for members of the teams. Practitioners identified as 'excellent' whilst working in unitary service delivery settings often found it particularly difficult to 'let go' of key aspects of their work. After all, their professional sense of self had been built around manifestations of excellence in their previous specialist roles. Yet activities deemed 'good' in, for example, school settings were likely to be inappropriate within the informal learning contexts of integrated settings. Teachers and health visitors found it particularly hard to adjust.

There was also the issue of the status of versions of knowledge – for example 'graduate' versus 'non-graduate' discipline (specialist psychology versus generalist education), speech therapist versus teacher, social worker versus health visitor. Staff whose specialist knowledge had in previous workplaces been accorded high status were more likely to defend its boundaries against 'dilution' to a generalist, 'lower' status.

In contrast 'lower status' practitioners seemed unaware of the strengths of knowledge they brought to the integrated teams. When asked to talk about their professional knowledge many seemed uncertain, even apologetic. This is not surprising. The knowledge of workers in the care sector (such as nursing or childcare) and early years sector (such as pre-school teaching or health visiting) has not been accorded high status. Workers are not used to being asked to articulate the knowledge implicit in their actions. But with probing they were able to articulate, and perhaps for the first time acknowledge, the depth of knowledge and expertise they had developed.

Eraut (1999) draws the distinction between 'C' or codified knowledge:

> defined in terms of propositional knowledge, codified and stored in publica-
> tions, libraries and databases and so on – and given foundational status by
> incorporation into examinations and qualifications

and 'P' or personal knowledge:

> defined in terms of what people bring to practical situations that enables them to
> think and perform. Such personal knowledge is not only acquired through the

use of public knowledge but is also constructed from personal experience and reflection.

(unpublished paper)

Most practitioners referred to 'P' knowledge, expressed in terms of practical, work-based experience; for example: 'I've built my knowledge through experience, for example from being alongside children when they've been on the receiving end of school systems. I've seen it through their eyes – fobbed off with dots to dots worksheets. It's believing in what you do that matters. And we've got support from our line manager now.'

Others responded in terms of their aptitude and emotional involvement rather than a knowledge base: 'I am passionate about my job. If people don't have commitment here they'll have to move on. I'm working from the front and I expect them to stand alongside me.'

In some cases personal life experiences of staff, such as lone parenting or financial struggles, gave them strong empathy with their clients/users and a practical knowledge of how to cope with the kinds of difficulties they were facing.

They rarely referenced 'C' knowledge, the vocational skills and knowledge gained through their training (National Vocational Qualifications (NVQ), Higher National Diplomas (HND), Nursery Nurse Examining Board (NNEB), BTECs, Qualified Teacher Status (QTS)), such as health and nutrition, family welfare and children's language development. It was even rarer for them to cite propositional knowledge such as psychology and sociology.

What is the message from this research evidence to pass on to policy-makers and service deliverers? The problem is that we have never articulated in an intellectually robust, but sensitive, way 'P' kind of knowledge. Nor have we been through a serious exercise of mapping qualifications (the 'C' knowledge) onto research into the effective delivery of children's services (though the EPPE study findings pointed clearly to the value of teacher involvement in promoting children's cognitive and social outcomes). We have little evidence about what kinds of vocational or 'work-based' training impacts on effective professional practice. At times of policy changes which require training programmes to prepare workers for dramatic shifts in working practices (such as in community rather than hospital based midwifery or teaching in educare rather than school settings or the rapid expansion of children's centres) this lack of any robust evidence base is problematic.

Work is ongoing at the DfES and National Children's Bureau to review qualifications for children's services, but the task is complicated by the plethora of qualifications currently accredited for universities, further education and private sector providers. A Children's Workforce Development Council is charged with developing a generic qualification framework for 'the early years professional'. It will include transferable units of core and specialist skills and knowledge. New employers will be expected to invest in training staff in additional specialist skills at point of need.

The brief for the staffs of the Centres of Excellence included networking with and learning from professionals outside the centres, but opportunities to do so were limited. Staff reported that contacts with speech therapists, health visitors, social workers and special education needs specialists were limited to the needs of a specific child or in response to a 'crisis (e.g. for a child protection review, for liaison about joint provision with a voluntary agency for a child with additional needs, to 'substitute' for working parents in encounters with speech therapists or social workers). This 'crisis' framework is not the concept of daily routine joint service delivery and sharing of knowledge espoused in policy documents. Yet with no time or funds built into contractual working hours to meet, work or train with staff from other agencies, the model was unable to progress beyond 'parallel' to 'joint' delivery of services. As one worker asked: 'Who minds the kids while we do that kind of networking?'

These findings have important resource implications for rolling out the policy of integrated services within Sure Start children's centres. Lessons learned from research need to be fed back into planning for the mainstreaming of multi-agency teamwork in reshaping all children's services to the Every Child Matters strategy agenda.

Curriculum and pedagogy in early childhood settings

I want to turn now to messages drawn from my research in implementing the radical changes to the curriculum and pedagogy for birth to 5-year-olds through the advisory guidelines, *Birth to Three Matters* (DfES 2002), and the statutory Foundation Stage Curriculum.

The innovative early learning, play and childcare services for under-3s which I have observed for research into the effectiveness of Early Excellence Centres and Sure Start local programmes have looked and felt radically different from traditional services (Anning *et al.* 2005). Services have often been planned and delivered by pairs or teams of professionals from different disciplines: speech therapists working with play workers, midwives working with nursery officers, health visitors working with librarians. The focus has been on *parents/carers and their children learning together*. Parents have been encouraged to work alongside professionals in interacting with babies and toddlers. There has been a genuine exchange of information about the children between parents and professionals, rather than the assumption that professionals were the guardians of all relevant knowledge. There has been an emphasis on having fun! The quality of relationships between parents, volunteers and staff has been key to parents returning to attend service sessions.

These features of service delivery resonate with the research evidence of what constitutes high-quality provision for young children reviewed earlier in the chapter. However, a constant dilemma for researchers is that the effects or outcomes of such reshaped services may take years to be detected (as was the case with the seminal research into the impact of the Headstart programme in the USA (Schweinhart and Weikart 1993)). Understandably a government needs to demonstrate value for money in children's services. They want evidence of results. It is to be hoped that the Labour Government has the courage to persevere with reforms even when early findings on their effectiveness, such as those from the Sure Start intervention, are equivocal.

We turn now to evidence of the effects of the implementation of the statutory foundation stage curriculum for 3- to 5-year-olds. In order to address the dilemma of 4-year-olds being offered a curriculum which was 'too formal too soon', many schools reorganised their nursery and reception classes into early years units (now foundation stage units). My research into the delivery of the foundation stage curriculum in such settings indicated recurring dilemmas (Anning 1998).

Where staff from nursery classes were incorporated into reception classes, there were often ideological clashes between 'pre-school' and 'school' approaches to educating 3- to 5-year-olds. Managers tended to favour the 'higher' status school knowledge, driven by the government agenda to demonstrate rising standards in literacy and numeracy. Parents of 4-year-olds who had been encultured into the idea of an early start to 'proper' school being in their children's best interests, were ill-informed and anxious about the impact of mixed-aged classes of 3- to 5-year-olds on their children's learning outcomes.

Staff were uncertain how to manage the complexities of planning for levels and coverage of the statutory foundation stage curriculum for the entitlement of 3-year-olds attending the units for half-day sessions as well as 4- and 5-year-olds attending school all day. Staff were also confused about appropriate forms of pedagogy, particularly for working with 3-year-olds. Activities were often ill-matched to children's learning capabilities – either too advanced for them or simply not stimulating enough. The planning for, management of, and monitoring of learning from outdoor activities was problematic. Units simply did not have enough staff to oversee outdoor areas. Units often included two sets of 25 children or more. Staff were challenged by the daunting task of managing the behaviour of so many young children together, particularly where children with additional needs were mainstreamed into the units.

The intended curriculum experienced by the children varied by age, gender and aptitude. Variations were compounded by uncertainties about how much choice children should have in managing their own learning. In general the older the child the less choice they were given in activities. Yet one might argue that the older children were more able to manage choices sensibly than the younger children.

Some primary school managers were diluting the entitlement of foundation stage children to trained teachers in early years units. To balance staffing budgets they were employing classroom support workers rather than teachers to staff early years units. Recent imperatives to implement workforce reforms in the UK early years sector, which involve assimilating nursery nurses into four levels of classroom assistant status and ensuring 10% of teacher hours as non-contact time by September 2005, are exacerbating this trend. The Government's require-ments for the implementation of the Children Act 2004 is that there should be only one qualified teacher (soon to be 'an early years professional') for every six settings providing pre-school education for under-5s. These policy changes will have a strong impact on the training and retraining of teachers in the early years sector.

What are the messages?

The research evidence reviewed in this chapter has implications for the radical restructuring of children's services promised in the UK for the next ten years and for the role of early years professionals in multi-agency teams. We have major workforce reform and training obstacles to overcome in order to deliver integrated children's services effectively. We need to set up joint training, funded into all business plans for children's services, for working in multi-agency teams. And we need to initiate at national level a radical reappraisal of staff training, development, career opportunities and salaries for those charged with delivering children's services.

The evidence implies also that we need more training for professionals working with young children, as childminders, in foundation stage units or in playgroups and primary schools, to help them understand the curriculum, pedagogy of play, and assessment of young children's learning. This means drawing together the separate empires of the Qualification and Curriculum Agency, Teacher Training Authority, National Primary Strategy and Ofsted to work together to agree how improvements in curriculum planning and pedagogy at the foundation stage may be implemented and monitored. Practitioners in the UK early years sector are weary of mixed messages from these separate empires.

Finally it is important that as a profession we draw on successful Sure Start local programme and early excellence centre expertise in redefining family support, play and early learning services for families with young children, learning from what has been achieved so far, rather than rushing on to another set of 'good ideas'.

Government policies of the last ten years have provided us with some commendable paper policies for early childhood services, but there is still a great deal of hard work to be done to turn those policies into effective practice.

References

Anning, A. (1998) An evaluation of the Kirklees early years units pilot programme. Unpublished Report, University of Leeds.

Anning, A. and Edwards, A. (2006) *Promoting Children's Learning Birth to Five: Developing the New Early Years Professional*, 2nd edn. Buckingham: Open University Press.

Anning, A., Cottrell, D., Frost, N., Green, J. and Robinson, M. (2004) *Report on the Multi-agency Teamwork for Children's Services ESRC Project.* http://www.esrc.ac.uk./ESRCInfoCentre/index.aspx (accessed 2 April 2006).

Anning, A., Chesworth, E. and Spurling, L. (2005) *Themed Study: The Quality of Early Learning, Play and Childcare in Sure Start Local Programmes.* London: NESS, Birkbeck College/DfES Sure Start Unit.

Anning, A., Cottrell, D., Frost, N., Green, J. and Robinson, M. (2006) *Developing Multi-professional Teamwork for Integrated Children's Services.* Maidenhead: Open University Press.

Atkinson, M., Wilkin, A., Stott, A., Doherty, P. and Kinder, K. (2005) *Multi-*

Agency Working: A Detailed Study. Slough: National Foundation for Educational Research.

Belsky, J. (1999) Interactional and contextual determinants of attachment security, in J. Cassidy and P.R. Shaver (eds) *Handbook of Attachment: Theory, Practice, Research and Clinical Applications.* New York: Guilford, 249–264.

Bronfenbrenner, U. (1979) *The Ecology of Human Development: Experiments by Nature and Design.* Cambridge, MA: Harvard University Press.

Dahlberg, G., Moss, P. and Pence, A. (1999) *Beyond Quality in Early Childhood Education and Care: Postmodern Perspectives.* London: Falmer.

Department for Education and Employment (DfEE) (1998) *Meeting the Childcare Challenge.* Green Paper. London: HMSO.

Department for Education and Skills (DfES) (2002) *Birth to Three Matters: A Framework for Supporting Children in their Earliest Years.* London: DfES.

Department for Education and Skills (DfES) (2003) *Every Child Matters.* London: HMSO.

Department for Education and Skills (DfES) (2004) *Every Child Matters: The Next Steps.* London: HMSO

Department for Education and Skills (DfES) (2005) *Ten Year Strategy for Childcare.* London: HMSO.

Eisendstadt, N. (2005) Director defends 'influential' Sure Start. Comment in Children's Services Section of the *Guardian* 16 February.

Eraut, M. (1999) Non-formal learning in the work-place: The hidden dimension of lifelong learning. A framework for analysis and the problems it poses for researchers. Paper presented at the First International Conference on Researching Work and Learning, University of Leeds.

Evangelou, M. and Sylva, K. (2003) *The Effects of the Peers Early Education Partnership (PEEP) on Children's Developmental Progress.* Report number RB489. Nottingham: DfES

Hutchins, J. and Webster-Stratton, C. (2004) Community based support for parents, in M. Hoghughi and N. Long (eds) *Handbook of Parenting.* London: Sage, 334–351.

Melhuish, E. (2004) *Child Benefits: The Importance of Investing in Quality Childcare.* Daycare Trust's Facing the Future Policy Paper No. 9. London: Daycare Trust.

Murray, L. and Andrews, L. (2000) *The Social Baby.* London: National Childbirth Trust.

Pugh, G. (2001) *Contemporary Issues in the Early Years: Working Collaboratively for Children,* 3rd edn. London: Paul Chapman.

Qualifications and Curriculum Authority (QCA) (2000) *Curriculum Guidance for the Foundation Stage. London:* QCA.

Sammons, P., Smees, R., Taggart, B., Sylva, K., Melhuish, E.C., Siraj-Blatchford, I. and Elliot, K. (2004) *The Early Years Transition and Special Educational Needs (EYTSEN) Project: Technical Paper 2 – Special Needs Across in the Early Primary Years.* London: DfES/Institute of Education, University of London.

Schaffer, H.R. (1992) Joint involvement episodes as context for cognitive development, in H. McGurk (ed.) *Childhood and Social Development: Contemporary Perspectives*. Hove: Lawrence Erlbaum.

Schweinhart, L. and Weikart, D. (1993) *A Summary of Significant Benefits: The High Scope Perry Pre-School Study Through Age 27*. Ypsilanti, MI: High Scope Press.

Smart, C. and Neale, B. (1999) *Family Fragments*. Cambridge: Polity Press.

Sylva, K. and Evangelou, M. (2003) *The Effects of the Peers Early Education Partnership (PEEP) on Children's Developmental Progress*. DfES/University of Oxford, 20 October.

Sylva, K., Melhuish, E., Sammons, P., Siraj-Blatchford, I., Taggart, B. and Elliott, K. (2003) *The Effective Provision of Pre-School Education (EPPE) Project: Findings from the Pre-School Period*, research brief no. RBX 15-03. London: Department for Education and Skills.

Williams, F. (2001) In and beyond New Labour: towards a new political ethics of care, *Critical Social Policy* 21(4): 467–493.

2

CAROL TAYLOR FITZ-GIBBON
Evidence-based education:
finding out what works and
what hurts

Introduction

Educational research, which informs both policy and practice, is a varied landscape. Recent initiatives by, among others, the Department for Education and Skills (DfES) and the Training and Development Agency for Schools (TDA (formerly TTA)) in England, have stressed the importance of developing a more robust evidence base to underpin changes in educational practices, particularly if they are to be applied on a large, system-wide scale. This evidence-based approach to education has rapidly become the gold standard for educational research.

The term 'evidence-based education' is now in widespread use, and sound evidence is sorely needed if educational professionals are not to lurch from one initiative to another without learning 'what works and what hurts'. Whilst there are many kinds of evidence, including qualitative descriptive data, it is arguable that, as in medicine, whence the phrase originated, the gold standard type of evidence for 'what works' is that derived from randomised controlled trials (RCTs), which identify the Effect Size of the impact of educational interventions. Effect Sizes indicate the difference an intervention makes. (See Figure 2.1 for a brief introduction to Effect Sizes.) For example, RCTs in education often compare a new way of teaching with an established way that has the same goals. To make the comparison of outcomes fair, students should be randomly assigned to either the new programme or the established one. Sometimes it might be that classrooms or schools are randomly assigned rather than individual students; such trials are referred to as 'place randomised trials' (Boruch *et al*. 2004). This chapter will present evidence relative to ongoing debates as to whether RCTs are necessary and useful for experienced educational practitioners.

Good intentions are no guarantee of good outcomes

For example, given that young males often suffer death in car crashes as witnessed

Einstein said that *'everything should be as simple as possible but no simpler'* and Effect Sizes are as simple as possible. The Effect Size provides a measure of the difference between the outcomes of two groups (which should have been formed by randomly assigning students to one group or the other). This requires knowing how to calculate four numbers:

- the number in each group (**N**)
- the **mean**, (or average) post-test score
- the **standard deviation** for each group
- the **Effect Size**.

The **Effect Size** is a measure of the extent to which the experimental group has scored higher than the control group (or vice versa if negative). Some examples of Effect Sizes can be seen in Table 2.2, which indicates large and small Effect Sizes.

The Effect Size for the post-test scores is simply calculated by (*the mean-of-the-experimental-group post-test scores*) minus (the *mean-of-the-control-group post-test scores*) divided by the average of the standard deviations from within the two groups. (It is, in effect, a z-score.)

$$ES = \frac{mean(e) - mean(c)}{SD}$$

Robert Coe of CEM has provided the formulae on http://www.cemcentre.org/ebeuk/research/effectsize/default.htm. Once the summary data (the number of students, means and standard deviations) are entered the ES will be automatically calculated.

Figure 2.1 The Effect Size

by the 50% increase since 2000 of young driver deaths (AA Motoring Trust 2006), can there be anything wrong with giving them driving lessons whilst they are still in school, particularly as 'being safe' is one of the five goals of the Every Child Matters strategy in England? A strong emphasis on safety and actual practice behind the wheel might reduce their deaths on the road. Analyses of RCTs of early driver education, however, showed that those randomly allocated to early training not only did not benefit but had increased accident rates (Roberts and Kwan 2001). There is now enough evidence to discontinue such well-intentioned but, sadly, harmful, even deadly, programmes. Guessing and good intentions are an insufficient guide to good practice, even when very well intentioned.

An examination of counselling in educational settings provides another example of how RCTs can provide evidence that is contrary to expectations. If there is a major accident or death in a school counsellors are often brought in to deal with posttraumatic stress disorder. However, no fewer than eleven RCTs have been conducted in which victims of stress were or were not counselled on a random basis (Rose *et al.* 2003). These controlled trials showed that the counselling actually made things worse; it prevented recovery. Those not counselled were better four months after the trauma but those counselled were still ill three years later.

It might seem reasonable to pay special attention to students who appear to have high ability but low aspirations. A test of this hypothesis was made when fifteen schools agreed to participate in an experiment. The Curriculum, Evaluation and Management (CEM) Centre at the University of Durham (see Coe in this volume; Fitz-Gibbon 1996; Tymms and Coe 2003), invited schools in the CEM Centre's ongoing yearly monitoring systems to participate in a test of the effects on a student of being identified to the school as an 'under-aspirer'. Fifteen schools chose to participate and the data identified a combined total of 120 under-aspiring pupils across the fifteen schools. For each of these schools only a random half of their under-aspirers were named to their school. The remaining under-aspirers were not identified to the school. Questionnaires to the schools found that the schools made efforts to mentor their under-aspirers in a variety of ways, including regular counselling, meetings with parents, and checking homework. Two years later external examination results became available for all students. The data showed an Effect Size of –0.38 for being on the named list. This indicated that the various kinds of mentoring had an adverse impact on the performance of the identified under-aspirers. One experiment is insufficient for broad conclusions and further work is needed but this finding was strong and surprising. A replication with a new set of schools showed mixed results, largely not statistically significant.

In Tennessee the hypothesis that reducing class size in elementary schools would improve achievement scores was tested (Ritter and Boruch 1999). For several years teachers and students were randomly assigned to small classes (fewer than 20 students) or larger classes. A random half of the large classes had a teaching assistant assigned in addition to the qualified teacher. The smaller classes made more progress than the classes with the worse teacher–pupil ratios. For reducing class size the Effect Size was about 0.20. The presence of a teaching assistant in a random half of the larger classes, however, did not affect the achievement levels in the large classes (Nye *et al.* 2000). These controlled trials provided the evidence which persuaded many school districts to reduce class sizes in schools rather than providing teaching assistants.

If the several hundred initiatives introduced in the UK (see Burton and Bartlett's examination of learning styles theories in this volume) had all been run as randomised trials we would now know something about what seems to work and what seems not to work. For example, teachers' associations could reasonably demand that policies be supported by research evidence before being imposed. Educational practitioners might be wise to be sceptical about new policies or practices that have not been subjected to rigorous research testing. For example, commercially developed programmes have all too often not been adequately tested (by published RCTs). Survey data have shown a large negative impact associated with the use of Integrated Learning Systems (ILS), for example, which were costing schools about £30,000 per year (Wood 1998).

Cost–benefit analysis as an evidence base

In most innovations costs are important but are often quite difficult to estimate. For one of the best examples of cost–benefit analysis in educational research Levin *et al.* (1984) collected data on the costs and the effects of four important interventions (see Table 2.1). (The computer-assisted instruction was quite different from the computer-controlled teaching in ILS systems.) All of the four interventions had positive effects but cross-age tutoring had exceptionally strong effects. Furthermore when the cost per $100 spent was estimated for each intervention, cross-age tutoring was exceptionally cost-effective.

Table 2.1 The cost-effectiveness of four interventions

Intervention	Cost-effectiveness
• Reducing class size from 35 to 20	0.09
• Increased time on basics	0.09
• Computer-assisted instruction	0.15
• Cross-age tutoring	0.34

It is possible to identify two very different types of tutoring programme: tutorial service projects, in which older students or college students help young students with reading or mathematics that the older students already know well, and learning-by-tutoring in which tutors are teaching work that they themselves need to learn (Fitz-Gibbon 1980). The fact that either project might be referred to as a tutoring project does not justify failing to analyse the two kinds separately since one (learning-by-tutoring) appears to be more reliably found to be effective for both tutors and tutees. For an example of a tutorial service project that did not improve the reading of tutees, who were tutored once a week by college students, see Ritter and Maynard (1999). However, why cross-age tutoring works may differ from student to student and site to site. Many of the effects postulated by the theories may well occur, but the important practical questions to ask are: how much improvement can you get, with which methods and at what cost? We will return to these practical questions in the section on quantitative evidence. The following section outlines some possible theoretical explanations as to why some kinds of tutoring work.

Using theories to design projects: an example of a tutoring project

Theories are only as good as the data on which they are based and the extent to which they match the situation to which they are being applied. Nevertheless it is useful to speculate as to what the psychological mechanisms might be, and whether or not the theories point towards particular kinds of projects or educational interventions that may be more effective than other kinds. I will now consider some theories from social psychology and apply these to several stages of implementing a cross-age tutoring project. Direct quotes from students arise from the author's RCTs conducted in the US and in the UK (Fitz-Gibbon 1975; 1980).

When the older students (tutors-to-be) are invited to tutor younger students in mathematics, those who are less successful than others in mathematics may be particularly surprised. Comments such as 'My mother will never believe it!' or 'I always fail mathematics!' indicate their surprise. When the organiser of the tutoring project is not concerned and continues to show confidence in them, tutors may then make the attribution that perhaps they are not as poor at the subject as they had thought. However, some may seek a way to avoid being a tutor (for example 'I'm not going to bring back my permission slip'). Attribution theory (Miller *et al*. 1975) would here suggest that they should be encouraged to participate voluntarily rather than be forced to participate. So the teacher might say, 'Well, bring back your permission slip and let's see how it goes for a couple of sessions.' Typically, all students give it a try and end up staying in the project as tutors. Their attributions and attitudes have already been changed.

When reluctant or insecure students do in fact participate and succeed, they can then again make the attribution that they are not so poor at mathematics or tutoring as they had imagined.

Forced compliance studies are very similar to these studies of attributions. These studies suggest that when students comply with a request believing themselves to be free to reject the request this changes their attitudes. Thus when they agree to tutor, having initially been reluctant, we can expect change in their perception of themselves (Festinger and Carlsmith 1956; Bem 1967; Malmuth *et al*. 1981). Counter-attitudinal behaviour leads to a change in attitudes when it is apparently freely chosen: hence the need to leave tutors able to refuse to tutor but to persuade them to 'give it a try'.

When students take on a teaching role, acting as tutors, this serves to increase tutors' empathy and understanding of their teachers. Such a process is indeed frequently reported by observers of tutoring programmes, and by tutors themselves. As one tutor put it, 'Now I know how teachers feel when we act up.'

The tutees' opinions about being tutored by an older student also need to be taken into account as a source of evidence about the efficacy of tutoring. An adult tutor, whether a teacher or not, may not seem like a good prospect to young tutees. Indeed Blank *et al*. (1972) reported 'extreme reluctance' on the part of tutees to receive tutoring from mothers in the community, whereas many cross-age, student-to-student tutoring projects have reported enthusiasm for participation. (Mohan 1972; Allen 1976; Goodlad and Hirst 1989; 1990; Topping and Ehly 1998).

Having considered, above, some of the social psychological mechanisms that might be brought into play by the use of cross-age tutoring I now want to turn to educational psychology for more theories as to why tutoring works so well. One theory is that of the impact of verbalisation. Merz (1969) showed that children learned much better when they were speaking aloud than when they were trying to learn the same material silently and Ausubel (1968) also reported this effect.

Wittrock (1974) and Osborne and Wittrock (1985) have identified 'generative learning' as a significant issue in tutoring programmes and have indicated that this would suggest that the lesson planning and the explanations developed by tutors help tutors themselves to learn to work more thoroughly than if they were simply studying from a textbook. Furthermore, when they are teaching younger children, tutors will move slowly through the work, probably keeping within what Vygotsky called the zone of proximal development (Wood and Wood 1996).

An important reason for using a long-term 'retention test', that is for testing students again some months after the short tutoring project has ended, is that it will often be found that the tutors still know much of the work but that those who studied the same material in normal classrooms have forgotten it (Fitz-Gibbon 1975, Chapter 8).

Clearly a successful experience in the tutoring project is important. This requires both good materials that are appropriate to all levels of expertise, and ongoing support throughout the project. Yet the support must not undermine the attribution of confidence in the tutor and must certainly not draw unnecessary attention to mistakes made. All this requires time with the tutors when the tutees are not around: time to praise the work done; time for tutees' work to be checked; time to quietly discuss errors and show how the topic can be re-taught. One study compared the progress made by tutees with the number of errors tutors made in their shared workbook; the more errors the tutor made, the greater was the tutee's progress (Fitz-Gibbon 1975).

Teaching is, essentially, an attempt to influence the learners. The various bases of social influence have been discussed by several authors, such as French and Raven (1959) and Raven and Kruglanski (1970). Using their classification, it is noticeable that, in normal schooling, the sources of influence are coercive, rewarding, informational, expert, legitimate and/or referent. It is quite difficult for a teacher to be seen as a source of referent influence given the differences in background and age between teachers and their students. However, when a student takes on the role of tutor, he or she is in an ideal position to exert referent influence on the tutee. When an older student is tutoring, referent influence can be expected to be powerful and compliance from the tutee tends to be high. Tutees report planning to become tutors themselves, thus showing strong identification with the older student (Fitz-Gibbon 1975). French and Raven (1959), in their taxonomy and theoretical analyses of social influence have suggested that referent influence has the most uniformly positive effects. A number of studies in educational settings have provided support for this theoretical proposition (for example Kelman 1958; Zander and Curtis 1972). Thus, in a tutoring project the referent power of peers is harnessed for the goals of the school.

Another social psychological effect of the use of one-on-one cross-age tutoring is that it counteracts the de-individuation which has been observed to be the rule rather than the exception in many secondary school classrooms. As pointed out by Zimbardo (1970) de-individuation encourages the development of situations in which anti-social behaviour can increase. The reverse situation exists in a room where cross-age tutoring is taking place. Each tutor is important to an individual tutee and each tutee is important to his or her tutor. They behave as individuals and tutors show an extraordinary dedication, even to difficult tutees, being unwilling to change their tutee even if offered the chance to do so. Tutors also display empathy with teachers once they are experiencing the role of being a tutor, as one tutor said: 'I know how you must feel sometimes: he didn't do his homework!'

The theory of cognitive dissonance (Bem 1967) suggests that cognitions must be consistent and that where there is dissonance or inconsistency, this results in uncomfortable tensions which may lead to changes that reduce the dissonance. These changes will be greatest when the dissonance is greatest. Thus when a difficult teenager takes on the role of a tutor and promotes the work of the school, the impact on the tutor is likely to be a change in his or her attitudes toward school, if only to reduce the dissonance of observing his or her own behaviour.

Some psychological studies have examined whether tutors should be paid for tutoring. If external rewards are given for behaviour, the attribution is made that the reason for the good behaviour, for example the tutoring, is to obtain the rewards. Many studies have shown that intrinsic interests can be undermined by extrinsic rewards (Kruglansky *et al.* 1975; Lepper and Green 1975). These studies suggest, then, that tutors should not be paid for being tutors. One dramatic example of the undermining of intrinsic motivation was provided by Gabarino (1975). A random set of tutors were offered a contingent reward if the tutee learned well. The other tutors were not offered any kind of reward. Observers, who did not know which tutors had been offered rewards, reported more criticism and more demands from tutors in the reward condition group. Gabarino (1975) asked whether rewards, inducements and pressure were effective. In order to answer this he considered whether the performance-related pay group got better results. He found that they did not. The contingent reward condition showed more than double the number of tutee errors! Pressure did not work. This is just one example of the frequently noted phenomenon that rewards undermine intrinsic motivation.

Thus numerous theories can be cited as reasons why learning-by-tutoring should be effective in producing learning in both tutor and tutee and also in developing other positive outcomes. I now want to consider whether the evidence from RCTs backs up or contradicts the studies reported on above.

Quantitative evidence

Evidence-based education will eventually be able to inform us not only about 'what works and what hurts' but how much benefit or harm is likely. In doing so it can provide educational professionals with power derived from having the best evidence. Even now, when we have far too few experiments to guide us, we can look at a collection of Effect Sizes from various kinds of projects (see Table 2.2).

From Table 2.2 we can see that Effect Sizes arising from controlled trials of tutoring are considerably larger than for the other interventions (computer-assisted instruction, class size reduction and more time, and Back to Basics).

I want to now consider whether other sorts of educational interventions work as well as cross-age tutoring. Data in Table 2.2 cast some light on this question by comparing the Effect Sizes from several tutoring projects with those from some popular and well-researched interventions: computer-assisted instruction, reduced class size (from two different studies) and more time on 'basics'.

Reducing class size is expensive but it is generally seen by teachers as a very important contribution to better education. However, opinions are an insufficient way to sway a legislature. In Tennessee, a teacher persuaded a sociologist, who was

Table 2.2   Some effect sizes in educational interventions

Author(s)	Year	Intervention	Effect Size
Fitz-Gibbon	1975	Tutoring	0.60
Cohen, Kulik and Kulik	1982	Tutoring	0.60
Levin, Glass and Meister	1985	Tutoring	0.60
Wang, Haertel and Walberg	1994	Tutoring	0.40
Levin, Glass and Meister	1984	Computer-assisted instruction	0.22
Nye, Hedges and Konstantopoulos	2000	Class size reduction	0.20
Levin, Glass and Meister	1984	Class size reduction	0.12
Levin, Glass and Meister	1984	More time/back to basics	0.03

on the legislature in the state of Tennessee, that this important question should be addressed by an RCT (Ritter and Boruch 1999). Thousands of primary school pupils and hundreds of primary school teachers were randomly assigned to classes of less than seventeen or to larger classes of over twenty. The progress of students was tracked for several years and the analyses indicated that smaller classes did indeed get better results than larger classes (Nye *et al.* 2000). The Effect Sizes were about 0.20, although larger effects were seen in those students most dependent upon the school because of their socio-economic status. Thus it was reliably and validly established, with far more evidence than that underpinning most initiatives, that there was a positive correlation between reduced class size and student achievement. Given a learner-focused criterion, such as the principles that underpin the No Child Left Behind federal programme in the US or the Every Child Matters strategy in the UK, the intervention was worthwhile because learners gained.

Table 2.3 summarises data on tutoring projects that are further disaggregated. It is arguable that patterns are emerging:

- Cross-age tutoring by students older than the tutees seems more effective than tutoring by same age or adult tutors.
- Tutoring in mathematics seems to yield much larger Effect Sizes than tutoring in reading.

A very strong pattern in Table 2.3 is that in all instances cross-age tutoring was more effective than tutoring by adults. However, this finding arose not within single studies using random assignment of tutees to adult or student tutors, but in a survey of many studies. This means the findings are only correlational, and correlation is not causation. The type of tutor (an adult or an older student) was not randomly assigned in these trials so the finding should be considered important but in need of further testing. However, the results are still strongly indicative of better results from cross-age tutoring than from involving adults.

Particular attention should be paid to the meta-analysis by Cohen *et al.* (1982). From reading 500 potential studies (many from academic dissertations) they found 65 studies that were usable studies with good data that would enable Effect Sizes to

Table 2.3   Data from projects and meta-analyses

Author(s)	Year	Effect Sizes: tutees		Effect Sizes: tutors		Type of tutor
		Reading	Maths	Reading	Maths	
Fitz-Gibbon	1975	–	0.58	–	0.60	Cross-age
Hartley	1977	–	0.54	–	–	Adult
Hartley	1977	–	0.52	–	–	Same age
Hartley	1977	–	0.79	–	0.58	Cross-age
Cohen, Kulik and Kulik	1982	0.29	0.60	0.21	0.62	Various (a meta-analysis)
Cook, Scruggs, Mastriopieri and Casto	1986	0.49	0.85	0.30	0.67	Cross-age
Levin, Glass and Meister	1987	0.48	0.97	–	–	Cross-age
Levin, Glass and Meister	1987	0.38	0.67	–	–	Adult

be calculated. The findings on cognitive tutoring are almost uniformly positive. In contrast, analyses of mentoring programmes are very mixed. Lucas and Liabo considered mentoring programmes for children at risk of developing severe behavioural problems in the UK. Their conclusion was that one-to-one, non-directive mentoring programmes have not been shown to improve behaviour in young people involved in offending or other anti-social activities (2003).

Tutoring should not be confused with mentoring. There is increasing evidence that mentoring not only does not work, but that it may make outcomes worse (Grossman and Tierney 1998; Scandura 1998; Piper and Piper 1999; Colley 2001; St James-Roberts and Singh 2001). The reasons might include dependency, self-labelling, and/or resentment.

The use of experiments for validating assertions and testing hypotheses is only slowly gaining ground in education. In the UK the EPPI Centre (www.ioe.ac.uk/eppi) in London has been trying to conduct meta-analyses of existing trials but there is a poverty of controlled experiments to analyse in educational research (Oakley 2004).

In the US, federal policy is now promoting the use of RCTs and a body called the What Works Clearinghouse produces meta-analyses and guidance on the systematic reporting of RCTs (see www.whatworks.ed.gov). Earlier I indicated that the Effect Size for cross-age tutoring in mathematics was generally 0.60 or higher. The Effect Sizes reported for mathematics on the What Works website, from studies they rate as 'meeting evidence standards' (well-conducted RCTs) have Effect Sizes reported as: –0.1, 0.41, 0.43, 0.11. (The last one met standards of evidence only 'with reservations'.) Almost without exception the developers were commercial and the programmes involved purchasing materials, often computer programmes. Having the teaching topic standardised in textbooks and computer programmes is an attempt to ensure fidelity of replication. However, this raises the question of whether standardising should be a goal regardless of cost. It may be that having tutors devise their own ways of explaining to their own tutee is a source of the effectiveness of cross-age tutoring. Tutors' language and explanations may in fact be better suited to the tutees than textbook language. Furthermore, having devised methods to teach the topic, tutors will know the work better as educational practitioners know when they try to explain or teach. A less structured and more discursive report from the US comes from the Northwest Regional Educational Laboratory (school improvement research series) (Kalkowski 1995). This concludes that research provides extensive evidence supporting the use of peer and cross-age tutoring. Achievement improves, and so do a host of social and affective outcomes.

Conclusion

Randomised controlled trials are important not only to show how great are the benefits that can be derived but also to demonstrate conclusively when treatments or interventions actually do harm. There is a need for thousands of RCTs because, as illustrated, many innovations have been praised and then found not only to be ineffective but to be actually doing harm. For further examples from programmes for at-risk young people see Dishion *et al.* (1999), McCord (2001) and Poulin *et al.* (2001)

Campbell and Stanley's best selling book, *Experimental and Quasi-experimental Designs for Research* was published in 1966 yet only in the last few years has the Campbell Collaboration (www.campbellcollaboration.org) begun to get attention drawn to the need for data from randomised controlled trials. Campbell and Stanley concluded that 'we must increase our time perspective, and recognise that continuous, multiple experimentation is more typical of science than once-and-for-all definitive experiments' (1966: 173). This raises the question as to who will conduct the 'continuous, multiple experimentation'.

Centralised decision-making may not be malevolent but it will often be ill-informed, and sometimes corrupted by political considerations or commercial interests. Deming (1986) argued that those who do the job are best placed to improve the job. This seems reasonable. Educational practitioners should be the innovators. However, those at the chalk face need data so that they can evaluate the effectiveness of their work.

There is a mass of sound evidence that cross-age tutoring 'works' better than other interventions. Furthermore, cross-age tutoring has the potential to address not only the cognitive goals of schooling but also many other goals as well. For example, it can address problems such as racism and social exclusion, by the direct experience of working on an important topic such as mathematics or foreign languages, as either a tutor or a tutee (Eisenberg *et al.* 1982; Datta and Singh 1994; Fitz-Gibbon 2000). Furthermore, it often reaches the most difficult students to an extent unmatched by any other intervention (Fitz-Gibbon 2006).

In a world distressed by conflicts, one hypothesis is that schools should not put undue academic pressure on students (for example by drilling, teaching to the test, relentless pressures, competition and excessive but undifferentiated homework), but should seek joy-in-work (Deming 1986). By using short bursts of learning-by-tutoring, schools can become effective learning communities, in which caring and helping are normal and prejudices are eroded by the pleasurable experience of older students tutoring younger students on topics that both need to learn.

References

AA Motoring Trust (2006) News at Views Issue 3, April. http://www.aatrust.com/ index.asp?pageid = 13 Accessed on 28th May 2006.

Allen, V.L. (ed.) (1976) *Children as Teachers: Theory and Research on Tutoring*. London: Academic Press.

Ausubel, D.P. (1968) *Educational Psychology*. New York: Holt, Rinehart and Winston, Inc.

Bem, D.J. (1967) Self-perception: an alternative interpretation of cognitive dissonance phenomena, *Psychological Review* 74: 183–200.

Blank, M., Koltuv, M. and Wood, M. (1972) Individualising teaching for disadvantaged kindergarten children: a comparison of two methods, *Journal of Special Education* 6: 207–219.

Boruch, R., May, R., Turner, H. Lavenberg, J., Petrosino, A., de Moya, D., Grimshaw, J. and Foley, E. (2004) Estimating the effects of interventions that are deployed in many places: place-randomized trials, *American Behavioural Scientist* 47(5): 608–33.

Campbell, D.T. and Stanley, J.C. (1966) *Experimental and quasi-experimental designs for research*. Chicago: Rand McNally.

Cohen, P.A., Kulik, J.A. and Kulik, C.L. (1982) Educational outcomes of tutoring: a meta-analysis of findings, *American Educational Research Journal* 19(2): 237–248.

Colley, H. (2001) Righting re-writings of the myth of Mentor: a critical perspective on career guidance mentoring, *British Journal of Guidance and Counselling* 29(2): 177–198.

Cook, S.B., Scruggs, T.E., Mastropieri, M.A. & Casto, G.C. (1986) Handicapped Students as Tutors in The Journal of Special Education 19 (4), pp. 483–492.

Datta, C.J. and Singh, B.R. (1994) Small scale study of the effects of cross-ethnic tutoring on inter-ethnic relationships, *British Educational Research Journal* 20(4): 407–428.

Deming, W.E. (1986) *Out of the Crisis: Quality Productivity and Competitive Position*. Cambridge: Cambridge University Press.

Dishion, T.J., McCord, J. and Poulin, F. (1999) When interventions harm: peer groups and problem behavior, *American Psychologist* 54(9): 755–764.

Eisenberg, T., Fresko, B. and Carmeli, M. (1982) Affective changes in socially disadvantaged children as a result of one to one tutoring, *Studies in Educational Evaluation*, 8(2): 141–151.

Festinger, L. and Carlsmith, J.M. (1956) Cognitive consequences of forced compliance, *Journal of Abnormal and Social Psychology* 52: 384–389.

Fitz-Gibbon, C.T. (1975) *The Role Change Intervention: An Experiment in Cross-age Tutoring, UCLA Graduate School of Education*. Los Angeles, CA: UCLA.

Fitz-Gibbon, C.T. (1980) Measuring time-use and evaluating peer tutoring in urban secondary schools. Final report for the Social Science Research Council.

Fitz-Gibbon, C.T. (1996) *Monitoring Education: Indicators, Quality and Effectiveness*. London: Cassell.

Fitz-Gibbon, C.T. (2000) Cross-age tutoring: should it be required in order to reduce social exclusion?, in G. Walraven, C. Parsons, D. van Veen and C. Day (eds) *Combating Social Exclusion Through Education: Laissez-faire, Authoritarianism or Third Way?* Leuven, Belgium: Garant.

Fitz-Gibbon, C.T. (2006) Affective and behavioural variables: reforms as experiments sto produce civil society. *Educational Psychology* 26(2): 303–323.

French, J.R.P. and Raven, B.H. (1959) The bases of social power, in D. Cartwright (ed.) *Studies in Social Power*. Ann Arbor: University of Michigan, 150–167.

Gabarino, J. (1975) The impact of anticipated reward upon cross-age tutoring. *Journal of Personality and Social Psychology* 323(3): 421–428.

Goodlad, S. and Hirst, B. (1989) *Peer Tutoring: A Guide to Learning by Teaching*. London: Kogan Page; New York: Nichols Publishing.

Goodlad, S. and Hirst, B.E. (1990) *Explorations in Peer Tutoring*. Oxford: Basil Blackwell.

Grossman, J.B. and Tierney, J.P. (1998) Does mentoring work? An impact study of the Big Brothers Big Sisters Program, *Evaluation Review* 22(3): 403–426.

Hartley, S.S. (1977) *A Meta-Analysis of Effects of Individually Paced Instruction in Mathematics*. Denver: University of Colorado Press.

Kalkowski, P. (1995) *Peer and Cross-age Tutoring*. School improvement research series; Close-up No. 1. Portland, OR: North West Regional Educational Laboratory. http://www.nwrel.org/scpd/sirs/9/c018.html (accessed 4 April 2006).

Kelman, H.C. (1958) Compliance, identification, and internalization, three processes of attitude change, *Journal of Conflict Resolution* 2: 51–60.

Kruglansky, A.W., Riter, A., Amitai, A., Bath-Sheva, M., Sghabtai, L. and Zabash, D. (1975) Can money enhance intrinsic motivation? A test of he content–consequence hypothesis. *Journal of Personality and Social Psychology* 31: 744–750.

Lepper, M. and Greene, D. (1975) Turning play into work: effects of adult surveillance and extrinsic rewards on children's intrinsic motivation, *Journal of Personality and Social Psychology*, 31: 744–750.

Levin, H.M., Glass, G.V. and Meister, G.R. (1987) Cost-effectiveness of four Educational Interventions in *Evaluation Review* 11/1: 50–72, Stanford: Institute for Research on Educational Finance and Governance, Stanford University.

Lucas, P. and Liabo, K (2003) One-to-one, non-directive mentoring programmes have not been shown to improve behaviour in young people involved in offending or anti-social activities, *What Works for Children Group Evidence Nugget*. http://www.whatworksforchildren.org.uk/docs/Nuggets/html/Mentoring.htm (accessed 4 April 2006).

Malmuth, N.M., Turcotte, S.J.C. and Fitz-Gibbon, C.T. (1981) Tutoring and social psychology, *Journal of Educational Thought* 15(2): 113–123.

McCord, J. (2001) Crime prevention: a cautionary tale. Paper presented to the Third Evidence-based Policies and Indicator Systems Conference, Collingwood College and CEM Centre University of Durham, July.

Merz, F. (1969) Der Einfluss der Verbalisierens auf die Leistung bei Intelligenzaufgaben [The effect of verbalization upon performance on intelligence tests], *Zeitschrift fur Experimentelle und Angewandte Psychologie* 16(1): 114–137.

Miller, R.L., Brickman, P., and Bolen, D. (1975) Attribution versus persuasion as a means for modifying behavior, *Journal of Personality and Social Psychology* 31: 430–441.

Mohan, M. (1972) *Peer Tutoring as a Technique for Teaching the Unmotivated*. Fredonia, NY: State University of New York, Teacher Research Center.

Nye, B., Hedges, L.V. and Konstantopoulos, S. (2000) The effects of small classes on academic achievement: the results of the Tennessee class size experiment, *American Educational Research Journal*, 37(1): 123–151.

Oakley, A. (2004) Who's afraid of the randomized controlled trial? Some dilemmas of the scientific method and 'good' research practice, in C. Seale (ed.) *Social Research Methods: A Reader*. London: Routledge.

Osborne, R. and Wittrock, M.C. (1985) The generative learning model and its implications for science education, *Studies in Science Education* 12: 59–87.

Piper, H. and Piper, J. (1999) 'Disaffected' young people: problems for mentoring, *Mentoring and Tutoring*, 7(2): 121–130.

Poulin, F., Dishion, T.J. and Harris, J. (2001) Three year iatrogenic effects associated with aggregating high-risk adolescents in cognitive-behavioral prevention interventions, *Applied Developmental Science* 5: 214–224.

Raven, B.H. and Kruglanski, A.W. (1970) Conflict and power, in D.G. Swingle (ed.) *The Structure of Conflict*. New York: Academic Press.

Ritter, G.W. and Boruch, R.F. (1999) The political and institutional origins of a randomized controlled trial on elementary school class size: Tennessee's Project STAR, *Educational Evaluation and Policy Analysis* 21(2): 111–125.

Ritter, G.W. and Maynard, R.A. (1999) *The Academic Impact of Volunteer Tutoring in Urban Public Elementary Schools: Results of an Experimental Design Evaluation*. http://policy.uark.edu/ritter/WPTP-EVAL5.html (accessed 4 April 2006).

Roberts, I., and Kwan, I. (2001) Cochrane Injuries Group Driver Education Reviewers. School-based driver education for the prevention of traffic crashes. *Cochrane Database Syst Rev* 2001; (3): CD003201.

Rose, S., Bisson, J. and Wessely, S. (2003) Psychological debriefing for presenting posttraumatic stress disorder (PTSD) *Cochrane Review*. The Cochrane Library, 2.

Scandura, T.A. (1998) Dysfunctional mentoring relationships and outcomes, *Journal of Management* 24: 449–467.

St James-Roberts, I. and Singh, C.S. (2001) Can mentors help primary school children with behaviour problems? Final report of the three-year evaluation of Project CHANCE carried out by the Thomas Coram Research Unit between March 1997 and 2000. London: Home Office.

Topping, K.J. and Ehly, S. (eds) (1998) *Peer-assisted Learning*. Mahwah, NJ: Lawrence Erlbaum.

Tymms, P. and Coe, R. (2003) Celebration of the success of distributed research with schools: the CEM Centre, Durham, *British Educational Research Journal* 29(5): 639–653.

Wang, M.C., Haertel, G.D. and Walberg, H.J. (1994). What helps students learn? *Educational Leadership*, 51(4) 74–79. (ERIC Document Reproduction Service No. ED461694).

Wittrock, M.C. (1974) Learning as a generative process, *Educational Psychologist* 11: 87–95.

Wood, D. (1998) The UK ILS evaluations: final report. Coventry: British Educational Communications and Technology Agency (BECTA).

Wood, D. and Wood, H. (1996) Vygotsky, tutoring and learning, *Oxford Review of Education* 22: 5–16.

Zander, A. and Curtis, T. (1972) Effects of social power on aspiration setting and striving. *Journal of Abnormal and Social Psychology* 64: 63–74.

Zimbardo, P.G. (1970) The human choice: individuation, reason and order versus de-individuation, impulse and chaos, in W.J. Arnold and D. Levine (eds) *Nebraska Symposium on Motivation*. Lincoln: University of Nebraska Press.

3

LISA MURPHY, DEREK KASSEM
AND GEOFF FENWICK
The politics of the National
Literacy and Numeracy
Strategies

Introduction

The National Literacy (NLS) and Numeracy (NNS) Strategies represent an attempt by the Government of large-scale reform that has been elusive (Earl *et al.* 2000) and largely unachievable by governments. The strategies are the product of both the present New Labour Government and the previous Conservative administration. The strategies developed from projects set up in the dying days of the Conservative Government in 1996. The National Literacy and Numeracy Projects (NLPs, NNPs) were separate initiatives but had the same key purpose of raising standards in the curriculum areas of mathematics and language in primary schools. Each project was to run for a period of five years in local education authorities (LEA) that had volunteered to take part in the projects. No LEA ran both projects at the same time.

New Labour came to power on 1 May 1997 with a political agenda committed to education and in particular to raising educational standards within the UK. For the new Secretary of State for Education, David Blunkett, the raising of standards was fundamental to his political credibility to such an extent that in 1998 he set primary schools targets for literacy and numeracy that had to be achieved by the year 2002. These targets identified the proportion of pupils to achieve Level 4 at the end of Key Stage 2, 80% in English and 75% in mathematics. Such importance was placed on these targets that Blunkett said he would resign if they were not met: they were not, but he moved office just before the date the results were due.

A state pedagogy

In an attempt to achieve these targets the Government implemented both the NLS and the NNS before their respective projects had completed their five-year trial period and before any results or evaluations were published. The curtailing and early implementation of the projects was to be repeated a few years later with the introduction of the Key Stage 3 Strategy. In effect, the Government was looking for a magic bullet that would raise academic standards in the State education system. The movement to increase State control of schools had progressed from the introduction of the National Curriculum by the Thatcher Government in 1987, which set a trend for educational reforms without prior research or evaluation, to New Labour's introduction of NNS and NLS. Both Strategies prescribe the pedagogy to be employed in schools by teachers, hence a state pedagogy.

The implementation of the NLS and the literacy hour (LH) came with the injunction, just in case anyone was unsure of its significance, that the NLS should be used by a school 'unless the school can demonstrate through its literacy action plan, schemes of work and performance in Key Stage 2 tests, that the approach it has adopted is at least as effective' (Literacy Task Force 1997: 5). This veiled threat demonstrates that the NLS is indeed a state-defined pedagogy and that few schools or teachers of literacy, given the threat of inspection and publicised results, would have the confidence to predominantly use other teaching methods. The NNS, introduced into schools a year later, took the same approach: implement unless you have the evidence to say you can do better. As with the NLS, the NNS had not completed the trial period and lacked evaluation of the proposed three-part daily mathematics lesson (DML).

The research basis for the NLS

One of the major influences in shaping the NLS was the claimed success of the NLP. However, the NLS adopted the LH after the NLP had been in place for a fraction of the originally intended five-year period and before an independent survey had been carried out. The National Foundation for Educational Research (NFER) who carried out the independent survey concluded that while the pupils involved in the NLP did make progress in literacy, there were concerns about the sustainability of improvement over a longer period of time (Sainsbury 1998).

As no control was conducted utilising other methods of teaching literacy, it could be suggested that it was the focus on literacy rather than the actual pedagogy of the NLP or NLS, which accounted for the rise in literacy standards. Any new initiative which gives teachers and pupils a united goal, introduces new methodology and is applied with great focus and energy will, in all probability, produce initially positive results (Wyse and Jones 2001).

Wyse (2003) traces what he considers to be abrupt changes in Ofsted attitudes to the teaching of phonics and suggests that this could be due to 'political expediency and the personal views of the chief inspector' (2003: 906). It is interesting to note that inspection comments on phonics collated in a table by Beard (1999: Appendix) do not always agree with the evidence cited by Wyse (2003). This in itself points to the fact that inspection evidence should be treated carefully. The Select Committee on Education and Employment in the House of Commons highlighted the need for extensive research into inspection evidence (Wyse 2003: 907). At best, inspection evidence, along with government-commissioned reports, is subjective, at worst it is a forum for promoting political dogma as can be seen in the current phonics debate.

Reading

The development of the NLS approach to the teaching of reading had come a long way since the great debate on reading (Chall 1967). The debate centred around whether reading is a top-down process based on meaning-getting in which readers start from the whole text or a bottom-up process in which readers start with the letters and build up meaning. Advocates of the top-down theories argued that phonics is subordinate to prediction (Smith 1978) while advocates of the bottom-up approach believed that the teaching of reading must begin with phonics (Morris 1979).

Researchers and educators agree that reading is a complex process in which the two systems work in parallel, though while learning to read one system may at times have precedence over the other. Therefore, a model for teaching reading which incorporates both processes is the most effective way of teaching reading (Adams 1990). Although the research basis for the NLS has been provided retrospectively (Beard 1999; Myhill and Fisher 2005), the 'searchlights' model for teaching reading in the NLS (DfEE 1998a) contains some sense in prescribing an interactive model combining top-down and bottom-up approaches.

However, there seems to have been a turn-around in Government policy. In an attempt to account for the fact that the 1998 target for literacy has still not been reached, the Government commissioned a House of Commons Select Committee investigation into reading in 2005 (HMC 2005) and subsequently, an independent report into reading to be carried out by Jim Rose, former Deputy Chief Inspector of Schools.

As Wyse (2005) points out, the committee was biased as it was composed of advocates of the synthetic phonic approach, such as the author of *Jolly Phonics*, a synthetic phonics reading scheme, and one of the co-authors of the study into synthetic phonics carried out in Clackmannanshire (Johnston and Watson 2005).

Careful reading of Rose's interim report (Rose 2005), reveals that the Government had an agenda. They did not commission a report into which method of teaching reading was most successful, or even which method of teaching phonics was most successful. The remit was to establish which method of teaching *synthetic* phonics is best practice.

Rose claims that having examined available evidence, and having engaged with teaching professionals and education experts, there is convincing evidence that synthetic phonics is the best approach (2005: 13). The only evidence that Rose cites, however, is HMI visits to schools and the Clackmannanshire study.

The Government has decided that after all, primarily on the basis of the Clackmannanshire study, a particular bottom-up approach to reading in the early years is the right and only way to teach reading. The Select Committee's investigation and Rose's report, which no doubt will be significant in the revising of the NLS framework, claim that the multi-strategy approach to teaching reading of the NLS should be replaced by a model which gives precedence to synthetic phonics.

In their search for a holy grail (Wyse 2005) for teaching reading, the Government appears to be carefully selecting evidence, and ignoring the common sense pointed out in the Bullock Report that 'there is no one method, medium, approach, device or philosophy that holds the key to the process of learning to read' and insistence on one method is 'no service to the teaching of reading' (DES 1975).

Policy, politics and teaching of literacy

John Stannard, former HMI inspector, who led the NLP, stated that its main purpose was to 'do something about the quality of teaching literacy' (Reid 1997: 3). When the NLS was implemented, the Government pulled off a master-stroke of marketing. They took some tried and tested teaching methods, repackaged and renamed them and sold them to us as new. It is generally accepted among the teaching profession that the teaching pedagogy outlined in the NLS is in fact derived from good practice and, as research has pointed out, that the teaching approaches advocated in the NLS were already being employed by effective teachers of literacy prior to its implementation (Wray *et al.* 2000). Moreover, research conducted since the implementation of the NLS found that in general teachers were supportive of the strategy and that the structure of the LH helped with planning and progression and promoted direct teaching and teacher–pupil interaction which was felt to be more effective than individualised teaching (Smith and Hardman 2000).

The problem

The problem is that the approaches advocated in the NLS are now being sold as the *only* right way of teaching literacy. In the past teachers could be creative in their planning and practice. They could choose from a variety of approaches at their disposal whichever they felt most appropriate to promote the learning of the topic in hand. The problem is that literacy is now presented to us a unified product. The NLS provides one method for teaching reading and writing – the LH – when developmental research shows that reading and writing involve different cognitive processes (Bissex 1980).

Moreover, the one-size-fits-all aspect of the strategy as a pedagogy to be applied in all classrooms nationally, what Reynolds terms the conflict of context specific versus the universality of effectiveness criteria (1998), does little to take into account the prior experience, background, interests and individuality of both teacher and pupil.

In fact, it is the removal of choice and the implicit we-know-best attitude of Government officials and academics with little experience of teaching literacy which has caused consternation among teaching professionals.

Hilton (1998) strongly asserts concerns at the swift and prescriptive implementation of the NLS which were shared by many in the teaching profession. It appears that much of her displeasure lay in the attitude of the politicians whom she implies were enforcing their top-down policies and political dogma upon the teaching profession with little respect for any previous practice, experience and wisdom and with little research basis. There is an implicit lack of faith in teachers' professionalism.

Lack of consultation and public debate does not encourage ownership of the NLS by the school or the teacher and can create a situation in which a teaching system is applied at odds with the teaching philosophy of the teachers (Beverton 2003). Teachers may deliver the NLS because they have to, but they may not believe in it. In this sense teachers may become technicians or production assistants delivering the set of skills, which the NLS outlines, in order that tests are passed, targets are met and the end-product of literacy is attained. In the process teaching is deprofessionalised.

The stress that teachers feel to cover NLS lesson objectives and to prepare pupils for SATs is well documented (Earl *et al.* 2000). English *et al.* (2002) record a further area of stress for teachers – the apparent contradictions in the rationale of the NLS and secondary strategy which describes effective teaching as interactive and discursive, but also requires fast-paced lessons which cover a set of defined objectives 'driven by the need to make progress and succeed' (DfEE 1998b: 8). Indeed, it is the pressure to cover all the objectives in the strategies, to prepare pupils for SATs and to cover the aspects of the NC English curriculum which are not catered for in the NLS, such as speaking and listening, individual reading and extended writing, which is deintellectualising the teaching of literacy.

Research carried out by Twiselton, exploring the impact of the NLS on the development of trainee primary school teachers, provides some evidence that the national strategies are deintellectualising and deprofessionalising teaching (Twiselton 2000). Twiselton compared the relationship between trainee teachers' practice in the teaching of literacy and their knowledge of child development underpinning it, prior to the implementation of the NLS and after its implementation.

Having outlined three basic teacher types – task managers, curriculum deliverers and concept/skills builders, Twiselton suggests that over the course of a four-year Initial Teacher Training (ITT) programme the tendency is for the majority of trainee teachers to begin as task managers and gradually, as their understanding of the literacy learning experience develops, for them to progress through the stage of curriculum deliverer to concept/skills builder. Not all trainee teachers become concept/skills builders able to help children develop their own understanding of literacy by adapting the learning experience, though this is the ideal.

Twiselton found that after the implementation of the NLS and changes to ITT to comply with the NLS (DfES 2002), more trainee teachers across the four-year course were classified as curriculum deliverers, but fewer progressed to become concept/skills builders. The suggestion is that the new curricula are so prescriptive and inclusive that trainee teachers, as long as they are following the script, needed to go no further in developing their underpinning knowledge of literacy learning. Further longitudinal research is required of the impact of the strategies on primary and secondary English teaching, but Twiselton's work provides some suggestion that the current curricula limit trainee teachers' understanding of the structures of subjects and may limit their ability to scaffold children effectively (2000: 402).

Research basis of the NNS

There has been less controversy and more acceptances of the NNS than the NLS, at least by teachers:

> While teachers in interviews are overwhelmingly positive about the NNS, and feel it has given them more knowledge about the curriculum and ways of teaching it, more control over learning , much more confidence, their teaching in the classroom seems to have changed in superficial ways, e.g. organisation of lessons and resources used.
>
> (Brown, *et al.* 2003: 668)

Brown *et al.* (2003), in their discussion of the role of academics in the development of the NNS, identify teacher attitudes to the NNS. Firstly, teachers, for the most part, are very positive about the NNS. Secondly, the degree of actual change that has occurred in the way mathematics is taught is superficial only. This is in part, it is suggested, because of the way in which the NNS was introduced on the back of the National Numeracy Project, as indicated above, that is, before there was any evaluation or published research.

However, the Numeracy Task Force, charged by the Government to design and oversee the implementation of an NNS claimed that all the recommendations they were making were based on sound research:

> [w]e have aimed throughout our work to look at the evidence to find solutions to any problems with mathematical achievement , and to make practical recommendations based on methods that have been shown to be effective in raising standards of primary mathematics.
>
> (DfEE 1998b: 7)

The NNS was the end-product of a process that began in 1982 with the publication of the Cockcroft Report into the teaching of mathematics spurred on by a general concern for mathematical education in the UK and the level of mathematical attainment. International comparisons, for instance Reynolds and Farrell (1996), indicated that the UK was not performing well in some key areas such as calculation. There is an element in the development of the NNS of 'something must be done'. It has been done, but is it based on research?

Some key issues

Calculators hit the headlines when it was announced by the NNS that children under the age of 8 would be banned from using them. It was as if there were an age of consent for the use of calculators. There does not appear to be any real reason for this ban other than the political views of the then Secretary of State. As there is very little evidence on the impact that calculators have on a child's ability to calculate, the biggest issue, in fact, is the teachers' inability to use the technology and to teach pupils how to use calculators. Ruthven concluded that:

the degree of calculator use remains modest in most schools and by most pupils ... however tempting it might be to cast the calculator as a scapegoat for disappointing mathematical performance at primary level, the available evidence provides scant support for this position.

(1997: 18)

What must also be borne in mind is that at the very same time the Government was banning calculators for the under-8s it was promoting the use of computers in schools and has done so ever since it came to power. The obvious question one might ask is, what exactly can a calculator do that a computer cannot?

The lack of research on calculator use is rather indicative of some of the other areas that are key to the NNS. This is of course not to claim that all aspects of the NNS lack a research base. It is not possible in the space available to review all aspects of the research that supports or opposes the NNS. Therefore, key aspects of the NNS will be examined not only from the research perspective, but also the extent to which the practice in schools has changed since the implementation of the NNS.

One of the key changes introduced by the NNS is described as whole class interactive teaching. This approach is in fact common to both the NLS and the NNS, though Brown *et al.* (1998) concluded that the evidence in support of whole class teaching was ambiguous and it was the quality of pupil–teacher interaction that made the difference rather than classroom organisation.

A fundamental aspect of whole class interactive teaching is the use made of questioning, the good use of pupil responses and the provision of clear instructions by teachers. However, teaching quality or the contribution made by individual teachers to primary numerical attainment was rather small (Brown *et al.* 1998). With the implementation of the NNS there must have been a change in the way mathematics is taught, and many claims have been made to that effect. McNamara and Corbin point out that the:

> extravagant claim that 'educational' reforms in Britain have hitherto [before the NNS] 'failed' may have more than a grain of truth. There was, for example, a perception in the late 1980s that the National Curriculum would compel teachers to change certain classroom management and teaching strategies; including that of increasing the amount of time spent on whole class and specialist subject teaching. Yet the consensus appears ... that there were only 'modest changes' in classroom practice as a result of its introduction ... the move to a more overtly specifying a pedagogy began in the early 90s and culminated in the launch of the NNP.

(2001: 268)

It would seem, therefore, that the NNS is one step down the ladder to enforce the introduction of whole class teaching, which has almost become the holy grail of academic achievement. Quite clearly it works in the Pacific Rim countries (Reynolds and Farrell 1996) so it must work here. Smith *et al.* (2004) point out that:

[i]t is suggested that more interactive forms of whole class teaching will play a vital role in raising literacy and numeracy standards by promoting high quality dialogue and discussion and raising inclusion, understanding and learning performance.

(2004: 395)

It would be safe to assume that in good, well-run classrooms where the NNS is being implemented, the above account of good practice should be taking place. Indeed, Smith *et al.* (2004) found that some 60% of the lessons they observed were taught by 'highly effective teachers'. This is important as they should be providing good NNS or NLS lessons. Unfortunately, they also found that while the whole class element of the lessons lasted for 60% of the lesson period, open questions made up only 10% of the questions asked by the teacher. They conclude that:

[f]ar from encouraging and extending pupil contributions to promote higher levels of interaction and cognitive engagement, most of the questions asked were of a low cognitive level designed to funnel pupils' response towards the required answer.

(2004: 408)

Moreover Smith *et al.* found that during the whole class part of the lesson, teachers spent the majority of the time either explaining or using highly structured question and answer sequences (2004: 408). In a similar vein, Burns and Myhill (2004) found that:

[g]iven that nearly 70% of all statements were concerned with teacher delivery and only 19% with response or encouragement of children to engage at a deeper level of thinking, there is some evidence here of a transmissive model of teaching, rather than an interactive one.

(2004: 46)

This research would tend to suggest that not only is the approach to teaching in the state-defined pedagogy of the NNS and NLS lacking in unambiguous research evidence to support the strategy but also failing in its attempt to micro-manage the teaching of mathematics in the primary classroom. The reality is that teachers are not actually implementing the interactive part of the lessons in the way they are supposed to. The changes that the NNS has brought into play are, therefore, rather superficial in nature. The change is one of form rather than substance. In part this might be due to the focus on teacher delivery and not how children learn.

The child has disappeared

Prior to the 1980s, government reviews and reports into education, such as the Hadow Reports (Board of Education 1931; 1933), the Plowden Report (DES 1967), the Bullock Report (DES 1975) the Cockcroft Report (1982), held the child learner as central to the education process (Wyse and Jones 2001). Since the 1980s comparison between literacy and numeracy standards in the UK with those of her international competitors has been the focus of much public debate and has been cited as a reason for international economic failure (Ernst and Young 1993; Reynolds and Farrell 1996; Barber 1996; Wyse 2003).

Literacy and numeracy has, to some extent, become a product or commodity promising potential increased opportunity both for the individual and for the nation as a whole (Hilton 1998). Within this model of literacy and numeracy the teacher's role is to deliver the product in regular and manageable chunks so that objectives are ticked off and targets are met. Once a child has attained SATs Level 4 at Key Stage 2 and Level 6 at Key Stage 3, the key skills have been delivered and literacy and numeracy have been achieved. Quantifiable literacy and numeracy standards, rather than educated children, have become the desired end product of the education process.

Conclusion

With the National Strategies, and more recently with synthetic phonics, or whole class interactive teaching, the Government has claimed to have found the magic bullet for raising national academic standards. It is worth remembering the advice of the Bullock Report that knowledge to improve reading 'does not lie in the triumphant discovery, or re-discovery, of a particular formula' (DES 1975: 77). Indeed, an HMI report, cited by Hilton, revealed that schools which used only one approach rather than a variety of methods had lower standards in reading and writing (1998: 5).

A revision of the strategies is proposed for 2006/7. In an ideal world, a revision of primary teaching would acknowledge that a single system can only improve standards for a time. While recommending effective ways of teaching literacy and numeracy, based on sound academic research and professional experience, it would give choice and ownership of the teaching process back to the professionals and would place the child as learner at the centre of the education process. Teachers need to become educators rather than their current status of technicians.

References

Adams, M. (1990) *Beginning to Read*. Cambridge, MA: MIT Press.

Barber, M. (1996) *The Learning Game*. London: Gollancz.

Beard, R. (1999) *National Literacy Strategy: Review of Research and other Related Evidence*. London: DfEE.

Beverton, S. (2003) Can you see the difference? Early impacts of the primary national literacy strategy on four secondary English departments, *Cambridge Journal of Education*, 33(2): 217–235.

Bissex, G. (1980) *GYNS AT WRK: A Child Learns to Read and Write*. Cambridge, MA: Harvard University Press.

Board of Education (1931) *The Primary School* (the second Hadow Report). London: HMSO.

Board of Education (1933) *Infant and Nursery Schools* (the third Hadow Report) London: HMSO.

Brown, M., Askew, M., Baker, D., Denvir, H. and Millett, A. (1998) Is the National Numeracy Strategy research-based? *British Journal of Educational Studies* 46(4), December.

Brown, M., Askew, M., Millett, A. and Rhodes, V. (2003) The key role of educational research in the development and evaluation of the National Numeracy Strategy, *British Educational Research Journal* 29(5): 655–672.

Burns, C. and Myhill, D. (2004) Interactive or inactive? A consideration of the nature of interaction in whole class teaching, *Cambridge Journal of Education* 34(1): 35–49.

Chall, J. (1967) *Learning to Read – The Great Debate*. New York: McGraw-Hill.

Cockcroft, W. (1982) *Mathematics Counts: Report of the Committee of Inquiry into the Teaching of Mathematics in Schools*. London: HMSO.

Department for Education and Employment (DfEE) (1998a) *The National Literacy Strategy: Framework for Teaching*. London: DfEE.

Department for Education and Employment (DfEE) (1998b) *The Implementation of the National Numeracy Strategy: The Final Report of the National Numeracy Task Force*. London: DfEE.

Department of Education and Science (DES) (1967) *Children and Their Primary Schools* (the Plowden Report). London: HMSO.

Department of Education and Science (DES) (1975) *A Language for Life* (the Bullock Report). London: HMSO.

Department for Education and Skills (DfES) (2002) *Qualifying to Teach: Professional Standards for Qualified Teacher Status and Requirements for Initial Teacher Training*. London: DfES.

Earl, L., Fullan, M., Leithwood, K., Watson, N., with Jantzi, D. and Levin, B. (2000) *Watching and Learning: OISE/UT Evaluation of the Implementation of the National Literacy and Numeracy Strategies*. London: DfEE.

English, E., Hargreaves, L. and Hislam, J. (2002) Pedogogical dilemmas in the National Literacy Strategy: primary teachers' perceptions, reflections and classroom behaviour, *Cambridge Journal of Education*, 32(1): 9–26.

Ernst and Young (1993) Literacy, education and training: their impact on the UK economy. Mimeo.

Hilton, M. (1998) Raising literacy standards: the true story, *English in Education* 32(3): 4–16.

House of Commons Education and Skills Committee (2005) *Select Committee Report: Teaching Children to Read*. www.publications.parliament.uk (accessed 31 March 2006).

Johnston, R. and Watson, J. (2005). *The Effects of Synthetic Phonics Teaching on Reading and Spelling Attainment*. Edinburgh: Scottish Executive Education Department.

Literacy Task Force (1997) *The Implementation of the National Literacy Strategy: Final Report*. London: DfEE.

McNamara, O. and Corbin, B. (2001) Warranting practices: teachers embedding the National Numeracy Strategy, *British Journal of Education Studies* 49(3): 260–284.

Morris, J. (1979) New phonics for old, in D. Thackray (ed.) *Growth in Reading*. London: Ward Lock Education.

Myhill, D. and Fisher, R. (2005) *Informing Practice in English: A Review of Recent Research in Literacy and the Teaching of English*. London: OFSTED.

Reid, M. (1997) An Interview with John Stannard, Director of the National Literacy Project, *English in Education* 1(3): 3–7.

Reynolds, D. (1998) Schooling for literacy: a review of research on teacher effectiveness and school effectiveness and its implications for contemporary educational policies, *Educational Review* 50(2): 147–163.

Reynolds, D. and Farrell, S. (1996) *Worlds Apart? A Review of International Surveys of Educational Achievement Involving England*. OFSTED Reviews of Research Series. London: OFSTED.

Rose, J. (2005) *Independent Review of the Teaching of Early Reading: Interim Report*. London: DfES.

Ruthven, K. (1997) *The Use of Calculators at Key Stages 1–3*, London: School Curriculum and Assessment Authority.

Sainsbury, M. (1998) *Evaluation of the National Literacy Project: Summary Report*. Slough: NFER.

Smith, F. (1978) *Reading*. Cambridge: Cambridge University Press.

Smith, F. and Hardman, F. (2000) Evaluating the effectiveness of the National Literacy Strategy: identifying indicators of success, *Educational Studies* 26(3): 365–378.

Smith, F., Hardman, F., Wall, K. and Mroz, M. (2004) Interactive whole class teaching in the National Literacy and Numeracy Strategies, *British Educational Research Journal* 30(3): 395–411.

Twiselton, S. (2000) Seeing the wood for the trees: the National Literacy Strategy and initial teacher education; pedagogical content knowledge and the structure of subjects, *Cambridge Journal of Education* 30(3): 391–403.

Wray, D., Medwell, J., Fox, R. and Poulson, L. (2000) The teaching practices of effective teachers of literacy, *Educational Review* 52(1): 75–84.

Wyse, D. (2003) The National Literacy Strategy: a critical review of the empirical evidence, *British Educational Research Journal* 29(6): 903–916.

Wyse, D. (2005) Is synthetic phonics really the holy grail? *Times Educational Supplement* 13 May.

Wyse, D. and Jones, R. (2001) *Teaching English Language and Literacy*. London: RoutledgeFalmer.

4

DIANA BURTON AND
STEVE BARTLETT
Shaping pedagogy from psychological ideas

Introduction

Current discourse about learning and teaching is redolent of a few ubiquitous and popular ideas from psychological research. The internet has been a powerful force in disseminating and globalising research into metacognition, multiple forms of intelligence, learning styles, learning preferences, brain functioning and emotional intelligence. This chapter explores the extent to which moulding pedagogy from a superficial reading of psychological ideas is educationally viable. It examines the widespread acceptance of such ideas and their apparent validation within Government documentation. The UK will provide the case study for this examination since its Government actively sponsors particular pedagogical approaches, packaging them currently under the label 'personalised learning' (Miliband 2004).

It is not possible to understand educational pedagogy without an appreciation of the political context within which certain strategies are developed. It is important, too, to distinguish between pragmatic arguments and 'educational' (political?) rhetoric constructed to justify these strategies. Harris and Ranson (2005), for instance, expose the contradictions in the Government's linking of personalised learning and social justice. It is the role of educators to apply a healthy scepticism to the provenance of new approaches, questioning their theoretical and empirical basis with precision. The task, perhaps, is to expose the 'emperor's new clothes' syndrome that currently besets education in respect of such constructs as 'personalised' or 'tailored' learning or 'learnacy' whereby sound bites become accepted into the educational lexicon, having been used in ministers' speeches or Government documents without anyone sharing an understanding of what they mean, much less a knowledge of their research basis. This chapter will explore some of these recent pedagogical trends, their research basis and the extent to which they might be applied in practice.

Pedagogy – a fashion garment?

The impact of fashions and trends is as keenly felt in education as on the high street. So too the power of the media to advertise, promote and interpret these trends, which is as powerful in relation to 'new' educational phenomena as it is to consumer goods. Witness the tabloid treatment of the return of 'synthetic phonics' or the debate around whether dyslexia actually exists or not. Education is important to everyone so new (or recycled) developments attract attention and, if packaged correctly, sell copy. It has always been the case that tabloids print the headlines not the full debate underpinning them, but latterly this 'tabloiding' of education policy, pedagogy and practice has led to ideas becoming popularised and even sensationalised within the education media themselves. There are annual teacher and lecturer awards ceremonies, often fronted by a media celebrity and sponsored by quality newspapers. Teachers and educators become the consumers of, and the audience for, this mediated expression of pedagogical or policy developments, whether through the educational press, the UK's Teachers' TV (what other profession has its own dedicated digital TV channel?) or even via Government websites.

This social phenomenon is fascinating as a manifestation of globalisation but it is important to understand the impact of it. The speed with which the internet and television can transmit ideas and information and appear to afford them (often spurious) validation should concern us as educators. We need to be interested in the way in which these ideas are researched and justified and not just in their utilitarian application. A sociological interpretation of this phenomenon is likely to lie in constructs of power and control wherein society is enabled to sustain and reproduce itself through the control and packaging of what people are taught and how they are taught it. Thus the control of the curriculum exercised by some governments via national curricula is being further extended via an even more insidious form of control: of pedagogical approaches. In England this takes the form of national strategies for literacy, primary and Key Stage 3. The format and approach of lessons are prescribed and, though not compulsory, have been adopted by almost all schools because of the force of the official support and government documentation behind them. The research underpinning these strategies is not well known and there is concern that limited learning gains have been achieved as a result of them (Wyse 2003).

Evidence-based practice and teachers' pedagogical research

In the 1990s educational research had been berated for its apparent lack of relevance to practical teaching and learning situations. The cry went up for research that would have a direct impact on practice in classrooms. Governments called for existing teaching approaches to be supported by practitioners' own research into 'what works' with learners. Thus the utilitarian value of research was sought and a mission to define 'evidence-based practice' was born. Simultaneously, in the UK the professional development of teachers has increasingly taken the form of 'edutainment', wherein charismatic, high-profile education consultants deliver courses on new pedagogies such as those embraced within Smith's accelerated learning (Smith 1996; Smith and Call 2002). High-energy presentations draw eclectically from a range of research findings thought to have practical benefits for learning. These are presented with a theatrical fervour and missionary zeal that is compelling. Teachers generally enjoy these stimulating sessions and the recipe approach to pedagogic techniques but they are not encouraged to look deeper into the research that underpins them.

Many teachers are keen to trial these techniques, tending to accept them at face value rather than to question their theoretical or empirical validity. Government money is directed at such trends so head teachers encourage their staff to explore their application in what can be an overly simplistic, mechanistic way, where short-term gains, possibly in the form of end-of-term test results, are the goal. When teachers meet for professional purposes within local, national or virtual communities of practice the new trends are discussed and the shorthand terms used to describe these ideas become generic, passing into educational discourse with a legitimacy and authority borne of practitioners' enthusiasm and partial application of the constructs. Consequently, many dissertations focus on the practical application of an increasingly narrow set of the latest popular ideas where the construct itself is not the focus of the investigation for its legitimacy is taken for granted. In this way the corpus of pedagogical research work is becoming self-referential and based on taken for granted assumptions with little attempt made to refer back to the original psychological research on which those assumptions may have been loosely based.

Psychological research and pedagogical developments

Research that has been influential during the last 25 years within educational pedagogy includes:

- constructivist theory which implies starting from pupils' existing conceptions
- social constructivist theory which reveals the importance of social interaction and scaffolded support in the learning process
- metacognitive theory which demonstrates the value of learners understanding and controlling their thinking and learning strategies
- learning style theories which imply not better/poorer distinctions between ways of learning but matching learning tasks to a preferred processing style
- learning preferences and the implications for conducive environmental conditions for learning
- multiple intelligence theory which suggests a multi-dimensional rather than a singular intelligence
- emotional intelligence theory which emphasises the potency of the learner's emotional state in learning effectively
- motivation and self-efficacy theory which exposes the higher value of intrinsic motivation rather than extrinsic reinforcement
- situated cognition theory which explains all learning as context-bound

- brain functioning and the implications of specific physical exercise on thinking skills.

(See Burton 2005 for more detail.)

Accelerated learning is an umbrella term for a series of pedagogical approaches that draw from a range of theories including many of those listed above. In many ways it coheres a set of principles that have governed effective teaching and learning for some time. Motivating learners is a key precept as is the expectation that all learners can achieve at a level normally considered beyond them. It stresses the need to understand how learning happens rather than what is learned. An assurance is given that all suggestions are based on sound research but little time is given to an examination of this research. Reference is made to VAK, the construct that there are predominantly three learning styles – visual, auditory and kinaesthetic (physical) – that pupils can be categorised into, with appropriate tasks matched to their individual styles. The emphasis on this single style construct is an example of the tendency to adopt the easiest or most attractive construct on offer rather than to properly examine the range of ideas available and their respective research bases. In educational circles VAK appears to have become synonymous with learning styles, virtually replacing it as the generic term; this is dangerously inaccurate.

Learning styles

Riding and Rayner (1998) reviewed a huge range of learning style constructs generated during the past 50 years, each predicated to differing degrees on empirical research. So why do teachers tend only to have heard of the VAK construct? It is easy to understand and internalise, easy to assess, useful as a labelling device to justify treating pupils in particular ways or having certain expectations of them. If we return to our argument that such new pedagogical ideas are promoted and paraded through universal media as a fashion garment might be, with one or two references to an original source providing the appearance of rigorous research legitimacy, we can apply this to a recent television appearance of VAK.

The construct was presented within a Channel 4 programme about how to teach 'difficult' children as *the* way in which to identify learning style rather than one of several discriminators that might help us understand learners' proclivities in different contexts and in relation to different stimuli. This is perhaps not surprising as the DfES and linked agencies, remarkably, promote this to be the case on their websites. Even when almost all the learners were found to favour kinaesthetic approaches to learning tasks, neither the award-winning (celebrity?) teacher nor the psychologist advisor queried the methodological validity of the construct, preferring to accept the very limiting notion that those learners only learned effectively when they could interact with the learning task in a physical way. It is interesting to consider how the exclusive use of kinaesthetic forms of learning could facilitate pupils' learning of the curriculum. Does this mean these pupils would never be expected to interact with visual or auditory stimuli in the form of reading a book or listening to one another? Emphasis on the identification of a single style attribute would certainly lead to this odd conclusion. The power of

Government and educational media endorsement of VAK is plain to see in schools where pupils walk round with labels identifying their VAK style. This is worrying on so many levels, from the lack of teachers' critical engagement in allowing such practice to the stultifying effect of labelling, and thereby limiting, learners' potential and opportunities. Is it actually possible, in any case, to use just one mode – don't we employ an interaction of seeing, hearing and doing in most things we learn? Doesn't learning require the use of different strategies according to the task and the context?

Curry (1983) developed a model which grouped learning style measures into strata which resemble the layers of an onion, distinguishing between a habitual and involuntary underlying feature of personality, the individual's intellectual approach to assimilating information and their instructional preference or choice of learning environment. One of the earliest researchers into learning or cognitive processing style (the inner layer of the onion) was Witkin (1978) who identified *field dependent* (FD) and *field independent* (FI) ways of approaching tasks. He found that people involuntarily used predominantly one or the other approach. FDs needed a greater degree of context in the processing of new stimuli whereas FIs found context distracting. Pilots are generally found to be field independent as they need to be able to land planes in the clouds or the dark without frames of reference that might be provided by landmarks, light, etc. It has generally been found that people cannot be trained to be naturally field dependent or independent although some small changes may occur with maturity and experience. Much of the cognitive processing style (now generally referred to as learning style) research which followed was built upon or was in some way related to Witkin's findings. Three distinct areas of investigation have emerged which can broadly be defined as follows and which align with Curry's three onion layers respectively:

Learning or cognitive style habitual way of representing and processing information; innate to learner; not susceptible to change
Learning strategy way of approaching and tackling tasks; learned; capable of change
Learning preferences environmental preferences for learning, such as place, light, sustenance, atmosphere, noise.

The important characteristic of each of these research areas is that learning is not better or worse depending on style, strategy or preference but is *different*. Whereas intelligence theory sets a limit on the capacity to learn, these theories describe the differences between learners' preferred or involuntary styles. This implies that a match between a learner's preference and the learning task will remove any such limits on learning potential.

The very fact that there are so many learning style constructs should set alarm bells ringing. We should question whether it is feasible that there can be so many different ways of describing aspects of learners' processing or thinking styles. Are these not just different manifestations of (and labels for) the same construct or at least different aspects of the same construct? Riding and Cheema (1991) argued that a whole host of style constructs reflected just two style dimensions: holistanalytic and verbaliser-imager. Most of the learning (or cognitive) style theorists deal in polar opposites and, whilst they argue that individuals may lie anywhere along a respective dimension and not necessarily at either end of it, the fact that they deal only in linear descriptions may suggest a failure to acknowledge the multi-faceted, context-bound nature of learning. Finally, it is probably worth considering just how helpful it actually is to be able to determine whether a learner is an innovator or an adaptor, reflective or pragmatic, etc. Once we recognise that learning style is not synonymous with the one simple, heavily promoted construct of VAK, the business of basing pedagogy on learning styles in their more multifarious forms becomes much more complex. Should educators define each learner across a range of style constructs and match tasks accordingly? Should teachers attempt to train learners not to use particular learning strategies or to need particular environmental preferences? Certainly a great deal of money has been made from the commercial application of style instruments in schools. Coffield *et al.* (2004) reviewed 71, concluding that most, including resources advocated by the DfES, were unreliable and of negligible pedagogical value. Teachers are probably better off providing varied pedagogy that reflects the host of ways in which learners interact with and process information rather than matching tasks to individuals that simply serve to reinforce the stereotypes assigned to them.

Metacognition

The knowledge society has generated a constantly expanding body of knowledge and ever more technological ways of accessing it. This requires people generally and learners in particular to develop more sophisticated ways of finding things out and greater confidence in filtering them for relevance and reliability. Claxton (2002) argues that learners need above all to learn to learn and that teachers' main focus should be teaching them how. This metacognitive approach, originated by Flavell (1979), has in some circles been dubbed 'learnacy', a product perhaps of the tendency to think that ideas are only accessible if they are reduced to sound bites or tabloid shorthand. This tendency is reinforced by some academics who infantilise teachers by creating gratuitous alliterative devices and metaphors to communicate their ideas as if they would not otherwise be understood. Thus Claxton talks about pupils needing to exercise their 'learning muscles' and to become 'resourceful, resilient, reflective learners', using these terms as organising vehicles for his arguments. This approach can lead to the publishing of polemic rather than detailed research accounts.

Research by Shayer and Adey (2002) have revealed that learning potential is increased if pupils are metacognitively aware, i.e. if they understand and control their own learning strategies. These strategies include techniques for remembering, ways of presenting information when thinking, approaches to problems and so on. They developed a system of cognitive acceleration in science education (CASE), which challenges pupils to examine the processes they use to solve problems (Adey 1992). In doing so it is argued that pupils are enhancing their thinking processes. A number of studies indicate learning gains as a consequence of metacognitive training. Namrouti and Alshannag's (2004) research in Jordan identified statistically significant differences in seventh grade students' achievement in science and the study of Black *et al.* (2002) in London, in which mathematics and science teachers were trained to use structured questioning and to encourage pupils to discuss their understanding of concepts, led to pupils of all abilities scoring higher in their national assessment tests or GCSEs than pupils in ordinary lessons.

Biggs' (1993) research has shown that successful learning, if defined in terms of understanding and permanence, is linked with deep and deep-achieving approaches to learning. It may be possible to foster these through metacognitive training that encourages learners to recognise surface or achievement-orientated approaches to learning. Differences in learning approaches between cultural groups can be a function of environmental and cultural factors. The achievement-driven context within which school and college students in England, the US, Japan and other 'developed' nations currently learn can militate against the possibility of teaching deep approaches which require reflection and plenty of time.

Brain functioning

Research into how the brain functions has enhanced our understanding of mental processes but research in this area is not well advanced in the sense that there remains a great deal we do not know. Neuroscientists revealed many years ago that the gaps between neurones (synapses) are traversed and new connections made when thinking and talking occurs. This means that challenging thinking opportunities will enable learners to 'grow' their brains by making new, strong connections. It is thought that meaningful learning will create longer term connections that can be refreshed even after long periods of disuse whereas rote learning is likely to lead to weak, temporary connections. However, brain scans have suggested that different brain patterns are activated when recalling facts learned in these separate modes which may explain why some rote learning, for example of arithmetical tables, persists but why problem-solving strategies appear to be transferable to new problems only following meaningful learning.

Hemispheric specificity, which indicates that the left side of the brain deals more with language and logic and the right side with spatial and visual awareness and emotion and creativity, is also well documented. Some attempts have been made to use brain function research to explain specific learning disorders such as dyslexia, a reading disorder thought to derive from sensory-perceptual processing delays which impede the brain's phonological representation. Controversy persists about its definition (Elliott 2005), prevalence and cause but explaining the condition using 'brain science' has reduced the stigma attached to it.

It was thought that certain parts of the brain were associated with the various processes of perception, attention, remembering, retrieval and language comprehension. This conflicted with the ideas of developmental psychologists and information-processing theorists who argue that mental processes are domain-general not domain-specific. More recently, however, doubts about this modularity or localisation of brain functioning have been expressed (Fodor 2000). Great popular interest in how the brain works, particularly in relation to consciousness, was created by the televising of Susan Greenfield's book *Brain Story* (Greenfield 2000). Greenfield cast doubt on the modularity theory, suggesting instead 'neuronal assemblies' in which millions of brain cells compete to create elements of consciousness, but provided limited evidence for this theory. Thus, psychologists are still trying to determine how subjective thought is derived from brain matter. Meanwhile the most persuasive bits of neuroscientific theory are culled for application in training teachers in the use of accelerated learning and other approaches to pedagogy. Novelty claims that are well known but not well substantiated by research include the beneficial effects of listening to music while learning, sipping water to 'hydrate the brain' and using neuro-linguistic programming to reveal how the brain codes experience in order to improve communication.

Brain gym, another popular brain improvement tool, is a set of exercises designed to improve concentration, reading ability and hand–eye coordination. These ideas were developed by the American Paul Dennison in the late 1960s who, as a dyslexic, was interested in the connection between physical activity and learning ability. More recently UK researchers have found that using simple movements improves learning. Exercise sessions usually last for a few minutes and are often used at the beginning of lessons to focus pupils' attention. They are sometimes related to the work that is being taught, for example letter sounds, arithmetical functions or handwriting; they may be used to break up passive learning or to refresh pupils, particularly those with attention difficulties. It is suggested that brain gym can help children become calm, alert and ready to concentrate by stimulating neurological pathways so that both sides of the brain work together. Mind mapping is a strategy copyrighted by Tony Buzan to facilitate this dual hemispheric functioning, which in turn enhances problem-solving, the generation of creative ideas and the organisation of thoughts. It has been suggested that stress causes people to overuse the right side of the brain leading to emotions obscuring understanding so attempts to balance this would be considered effective pedagogical strategy. Studies authenticating long-term benefits, however, are not easy to find.

Related to this is the construct of *emotional intelligence* (Salovey and Mayer 1990; Goleman 1995), which has received a good deal of attention within both management and education studies. Teachers have long known that emotional state can impact on educational performance. The brain science explanation (OECD 2005) is that the amygdala, part of the limbic system that controls and processes emotional experience and behaviour, takes over when someone is frightened or stressed (this is the well-known fight or flight mechanism that ensures survival). The amygdala also controls the routing of information to the cortex, where it is stored as long-term memory; if a learner is frightened, perhaps of failure or reprisals, this transfer stops and long-term learning is prevented. Goleman's popular work related the ability to control impulses, motivate oneself, and regulate moods to improved thinking and learning and to better self and people management. Subjecting emotional intelligence to research is problematic, however, because it is not easy to isolate such a nebulous variable within a research context. Ecclestone (2004) criticises the elevation of emotions within education, arguing that it detracts from risk-taking and pointing to a lack of systematic research evidence to support claims made about the damaging effects of poor emotional literacy.

Multiple intelligences

Educators and psychologists continue to hotly debate whether a single intelligence can be identified or whether intellectual power is better characterised as multiple intelligences. The most popularised theorist in this area is the American Howard Gardner (1983; 1993), who postulates that eight distinct intelligences exist independently of one another: linguistic, spatial, logical-mathematical, musical, bodily-kinaesthetic, interpersonal, intrapersonal and naturalist. Gardner contends that individuals have different entry points to learning depending on the strength of their various intelligences. Robert Sternberg, also working in the US, developed a multiple model of intelligence that describes intelligence in relation to its cognitive components. Sternberg's (1985) triarchic model comprises three major aspects that interact with one another: analytical, creative and practical thinking. Analytical or *componential* intelligence is what is normally measured on IQ and achievement tests – planning, organising and remembering facts then applying them to new situations. Creative or *experiential* intelligence is the ability to see new connections between things and to develop original ideas. Practical or *contextual* intelligence is the ability to read situations and people and manipulate them to best advantage. Neither experiential nor practical intelligence is measured in IQ tests according to Sternberg.

Clearly these models are significantly different from one another and although developed around the same time, fewer educators have heard of Sternberg's model than Gardner's. It is interesting to consider why this is the case. It is easy to see how Gardner's model could gain currency at a common-sense level since people often display particular talents or tendencies. Indeed the school curriculum and Hirst's (1975) forms of knowledge use similar categorisations. However, if one sees cognition as the processing of information using fairly universal sets of mental strategies it is difficult to conceive of separate, discrete intelligences. Sternberg (1999) points out that although Gardner cites evidence to support his theory he has not carried out research directly to test his model. Gardner's work has become popular in educational circles across the world, possibly because it offers an alternative to the unitary view of intelligence which suggests a ceiling on ability, encouraging instead a focus on developing particular individual capabilities to their highest potential. White (1998) has critiqued Gardner's theory in detail, questioning the criteria on which the designation of an intelligence is based and pointing out that much intelligent behaviour can often rely on more than one of Gardner's intelligences at once. His critique does not seem to have registered with educators as reliance on Gardner's problematic explanation of intelligence persists in schools in many countries.

Personalised learning

Each of the areas we have looked at are embraced within the current trend for 'personalised learning' (Leadbetter 2004) which has its pedagogical and political roots in the 1990s vogue for differentiated learning, 'a shorthand for all the methods which teachers try to use within the classroom to enable each pupil to achieve intended learning targets' (Weston 1996). The pedagogical discourse of the 1990s established 'differentiation' as a seminal term; just as inspectors currently look for evidence of teachers' personalising learning, no inspection report was complete without a reference to it and it was the key focus for professional development.

The Labour Government's 2001 description of individualised learning resonates both with definitions of differentiation and with the current preoccupation with personalised learning.

It is becoming possible for each child to be educated in a way and at a pace which suits them, recognising that each is different, with different abilities, interests and needs (DfES 2001: 20).

The 2001 White Paper described a range of ways in which pedagogical diversity was to be pursued. These included the use of different types of adults in classrooms, for example classroom assistants and learning mentors, investment in ICT equipment, online curriculum materials 'catering for children of all abilities' (2001: 5) and the facility for the most able pupils to progress at a faster pace. These workforce-remodelling initiatives have since been implemented and there is now much more emphasis in schools and colleges worldwide on developing the learning technologies and software to support personalised learning. Sophisticated hypermedia systems can identify learners' interests, preferences and needs, and adapt the content of pages and the links between them to the needs of that user (Triantafillou et al. 2004). Social constructivist research has repeatedly demonstrated the necessity, however, for group interaction in consolidating learning and extending thinking. Vygotsky (1978) described a 'zone of proximal development' – the gap between a pupil's current level of learning and the level s/he could be functioning at given the appropriate learning experience and adult or peer support. Research using the ideas of psychologists such as Vygotsky (1978) has testified to the learning gains which can be made when talking is facilitated amongst pupils working in pairs and groups (Bartlett et al. 2001) and when adults intervene to challenge and scaffold the talk. Many teachers are familiar with these key ideas but Kutnick et al. (2002) caution that they may not think strategically about the size and composition of groups in relation to the tasks assigned, calling for educationalists to pay attention to the social pedagogy of pupil grouping.

Personalised learning was further promoted in the subsequent White Paper (DfES 2005) with an explicit call for setting pupils. Yet research provides no clear evidence that setting creates greater learning gains for pupils. In 1997 Boaler's review of research into setting revealed that whilst there was a small advantage for the most able pupils if they were set, the losses for the less able when set were great. Their attainment was significantly lower than the attainment of the less able who were in mixed-ability groups. Boaler's own three-year study compared the

GCSE mathematics results of 310 pupils in two schools, one of which set the pupils whilst the other taught pupils in mixed-ability groups. She found that results were significantly better amongst the latter group even though test results from Year 7 indicated the pupils were of similar ability. Research has revealed that attempting to match tasks to learners' abilities may be less effective than providing differentiated, individualised teacher support to pupils working on the same task (see Burton 2003 for a review). The key determinant is the extent to which the teacher has a detailed knowledge of each learner's progress, strengths and challenges in a particular learning context. Given the time to target individuals who are engaged in common tasks, teachers can facilitate a greater match between learners' needs and their instruction, which in turn can lead to greater cognitive gains. So, whether we call it personalised learning, differentiation or a learner-centred approach, the issue is not one that can be simply dealt with by Governmental injunctions to setting, since in both set and mixed-ability groups the individualised nature of pupil learning and teacher response is paramount.

Conclusion

In recent years psychological research has facilitated new understandings amongst educators about how people learn, from which pedagogical implications have been derived. The varying influence of these theories is linked to shifts within both policy imperatives and pedagogical 'trends' and the extent to which these are championed and globalised within the ever more sophisticated education media sector. Psychological research continues to develop and refine theoretical ideas about learning. Students of education will enjoy a fascinating perspective on them as long as a critical, enquiring approach is taken to their theoretical or empirical basis and their political provenance.

References

Adey, P. (1992) The CASE results: implications for science teaching, *International Journal of Science Education* 14: 137–146.

Bartlett, S., Burton, D. and Peim, N. (2001) *Introduction to Education Studies*. London: PCP.

Biggs, J.B. (1993) What do inventories of students' learning processes really measure? A theoretical review and clarification, *British Journal of Educational Psychology* 63: 3–19.

Black, P., Harrison, C., Lee, C., Marshall, B. and William, D. (2002) *Working inside the Black Box: Assessment for Learning in the Classroom*. London: King's College, University of London.

Boaler, J. (1997) Setting, social class and survival of the quickest, *British Educational Research Journal* 23: 575–595.

Burton, D. (2003) Differentiation of schooling and pedagogy, in S. Bartlett and D. Burton (eds) *Education Studies: Essential Themes and Issues*. London: Sage.

Burton, D. (2005) Ways pupils learn, in S. Capel, M. Leask and A. Turner (eds) *Learning to Teach*, 4th edn. London: Routledge.

Claxton, G. (2002) *Building Learning Power: Helping Young People Become Better Learners*. Bristol: TLO.

Coffield, F., Moseley, D., Hall, E. and Ecclestone, K. (2004) *Learning Styles: A Systematic and Critical Review*. London: Learning and Skills Development Agency.

Curry, L. (1983) An organisation of learning style theory and constructs, in L. Curry (ed.) *Learning Style in Continuing Education*. Halifax, Canada: Dalhousie University.

Department for Education and Skills (DfES) (2001) *Schools Achieving Success*. Nottingham: DfES Publications.

Department for Education and Skills (DfES) (2005) *Higher Standards, Better Schools for All*. Nottingham: DfES Publications.

Ecclestone, K. (2004) Learning or therapy? The demoralisation of education, *British Journal of Educational Studies* 57(3): 127–141.

Elliott, J. (2005) Dyslexia myths and the feel-bad factor, *Times Educational Supplement* 2 February.

Flavell, J.H. (1979) Metacognition and cognitive monitoring, *American Psychologist* 34: 906–11.

Fodor (2000) *The Mind Doesn't Work That Way: The Scope and Limits of Computational Psychology* Cambridge. MA: MIT Press.

Gardner, H. (1983) *Frames of Mind: The Theory of Multiple Intelligences*. New York: Basic Books.

Gardner, H. (1993) *Multiple Intelligences: The Theory in Practice*. New York: Basic Books.

Goleman, D. (1995) *Emotional Intelligence*. New York: Bantam.

Greenfield, S. (2000) *Brain Story*. London: BBC Worldwide.

Harris, A. and Ranson, S. (2005) The contradictions of education policy: disadvantage and achievement, *British Educational Research Journal* 31(5): 571–588.

Hirst, P.H. (1975) *Knowledge and the Curriculum*. London: Routledge and Kegan Paul.

Kutnick, P., Blatchford, P. and Baines, E. (2002) Pupil groupings in primary school classrooms: sites for learning and social pedagogy?, *British Educational Research Journal* 28(2): 87–206.

Leadbetter, C. (2004) *Personalisation through Participation: A New Script for Public Services*. London: DEMOS/DFES Innovations Unit.

Miliband, D. (2004) Child and voice in personalised learning. Paper presented to DfES/DEMOS/OECD Conference 18 May.

Namrouti, A. and Alshannag, Q. (2004) Effect of using a metacognitive teaching strategy on seventh grade students' achievement in science, *Dirasat* 31(1): 1–13.

Organisation for Economic Cooperation and Development (OECD) (2005) *Learning Sciences and Brain Research Project*. http://www.oecd.org/department/0,2688,en_2649_14935397_1_1_1_1_1,00.html (accessed 4 April 2006).

Riding, R.J. and Cheema, I. (1991) Cognitive styles – an overview and integration, *Educational Psychology* 11: 193–215.

Riding, R.J. and Rayner, S. (1998) *Cognitive Styles and Learning Strategies.* London: David Fulton.

Salovey, P. and Mayer, J.D. (1990) Emotional intelligence, *Imagination, Cognition, and Personality* 9: 185–211.

Shayer, M. and Adey, P. (eds) (2002) *Learning Intelligence: Cognitive Acceleration across the Curriculum from 5 to 15 years.* Buckingham: Open University Press.

Smith, A. (1996) *Accelerated Learning in the Classroom.* London: Network Educational Press.

Smith, A. and Call, N. (2002) *The ALPS Approach.* London: ALITE.

Sternberg, R.J. (1985) *Beyond IQ: A Triarchic Theory of Human Intelligence.* New York: Cambridge University Press.

Sternberg, R.J. (1999) Intelligence, in R.A. Wilson and F.C. Keil (eds) *The MIT Encyclopedia of the Cognitive Sciences.* Cambridge, MA: MIT Press.

Triantafillou, E., Pomportsis, A., Demetriadis, S. and Georgiadou, E. (2004) The value of adaptivity based on cognitive style: an empirical study, *British Journal of Educational Technology,* 35(1): 95–106.

Vygotsky, L.S. (1978) *Mind in Society: The Development of Higher Psychological Processes.* London: Harvard University Press.

Weston, P. (1996) *Learning about Differentiation in Practice,* Topic 16, no. 4. London: NFER.

White, J. (1998) *Perspectives on Education Policy: Do Howard Gardner's Multiple Intelligences Add Up?* London: Institute of Education.

Witkin, H.A. (1978) *Cognitive Styles in Personal and Cultural Adaptation.* Heines Werner Lecture Series, Volume 11. Worcester, MA: Clark University Press.

Wyse, D. (2003) The National Literacy Strategy: a critical review of empirical evidence, *British Educational Research Journal* 29(6): 903–916.

5

MICHAEL NEWMAN
When evidence is not enough:
freedom to choose versus
prescribed choice: the case
of Summerhill School

Introduction

The New Labour Government in England has indicated that the school system needs to develop towards one that allows for greater diversity and choice in respect of school type and provision in order to raise educational standards. This movement manifests itself through the development of a range of schools such as city academies, specialist schools, school trusts and faith schools. There is also a growing impact of a diverse range of providers of education, including private and corporate sponsors, some of whom appear to have no previous direct link to educational developments. Choice and diversity, within a framework of public accountability through auditing by inspection and examination tables, have become ciphers for improvement and academic achievement. (See Hill and MacDonald in this volume for a fuller discussion of these developments.) Given the strong political commitment to choice and diversity in education it can be seen as ironic that when one school – Summerhill – manifests and represents these qualities through an alternative approach to schooling it was these very values that were the source of its potential closure as a result of an Ofsted inspection in 1999. This chapter provides a personal account of the inspection processes and the political and educational ramifications following the publication of the inspection reports. This chapter is about a government attempt to impose on a school, A.S. Neill's Summerhill, founded on democracy and children's rights, its own values of public accountability, and in doing so threaten to close it down. The 1999 Ofsted inspection of Summerhill led to a court case in 2000 through which the school fought for its existence against an array of witnesses, including the Chief Registrar for Independent Schools in England and Wales (DfEE), Michael Phipps, Ofsted's inspector responsible for independent schools, Neville Grenyer, and Professor John McBeath, an expert and promoter of school self-evaluation.

Summerhill

Summerhill is a small boarding school on the outskirts of Leiston, Suffolk, situated in approximately 12 acres of land including woods and fields. Summerhill was founded in 1921 by the ex-teacher and education writer A.S.Neill. It was his response to the barbaric and senseless state school system of corporal punishment and payment by results that not only brutalised the children, but failed the peasant farm labourer pupils whom he taught in Gretna Green, Scotland, in the early 1900s (as told in his first book, *A Dominie's Log* (1915). It has up to 90 students aged from 6 to 17, most of who live on site, along with the staff, some eleven teachers and four houseparents. The students are mainly from abroad, including Japan, Germany, Taiwan, Korea, France, Switzerland and America, sometimes starting the school with very little English. (See the *Brief History of Summerhill* (www.summerhillschool.co.uk) and Neill (1968) for more detail.) The school lives as a democratic community, holding three meetings a week, chaired by elected students, which create the laws of the school and make decisions about its justice. Everyone has a vote, people put up their hands to speak, and all decisions are made by majority vote. The meeting can vote to get rid of any or all of its laws, except those that are required by British law, or even to get rid of itself. Staff and students are equals in the meeting. The children are woken in the mornings by elected 'beddies officers', who also ensure they are in bed at night. The bedtime laws and structures are created by the community. During the day the students can choose to go to lessons, or not. If they are older than 12 they will have a personalised timetable created for them at the beginning of term, depending on what they want to study, but they can freely choose to attend the lessons or not.

This control over their own learning, manifested in the right to choose whether to attend lessons or not, was one of the main factors that Her Majesty's Inspectors decided in 1999 should be changed or the school closed (Stronach 2006). They believed it denied the right of the child to a broad and balanced curriculum, the National Curriculum.

Summerhill is a school based on the concept that emotional learning is necessary to create a foundation that permits academic learning to be transformed into self-managed learning. It is a school in which the students define their own objectives for their school life. They can choose to learn to read and write, to study academic subjects and to gain GCSEs. Yet their choice is framed within a living community in which they create their own laws, run their own justice system, and decide what to do during the day. This was Neill's vision:

And we must be optimists in our planning; we must be broad and big, striving to see the deep things in education, and not being limited in our vision to classrooms and textbooks. Education is much wider than school subjects. Our plans must be founded on the fact that the emotion is of greater moment than the intellect, that the unconscious of the child is infinitely greater than his conscious. It is concerned with turning out professors and mechanics, but it does not ask how schools are to make people happier, more sincere, less neurotic, less prejudiced. A university graduate can be an emotional wreck: a skilled mechanic can be a dangerous sadist, and unless our planning for education is to aim at producing balanced individuals rather than educated men, education will continue to be merely a matter of heads and not hearts.

(1944: 7–8)

A.S. Neill and Summerhill have been acknowledged as major influences on education throughout the world. UNESCO lists Neill as one of the world's 100 most important educationalists. *The Times Education Supplement* put him as one of the twelve most important for the UK in the last millennium. Summerhill has been recognised as at the forefront of children's rights and progressive education; it is even used as an example of the use of the word democratic in the *Oxford Shorter Concise English Dictionary Volume 1*. Amity Shlaes (2000) in the *Financial Times* wrote: 'As Diane Ravitch (2000), the academic and former Assistant Secretary of Education, points out in *Left Back: A Century of Failed School Reforms, a History of Progressive Education*, "America is now a nation of Summerhills".'

Democratic schooling

Summerhill was founded as a democratic school. Aspin (1995) describes the principles of democratic schooling as:

- Policies and actions based on decisions and not arbitrary nor autocratic acts of will.
- Decisions will be arrived at by rational discourse and on the grounds of the objective and convincing character of arguments advanced to support them.
- Universally extended suffrage, full powers made available to all, subject to limitations of age.
- All act freely without being subject to duress.
- Majority will prevails.
- Minority rights are preserved, respected and allowed full and proper hearing and given due consideration.
- Regular periodic review of policies and practices.
- Reversibility shall obtain.
- All are guaranteed rights of access, equity and participation.
- Those responsible for the implementation of policies are accountable to all.
- All count equally.
- There are checks and balances built in to the institutional systems.
- Arrangements are operative rather than rhetorical.
- Social justice obtains (1995: 33–34).

The procedures and principles of a democratic institution include:

- equality
- freedom
- tolerance

- consideration of other people's interests
- respect for other people (1995: 35).

Summerhill maintains its founding principles as a democratic school because of:

- students having a majority say in the running of the school
- no authority figures
- optional attendance
- adult imposed discipline and punishment replaced by community democracy
- emphasis on play
- letting children develop and follow their own interests
- nothing being compulsory (1995: 46).

Inspecting Summerhill

The issues of accountability and open government have been allied to methods of evaluation, and the use of measured outcomes not just as an input into management decisions but through their public openness to inform the choice of the relevant consumers. These arguments for target-based management and market choice are being used equally in the health service and in education (see Hill, this volume, for a further discussion of this issue).

The use of SATS, GCSEs and league tables allows parents, the customers but not the consumers, to create a view of a school's success, and thus to enable them to make an informed choice. With schools seeking match funding to become specialist schools in business, performing arts, arts, humanities, languages, science, there is a sense of greater publicly defined diversity between our schools and therefore greater choice.

Summerhill was failed in a 1999 Ofsted report despite its above average examination achievements and the unusually high, nearly 100%, satisfaction of its students and parents. It had been the most prepared it had ever been for an inspection, with policy statements, an ongoing action plan, a peer teacher review system, handbooks for staff, parents and children, an evidence base showing activities outside lessons, and interviews with student leavers and ex-students.

It had had a successful registration inspection the previous year, and the team leader was one of the previous registration inspectors. As part of the school's attempts to improve the inspection process it had suggested different forms of evidence that it could provide and had requested that there be continuity between inspections, as was the process of its successful social services inspections. A social service's inspection within a few weeks of the Ofsted inspection expressed no concerns with the school.

Ofsted inspects private schools to ensure they are fulfilling the minimum requirements for their continued registration as schools. If they lose this registration they close. As well as reporting inspections that allow the public access to a published school evaluation, they carry out registration inspections whose outcomes are a private report to the DfES, a school profile document and a confidential letter to the school principal summarising the findings and giving recommendations for changes.

For ten years, up until its court case in March 2000, Summerhill was inspected nearly every year, despite the fact that during the court case Michael Phipps asserted that the school had been subject to a 'routine inspection regime' (Stronach 2006).

The question is not why the school was threatened in 1999 but why it had taken so long. The school was seen to be one in need of frequent inspections since the creation of the National Curriculum in the 1989 Education Reform Act, and the implementation of inspections based on the new national standards. In fact it came out during the court case, to the consternation of one of the judges, that the school had been designated TBW ('to be watched'), as early as 1990, a status that led to near-yearly inspections. This status was kept secret despite repeated attempts by parents and staff, who complained about the effect of institutional bullying felt by the school through the frequent inspections, to find out why.

When asked why the inspection was such a contrast to the one in 1949, when the inspectors had advised all educationalists to visit Summerhill to learn from it (Neill 1968), the inspection team leader simply cited the National Curriculum. Nearly all the inspections since 1990 expressed concern at the right of students to choose to attend lessons. It was felt that they were receiving a narrow and fragmented curriculum. The attitude of the inspectors was hostile, reducing a teacher to tears, inspectors stood up from their chairs in defiance when their values were challenged, dismissing opportunities and requests to inspect the school according to its own values. This was reflected in the language of Summerhill's 1999 Ofsted report. The school strongly pointed out to Ofsted that the way the press had represented reports in the past required the careful and precise use of language for the school to be treated fairly. The published report included the phrases: 'foul-mouthed', 'to mistake the pursuit of idleness for the exercise of personal freedom', 'an abrogation of educational responsibility', 'the school has drifted into confusing educational freedom with the negative right not to be taught'.

As was stated earlier the main locus of the tension between the school's philosophy and the inspection regime was around the non-attendance at lessons. This exchange during the court case whereby the school challenged the notice of closure is illustrative of the importance of this issue:

Question (Rt Hon Geoffery Robertson QC) But nonetheless, none of these reports 1990 1991, or 1992 are indicative of a school that is failing. It is indicative of a thriving community and a continuing concern by inspectors about the policy of non-attendance at lessons?
Answer (Michael Phipps) That is correct.
(Court transcript, Independent Schools Tribunal Case No. Ist/59,
Zoe Redhead and the Secretary of State for Education
and Employment (2000) Tuesday 21 March, p. 36)

After the 1997 registration inspection Summerhill received the confidential DfEE letter to the principal stating the need for change on seven key issues. These included raising overall standards of achievement, especially in literacy and numeracy for the younger children, teachers' lesson planning to take into account individual needs and stages of learning, consistent procedures for record-keeping and report-writing ... The school responded with a three-year action plan that included the creation of the school's first ever policy statements – general policy, literacy and numeracy policies, and a policy on assessment and record-keeping. These were all written with the aim of stating and defending the aims and values of the school. They were written with the assistance of external advisers including local Ofsted inspectors and with the participation of the students.

The following inspection in 1998 was positive, acknowledging the success of the action plan, that teaching was satisfactory or above, with positive student responses. As stated in the court case:

> **Question (Rt Hon Geoffery Robertson QC)** Overall, the result of this June 1998 visit is that the statute was being complied with, that Summerhill School in June 1998, after eight inspections throughout the last eight/nine years, is providing suitable and efficient instruction. Correct?
> **Answer (Michael Phipps)** That is correct.
> **Question (Rt Hon Geoffery Robertson QC)** Why then is this school subject to a full reporting inspection with all the problems of press publicity and the like only eight months later?'
> **Answer (Michael Phipps)** [précised from a longer response] Correspondence from the school following the June 1998 visit threw doubts on its commitment to implement the 1997 action plan.
>
> (Court transcript (2000), Tuesday 21 March, p. 68)

The Summerhill 1999 inspection was conducted by highly qualified, experienced and senior inspectors. This was not an error-ridden inspection and report by stumbling beginners. Its quality reflected on the very reputation of the closest colleagues of the then Chief Inspector, Chris Woodhead. Its content displayed the philosophy and values of Ofsted. Ofsted stood by the accuracy of the inspection grades (Stronach 2006). The 1999 inspection led to a 'Notice of Complaint', a legal document that required the school to make six changes, three of which it agreed to, and three which it refused to implement. The three it refused to agree to were ensuring children were at lessons or undertaking private study; assessing children throughout their school life; and organising separate toilets for staff, children, male and female. Ofsted wanted Summerhill to have compulsory lessons, as written in their recommendation for the Notice. The Notice of Complaint had been redrafted by the DfEE to include the option of private study, as they thought this would be seen not to threaten the school's philosophy of voluntary lesson attendance.

In order to refuse to implement the Notice of Complaint the school had to appeal to an Independent Schools Tribunal, heard by three judges at the Royal Courts of Justice, and with QCs for both the school and the DfES, and with witnesses, including experts, on both sides. This allowed the school's legal team access to all the documents produced by Ofsted during its inspections of the school. Contesting the case cost Summerhill over £120,000 (not including the support of the research of the expert witness for Summerhill, Professor Ian Stronach, who was supported by the Nuffield Foundation and Manchester Metropolitan University). Few schools could afford such a case, raising issues of social justice and fairness (Hansard 2002). After three days, with the DfEE accepting an agreement written by the school and voted on in the courtroom by the children, the result was effectively a victory for the school, and genuine choice in education – choice created by freeing auditing from the framework of national standards defining a broad and balanced curriculum through the National Curriculum, and education as being solely teacher delivered.

Values and measurement

Evaluation is often portrayed as if it is equivalent to measurement and decisions about ease, accuracy and interpretability are seen as key to its use. This means thinking not only about what is measured and how but also how it affects the values and meaning of what is being measured. This was one of the key debates within Summerhill in response to the repeated inspections and the requirement to write school policies and a three-year action plan.

The process by which we at the school decide what we are to measure, how and why, is not simply a matter of choosing from an array of neutral tools. There are three main problems that can arise from evaluation.

We can unknowingly redefine the original objectives and values of our actions by narrowly basing them on measurable outcomes. We can give our evaluations unwarranted authority because they are expressed in numbers, in a format that appears objective, and where the underlying assumptions can be well concealed hindering scrutiny and discussion of their meaning and reliability. Most problematically if the evaluation methods become embedded in the structure, processes and values of the institutions being reviewed then they can redefine or corrupt the organisation's values and especially its members' sense of what is important and why things are done.

In debates about the influence of evaluation there are references to the need for a balancing act between the measurable and the immeasurable, and that this balance may not have yet been achieved. This defence does not address the issue of how evaluation effects the values, framework and meaning of education. Indeed, this is a superficial avoidance of the debate.

An Ofsted inspector and adviser to the European Council on democratic education, who resigned publicly over the Summerhill case, angrily asked the then Minister for Children, Margaret Hodge, why English schools, in a culture of assessment, fail so many of our children. She answered that on the back of her office door was a graph with two lines showing the gap between the health and achievements of the haves and have-nots. Her motive in education was to close the gap (spoken answer at Children's Rights Alliance for England, Annual Conference 24 November 2003).

In order to achieve a more universal application of social justice it is necessary to promote the culture of institutional education as a doorway out of poverty. The assessment culture can be used as a tool for focusing on underachievement. In promoting schemes, projects and systems that contribute to the 'value added', encouraging the acceptance of examinations as necessary and valuable objectives and evidence of achievement needed to access higher income jobs, success being linked to staying on as long as possible in institutional education, government can thereby use free market opportunity to break the cycles of poverty. Child-centred education that rejects the values of examinations is seen as the enemy of achieving social justice and equity in our society.

Nature of evidence

Peters (1981) dismissed Summerhill because its founder uses anecdote to describe the school and did not use records as evidence that Summerhill works. Peters wrote that:

> A.S. Neill is actually very guarded in his claims for the long-term effects of Summerhill on its inmates. And what he does claim is based on selective impressions. He had conducted no surveys ... and, I suspect would be absolutely unconvinced by negative evidence of this mundane sort.
>
> (1981: 116–7)

For Summerhill the nature of evidence of whether it works or not and what it does has always been problematic. In its defence Summerhill had to look at demonstrating how it works to inspectors and finally in the courtroom to the Tribunal.

The evidence discussed by the staff included student leaver interviews, ex-student questionnaires, research projects by external professionals (Stronach 2002a; 2002b; 2006), a comparison of achievement to base-line assessments, portfolios of work, individual tracking of students, independent learning computer assessments, literacy assessments, termly reports to cover all lessons and possibly out-of-lesson activities. As a result of the impending court case two independent inspections were conducted and reports published, one funded by Nuffield and led by Professor Ian Stronnach with a team of five researchers, the other led by Professor Ian Cunningham with a team including three Ofsted inspectors, two senior managers of large independent schools, a psychologist, and the educationalist and writer Michael Rosen.

The relationship between collecting the evidence and the values of education of the school were discussed. At Summerhill informal learning is dependent upon being defined by the student, dependent on their relationship with their world, their lives. This would be changed through imposed assessment and reporting.

Within the staff it was argued that to report only on academic achievement, to collect evidence on lessons, might be seen to give this priority over informal learning. A written report or assessment could be perceived as somehow to give status to the activity being written about. In Ofsted inspections written documents appear to be treated, alongside direct inspector observations, as high-status evidence. Without Summerhill recording the non-academic it could be a feature of the school invisible to the inspectors.

Despite the provision of evidence, as listed above, and numerous invitations to out-of-lesson activities, the team of eight inspectors over three days in 1999 attended and reported on only one activity apart from a community meeting. During the feedback they apologised for the lack of inspection of this area of the school. Subsequently, in their evidence to the court, their response to the school complaint and to the Independent Adjudicator, they claimed to have done their utmost to inspect all aspects of the school. They belatedly realised that to inspect Summerhill according to its own values required the inspection of the space outside the classroom.

The difference between formal and informal learning, the boundary between classroom and outside the classroom, became a focus of debate at Summerhill. The final, published policy documents define this boundary as a part of the value of the school, as the following extracts from school policy statements indicate:

1. To provide choices and opportunities that allow children to develop at their own pace and to follow their own interests.
2. To allow children to be free from compulsory or imposed assessment, allowing them to develop their own goals and sense of achievement.

(Summerhill School General Policy Statement 1998)

The policy divides the child's space into 'the classroom' and 'outside the classroom' as Summerhill philosophy relies upon the 'classroom wall' as a boundary defining choice.

(Summerhill Policy on Assessment, Record-keeping and Report Writing,
4 June 1998 (later amended))

Within the classroom, assessment is seen as a necessary part of teaching. Formal testing needs the consent of the child, but by attending lessons the student has agreed to the values of formal teaching and evaluation as a tool to assist their learning. The small size of the teaching groups, and the school itself, means a high level of familiarity of the staff with their students' attitudes, skills, knowledge and understanding. Most of the assessments are therefore practical and spoken, with no normal need to record them. This left little evidence for the inspectors. Tests, mock examinations, corrected and marked work, summarised termly reports, and class registers provide 'evidence'. This is dependent on classroom attendance.

The outside-of-the-classroom, informal learning, was seen as in need of protection from the values of academic learning. A space to be protected from adult-defined objectives, adult assessments, adult manipulation into more productive learning experiences that can be recorded.

It was proposed that the act of assessing and recording could simply be done by the staff without the awareness of the students, and therefore without influencing the children's attitudes and perception of their lives in the school. This would lead to a necessary hypocrisy of values, a hidden agenda by the staff. This agenda would be further problematic because the skills, attitudes and knowledge assessed and recorded would be chosen and defined by the adults. The concept of children learning what they want, when and how they want, and defining their own success, defining who they want to be, would be their world, whilst the staff would be in a parallel world, observing, evaluating and recording according to their own list of objectives defining success. This was rejected by Summerhill staff.

As evidence for the inspectors the principal, with help from staff and students, agreed to create a list of all the activities that children could and have done. Event posters and a calendar were kept. A list of all the roles children could take was made, and each role broken down into its required skills, attitudes and knowledge – this is used for writing references for children on application to schools, colleges or employment, along with a statement about living in the school that describes the challenges, responsibilities and experiences.

Values and learning

Public assessments have moved from such beginnings as the IQ test, created to identify special needs children who would need extra help and then corrupted as a measure for comparing the whole population (Gould 1981), or examinations linked to discriminating for university education and to certify the capacity to do specific professional work, to become national levels of assessment (Standardised Assessment Tests) for set ages of children. Learning and teaching have become defined through the achievement of levels within a national curriculum. Learning as an act in response to personal inquisitiveness, as part of our developing humanity, has become lost in discussions about relevance, public rewards, punishments, value for money and expected outcomes. One of the consequences of a utilitarian approach to education which manifests itself in an 'outcomes approach' is that the learner's sense of self becomes shaped by the framework of learning, in England the National Curriculum and competitive examinations. Perception and understanding of the world, of oneself and each other is about an individual's relationship with language, classification, definitions and the normally inexplicitly examined concepts of evidence and knowledge.

Summerhill was and is an attempt to allow children to develop into human beings who would help to create a peaceful world, to help create citizens who had developed their own values through democratic community living, and whose autonomy would prevent them from blind obedience to authority. The following extract from the court transcript illustrates the problematic nature of this position:

> **Question (Rt Hon Geoffery Robertson QC)** Did you know by the way that when Rab Butler introduced the 1944 Act he said that the prime purpose of education was to fit the person for citizenship?
> **Answer (Michael Phipps)** I did know that, yes.
> **Question (Rt Hon Geoffery Robertson QC)** But insofar as the ministerial statement introducing the act which sets up the Independent Schools Tribunal, if indeed the prime purpose of education is fitting students for citizenship, then Summerhill passes with flying colours, does it not?
> **Answer (Michael Phipps)** If that were to be the proposition, then yes ...
>
> (Court transcript (2000), Tuesday 21 March, p. 70)

Outcomes of the inspection and court processes

After three days of examination of the civil servant Michael Phipps, the Registrar for Independent Schools, the DfES agreed to a statement drafted by the school. The Notice of Complaint was withdrawn, the DfES agreed to respect the philosophy and values of the school, and a new process of school inspection for Summerhill was created. The DfES agreed that the school would not be inspected within the next five years except for a review inspection to determine the implementation of the three parts of the Notice that had not been contested and that Summerhill had agreed to do from the start.

Much to the anger of the school, the DfES issued a press release stating Summerhill had conformed to its wishes. The release had three points that were contradicted by written evidence, and was therefore covered by the *Observer* and BBC Radio 4 as 'spin' becoming deceit. This even lead to the Rt Hon David Blunkett, the then Secretary of State for Education, responding with a defensive personal letter to the *Observer* which was countered by further letters and an *Observer* journalist (*Observer* 2 April 2000).

The school continued its fight, as the Ofsted report is still officially published. Staff and students lobbied the Chief Inspector of Schools twice a year at his regular cross-examinations (Select Committee in Education 2000–2001). MPs from all parties have addressed the issue, especially that of Ofsted accountability and school diversity (Hansard 2002). Summerhill has lobbied for the report to be withdrawn and for children in every school in England to have the same rights as Summerhill children (Education and Employment Committee 2000–2001). An official complaint was made to Ofsted and then to the Independent Adjudicator. The Adjudicator wrote a fourteen-page report that criticised Ofsted for failing to sufficiently take into account Summerhill's philosophy, for not acting clearly and openly, for not collecting enough evidence, for drawing conclusions that were not backed up by their written evidence, but stated in conclusion that they were acting correctly within their framework and therefore did not demand a withdrawal of the report. The report still stands and Summerhill has to wait for a new inspection and subsequent report being published before it will no longer face the prospect of being judged as a 'failing school' (Education and Skills Committee 2004).

The consequences of an inaccurate, public negative evaluation of Summerhill are significant. Two special educational needs (SEN) appeal tribunals refused to name Summerhill on a special needs statement for a child diagnosed with severe attention deficit hyperactivity disorder (ADHD). Both referred to the 1999 Ofsted report. When the parents' team referenced submitted evidence – a successful complaint to the Independent Adjudicator, a successful court appeal, and a successful last review inspection, the chair of the tribunal responded by indicating that the most recent published evidence was the 1999 report. In one tribunal the chair claimed Summerhill could not be democratic because of its Japanese students. In the final appeal, in which the school's expert witness was Mark Vaughan, an ex-Summerhill student and founder of the Centre for Inclusive Education Studies, which publishes the *Index on Inclusion*, it was reported by the county chief educational psychologist that the boy was no longer displaying

ADHD symptoms. It was pointed out that he had been at Summerhill for two years and that his behaviour at home and school had changed remarkably. The report of the appeal, written by the chair to justify their decision, comments that ADHD symptoms were no longer displayed because the child could do what he wanted at the school.

Summerhill's first review inspection after the court case was not only a very successful one, but was the first inspection in the country to have two observers on behalf of the school, an expert educationalist in the form of Professor Ian Stronach, and a representative of the school, an ex-student and ex-parent of Summerhill, Dane Goodsman, alongside an observer from the DfES, Professor Paul Hirst. These observers scrutinised the inspection process, advised the inspectors on what they were doing, and made verbal reports during the HMI feedback session. This was a legal requirement of the agreement that concluded our appeal in the Royal Courts of Justice. The inspectors also legally had to meet with the students to discuss their views of the school, something that the HMI team of the damning 1999 report inspection had been repeatedly invited to, but had refused. Summerhill was the first school in this country in which the students had a legal right to a formally organised meeting with the inspectors to present their views. A team of students at their own suggestion helped the inspectors by walking with notebooks in hand to record, by tally, where students were and what they were doing outside the classrooms, at regular intervals throughout the two days. At the inspection, when asked by a student what a broad and balanced curriculum meant, one of the HMI stated, 'the National Curriculum', but the DfES observer, Professor Hirst, stated he had never seen such a broad and balanced curriculum as he had seen at Summerhill. The issues of 'a broad and balanced curriculum', 'progress is monitored appropriately' and 'acceptable levels of achievement' are all 'an attack on the principles of the school'. Such common sense statements appear deceptively simple and unproblematic but they struck at the heart of Summerhill.

Conclusion

What this account of the inspection and reporting of Summerhill, and the subsequent challenge to the published outcomes of that process by the school, shows is that in a culture of public auditing, when the auditors fail to abide by their own rules there is no right of redress. Ofsted are required to assess the achievements of a school against the aims of the school. By using the National Curriculum as a universal standard for education, as the definition of a broad and balanced curriculum, it decided that one of the principles which underpins Summerhill's aims, namely the voluntary attendance at formal lessons, was a sign of the school's failure. The school failed to provide a broad and balanced education for its students. This definition of education, one repeatedly questioned by the appeal judges and independent researchers, led the inspection team to appear to ignore its own protocols, failing to inspect the school properly and defensively trying to save appearances. The values of the audit culture are revealed when it must measure the extreme examples of provision. Summerhill, founded as a democratic school, upholds the principles of a democratic education with some considerable vigour. Whilst the New Labour Government in England was implementing changes to the curriculum to introduce citizenship, participation and children expressing their voices, values that reflect and have been fought for by Summerhill, it was attempting to close Summerhill down. Summerhill held on to and continues to hold on to a principle of genuine choice. It appears that the choice which New Labour offers to learners and their parents is a prescribed, illusory choice – the opportunity to choose what is acceptable to the paternalistic State.

References

Aspin, D.N. (1995) The conception of democracy: a philosophy of democratic education, in J. Chapman, I. Froumin and D. Aspin (eds) *Creating and Managing the Democratic School*. London: Falmer Press, 30–59.

Education and Employment Committee (2000–2001) *Eighth Report*. http://www.parliament.the-stationeryoffice.co.uk/pa/cm200001/cmselect/cmeduemp/362/362ap10.htm.

Education and Skills Committee (2004) *Minutes of Evidence*. http://www.publications.parliament.uk/pa/cm200304/cmselect/cmeduski/426/4030812.htm.

Gould, S.J. (1981) *The Mismeasure of Man*. New York: W.W. Norton.

Hansard (2002) Thursday 4 July, Vol. 388, No. 171, 126WH, Paul Homes MP.

Neill, A.S. (1915) *A Dominies Log*. London: Herbert Jenkins.

Neill, A.S. (1944) *Hearts not Heads in the School*. London: Herbert Jenkins.

Neill, A.S. (1968) *Summerhill*. Harmondsworth: Penguin.

Peters, R.S. (1981) *Moral Development and Moral Education*. London: Unwin Education Books.

Ravitch, D. (2000) *Left Back: A Century of Failed School Reforms*. New York, Simon and Schuster

Shlaes, A. (2000) When progressiveness leads to backwardness, *Financial Times* 23 October. http://www.hooverdigest.org/011/shlaes.html (accessed March 31 2006).

Stronach, I. (2002a) *The OFSTED Response to Summerhill's Complaint: An Evidence-based Appraisal*. Manchester: Manchester Metropolitan University.

Stronach, I. (2002b) Progressivism versus the audit culture: the continuing story of Summerhill and the OFSTED Inspectors. Paper presented to the European Educational Research Association Annual Conference, September, Lisbon.

Stronach, I. (2006) Progressivism against the audit culture: the continuing case of Summerhill School versus Ofsted. http://www.mmu.ac.uk/research/esri (accessed 4 April 2006).

Section 2

Policy, politics and education

Section introduction

The formulation, ideological perspectives and impact of educational policies should not be underestimated in any discussion concerning issues relating to educational provision. As Dave Hill (this volume) points out, educational policy should be subjected to a range of questions. Hill categorises these questions into three main areas:

- aims
- context
- impact.

It is important, as a student or educational practitioner, to examine the reasons behind the development of a new policy as it is through questioning, on a range of levels, that a clearer idea of the overall intention of that policy emerges:

- For what reasons has the policy been created?
- What issue is it attempting to address?
- What are its intended outcomes?
- What is the policy's actual impact on *all* learners and educational institutions? (see Hill in this volume).

Ideological perspectives

In order to fully understand the direction of policy design it is crucial to gain a sense of the political ideologies that policy creators adhere to. Arguably the main ideologies relevant to the political scene in England and Wales today are: (a) social democracy; (b) neo-liberalism; and (c) neo-conservatism. A more detailed overview of these and other ideologies can be found in Fielding's (2001) book *Taking Education Really Seriously: Four Years' Hard Labour* in addition to the chapters within this section. But in (brief) summary they are:

Social democracy

Social democratic policies are characterised by aims of full employment, a strong welfare state and a progressive taxation policy that distributes resources downwards through high-quality, well-funded public services. In terms of education, social democratic policies manifest themselves through a comprehensive education system which allows access to all and has little or no selection by ability, and an expansion of education, for example widening participation within higher education. Additionally, there is a commitment to ensure equal opportunities, for all, regardless of race, sex or socio-economic status and a (largely) un-prescribed curriculum within schools which seeks to focus upon the individual needs of the child to enable them to take part in a functional 'meritocratic' society.

Neo-liberalism

Neo-liberalist policies promote the involvement of private enterprise within public services in terms of both finances and structures; effectively a marketised state. Further to this, neo-liberalist policies suggest that public services are best served by being opened up to general market forces, for example competition. In order to provide true competition, consumers (in the case of education, parents and children), need to be able to compare results through the publication of league tables and Ofsted reports. Furthermore, for those results to have any meaning education needs to be under a strict inspection regime so that results can be compared on a like for like basis. This results in strict controls over standards, teacher training and school performance. The publication of league tables necessitates frequent testing of pupils at various prescribed ages regardless of the individual child's readiness for any test. Neo-liberalist policies suggest choice and freedom in education and allow for a range of schools including academies and independent trust schools. However, the testing within schools, and the subsequent publication of those results, frequently mean that schools are less likely to offer a true alternative education (in much the same way that supermarkets are reluctant to differ greatly from each other) for fear of 'losing out' to the competition. For a more detailed discussion of neo-liberalist policies see Hill (2003).

Neo-conservatism

Neo-conservative policies share some key philosophies with those of the neo-liberalists in terms of high levels of control over schools and in fact go further by enforcing a prescribed curriculum (the National Curriculum) and pedagogy. The prescribed curriculum aims to ensure that neo-conservatives' desire for a 'moral' education are at the foreground of content including family values, respect for authority, heterosexual relationships and 'respect'. The prescribed pedagogy suggests a homogeneous group of pupils who will benefit from similar teaching methods, most notably teacher-centred approaches. The promotion of Britishness and assimilation in regards to issues of race, gender and class are given priority. In essence schools would be governed via strong State control.

The development and impact of policy

Robert Coe, in his chapter, discusses the lack of critical engagement in evidence which supports policy decisions. He bemoans the obviousness of research which indicates the characteristics of an 'effective teacher' and the continuing suggestion that policies to improve schools can be made at a national level. Coe suggests that school improvement needs to take account of local needs of communities and individual pupils and as such what works in one school may have little impact on another. He argues that as we have little real evidence as to what works within all schools then excessive control through policy is at best misguided and in many cases dangerous to educational achievement.

Arguably the true test of any policy, rather than its development, is in its implementation and the intended or unintended impact it has on any given group within society. For example, Michael Apple in his chapter demonstrates that policies which have led to an increase in home schooling are drawing on neo-conservative concerns about the secular nature of American education together with a sense that 'home schoolers' children need to be protected from 'the Other'. In this case 'the Other' are those class and race groups which are seen as a negative influence on the moral compass of the home schoolers. Apple goes further by demonstrating that home schoolers are able to, through loopholes, use public money to purchase overtly religious materials (forbidden in the state school system) to use in the education of their own children. Thus money which was intended to contribute to equality is being used in such a way as to ensure that racial and religious divisions in American society are strengthened and legitimated.

Dave Hill within his chapter provides a wide-ranging critical overview of New Labour's educational policies that demonstrate New Labour's 'class war from above'. Effectively, New Labour's policies have resulted in further and deeper divisions between the most affluent within society and those groups who have traditionally lost out in terms of educational progression and achievement. As Mike Baker (2006) points out, of the ten top schools in Essex (according to the *Good Schools Guide* 2006) eight are either fee-paying schools, selective stage grammar schools (control over admissions) or have complex admission require-ments. The two remaining schools are in affluent areas, and have significantly fewer children receiving free schools meals or with special educational needs than the national average.

Kate MacDonald in her chapter provides a detailed examination of how educational policy, through its development of competition and links to economic growth and reform, has consistently maintained inequalities within society. MacDonald argues that choice is available only to those who have the economic and social resources to benefit from it resulting in a situation whereby identifiable sections of society are left with no real choice within education. MacDonald argues that 'parentocracy' has ensured the retention of a historical pattern of elite schools, as within competition it is impossible to create winners without there also being losers.

Emmanuel Mufti in his chapter demonstrates that a move to widen access within higher education has resulted in a lack of awareness of the needs of students entering institutions. The policy, thus far, has not resulted in a reduction of the significant gap between those from the opposite ends of the socio-economic spectrum attending higher education. Furthermore, it has ensured that the quality of provision and support that students receive is restricted as increased numbers of students have not led to sufficient investment in modes of working and numbers of tutors. Mufti argues that traditional methods within higher education are no longer suitable if we are to ensure that true equality of access is to be achieved.

This section, 'Policy, politics and education', links closely to the previous section, 'Inside the school', as an understanding of the development and impact of policy is crucial in order to understand the day-to-day activities which take place within educational institutions. These inequalities, primarily based on socio-economic status, that exist within our educational system are not new issues. However, through the reading of the chapters one message becomes clear, recent educational policies have done little to challenge those inequalities and, for a variety of reasons, have often strengthened them.

References

Baker, M. (2006) How do you create a good school? BBC News/Education 28 January. http://news.bbc.co.uk/1/hi/education/4655378.stm.

Fielding, M. (ed.) (2001) *Taking Education Really Seriously: Four Years' Hard Labour*. London: Routledge.

Hill, D. (2003) Global neoliberalism, the deformation of education and resistance, *Journal for Critical Education Policy Studies* 1 1. http://www.jceps.com/index.php?pageID=articleandarticleID=7.

6

DAVE HILL
New Labour's education policy

Introduction

This chapter sets out a series of questions in Part One, to enable policy to be analysed. In Part Two, New Labour's 1997–2006 education policies are described and analysed with a particular focus on schooling and teacher education. These policies are compared with the Conservative education policies of 1979–1997. New Labour's policies are then analysed into six themes.

Part Three contains an evaluation of the impacts and ideologies of New Labour's education policies. They are a mix of traditional, social democratic and neo-conservative ideologies/policies. New Labour's social democracy is suffocated by the third ideology and its policies, the neo-liberal policies of marketising, competition, differentiation, pre-privatising and apparent 'choice' in education. New Labour's education policies are overwhelmingly neo-liberal.

Part One: Policy analysis

One way of analysing policy is to subject it to the following questions:

Aims:
1. What do its originators claim are the reasons for it?
2. What do they claim are its intended aims and what are its likely effects?
3. What do others (e.g. its opponents) say are the aims of the policy?
4. What do others (e.g. its opponents) say are the likely effects of the policy?

Context:
5. How does the policy relate to wider social trends, ideological developments and government policies – what is the wider context, nationally and internationally?

Impacts:
6. What are the consequences of the policy? Which societal groups (class/race/gender) actually benefit and who loses as a result of the policy?

7. Who resists the policy, why and how, and how successfully – in the short term (the policy proposal stage), medium term (the policy implementation stage) and the long term (the policy consolidation stage)?
8. What, if any, are the *unintended* consequences of the policy?

This chapter will address these questions in relation to New Labour's education policies.

Part Two: New Labour education policy 1997–2006

In this first part of this section New Labour's promises are *uncritically* set out followed by its claims of achievement.

New Labour promises in 1997

In 1997, the six 'promises' in the New Labour general election manifesto were:

- to cut class sizes to 30 for under for 5-, 6- and 7-year-olds
- to provide nursery places for all 4-year-olds
- to attack low standards in schools
- to provide access to computer technology
- to provide lifelong learning through a new University for Industry
- to spend more on education as the cost of unemployment falls (Labour Party 1997).

New Labour achievements by 2005

The October 2005 White Paper (DfES 2005) and the accompanying Press Briefing (Labour Party 2005) detail New Labour's claims about what it calls 'increased standards' in education.

Early years
'Labour is undertaking a revolution in early years education and care – with a guarantee of a free part-time nursery place for every 3- and 4-year-old' (Labour Party 2005). New Labour's 2001 Green Paper on Education had noted that 'universal nursery education for all 4-year-olds is now in place. There has been a significant expansion for 3-year-olds. In total there are 120,000 more free nursery places than in 1997' (DfEE 2001: 9). It also promised to 'expand Sure Start (a programme aimed at helping pre-school children and their families in poorer areas) to a total of 500 programmes, to support 400,000 under-4s, one-third of under-4s living in poverty, by 2004' (2001: 6). The October 2005 White paper notes that there are 'more than 500 Sure Start centres and they are increasing the number of children's centres'.

Standards overall
    Remarkable progress in education has been made so far with standards up

across the board including the best ever primary school results. In education, the hard work of pupils and teachers has delivered the best ever results at ages 11, 14, 16 and 18.

(Labour Party 2005)

In 2005 schools secured a record rate of improvement in GCSE with some 56% of 16-year-olds achieving 5 or more good GCSEs, up from 45% in 1997.

(DfES 2005)

Standards in poor areas

The 2001 Green Paper also promised to 'ensure that every school with fewer than 25% achieving 5 or more A*–C at GCSE or more than 35% on free school meals receives extra targeted assistance' (DfES 2005: 9). By 2005 'schools in the most deprived areas have seen the greatest improvement in performance' (Labour Party 2005). 'Over 50% of pupils in Inner London now get 5 or more good GCSEs, compared with a third in 1997 and 55% do so in Birmingham, compared with 35% in 1997' (DfES 2005: 14–15).

Expansion of further and higher education

Over a quarter of young people start Apprenticeships and we now have the highest number ever going to university. The proportion of 18 to 30-year-olds going into higher education has risen from an elite few of around 6% in the 1960s to 44% in 2004.

(Labour Party 2005)

Staffing and spending: more teachers and support staff

There are more teachers in schools than at any point in the last 20 years – 28,000 more than in 1997 and 105,000 new support staff. Every secondary school will be rebuilt or refurbished over the next ten to 15 years.

(Labour Party 2005)

Teacher numbers have risen from 399,200 in January 1997 to 431,900 in January 2005, with much higher numbers of well-qualified graduates joining the profession through programmes such as Teach First. School support staff numbers have doubled since 1997, to 269,000.

(DfES 2005: 13)

Spending on schools

Substantial and sustained investment has underpinned all these reforms. Spending on education in England has risen from £35 billion in 1997/98 to £51 billion in 2004/05, allowing a real-terms increase in funding of 29% per pupil and significant investment in the workforce, in books and technology and in the fabric of the school estate. By 2007/08, at the end of the current spending review period, this figure will have risen to £60 billion in today's prices.

(DfES 2005: 13–14)

Furthermore, (teachers') pay has increased 20% in real terms; and pay and promotion are increasingly linked to results and pupil progress.

(DfES 2005: 92)

Education maintenance allowances

Already over 250,000 people are benefiting from Labour's Education Maintenance Allowance. The earn-asyou-learn allowances, for 16–20 year olds staying on at school or FE college after the age of 16, offer a financial incentive to help combat the culture of 'dropping out' at 16 (Labour Party 2005).

Six themes in New Labour's education policy

In this next section New Labour's education policies are analysed in terms of six themes, and analysis/comment is provided on those developments in addition to a critique on their impacts and ideologies.

Theme 1: a social democratic theme: 'inclusion'; targeted expenditure, redistribution and spending

New Labour promises to 'benefit the many not the few'. Expenditure has been targeted at areas of social exclusion, in particular city areas, through a number of targeted redistributionist funding schemes such as Education Action Zones, Excellence in Cities, Education Maintenance Allowances, and the 'New Deal' for 18–24-year-olds to ensure that young people without qualifications are in work, education or training.

Education Action Zones (EAZs) and Excellence in Cities
New Labour instituted a number of interventionist measures such as university summer school places for 'gifted and talented' children, mentoring projects, learning support units, city learning centres with state of the art ICT, and school–post-school links, as well as extra funding for schools (DfEE 2001: 45). These classic social democratic policies were married to neo-liberal policies of involving 'new partners', industry, charities and religious groups, in their funding and governance.

Ending per capita funding
New Labour stopped the per capita funding of the Conservatives. Per capita funding was introduced by the Conservatives under the 1988 Education Reform Act. It meant that in any LEA all children of the same age had a similar level of funding, regardless of their needs, to be given to whichever school took them. This had virtually halted the previous Labour/social democratic policy of extra funding in favour of schools with the poorest intakes.

Increased funding
New Labour also increased funding for schools and local education authorities' capital and revenue budgets. For example, primary school class sizes have been reduced, and there is a large scale programme of repairing and rebuilding schools.

This is, however, mainly funded via the Private Finance Initiative (PFI), a neo-liberal handing over of public works to private companies.

Education Maintenance Allowances (EMAs)
These are paid to 16–19-year-olds from poorer families, to encourage working-class children to stay on in further education.

Expansion of higher education
New Labour aims to have up to 50% of 18–30-year-olds attending university. This has become 'universities for the masses', rather than 'massification of universities'. The third and fourth tier universities, which are most working class in intake, have less contact time, and more vocational and skills training-type courses than traditional universities, and, in comparison with the 1960s, the 'unit of resource' (money spent per student), has more than halved (see Mufti in this volume for a fuller discussion around this issue).

Ending of student grants for higher education
New Labour is now introducing variable fees to be paid back through the tax system. Students will, increasingly over the coming years, choose university courses based on price. This is likely to be class based, as it is in the USA.

Public expenditure
From 1999/2000 to 2005/2006 public spending on education will have risen by 4.5 percentage points of GDP, from 37.4% to 41.9% (IPPR 2005). It will be held at that level to 2007/2008. This, it should be noted, is a smaller share than in most other developed countries, and is 'less than the 49.9% in 1976' (Toynbee 2000).

Theme 2: a neo-conservative theme: 'Back to Basics'; curriculum, pedagogy and traditionalism

Curriculum
The 'standards' to be maintained and improved are, for the most part, traditional ones. *Traditionalism* is sustained through the continuation of the Eurocentric and traditionalist Conservative National Curriculum for schools, accompanied by concentration on 'Back to Basics' in the literacy hour and numeracy hour primary school curriculum:

> If teachers, in the Conservatives' and in New Labour's view, need to be controlled (by having to stick to the National Curriculum), then, even more so, do those who teach the teachers – the 'teacher trainers'. Prior to the 1997 general election, the message from Tony Blair and Education spokesperson David Blunkett was that 'the Labour Party intends to launch a back to basics drive in the classroom. More emphasis on basic skills, classroom discipline and whole class teaching will become part of a drastic overhaul of teacher training'.
>
> (*TES* 1996)

Pedagogy
It is not only through the formal, or subject, curriculum that school students and student teachers are conditioned into conservatism, it is also by the hidden curriculum, the covert expectations about behaviour, ambition, validity and acceptability of home/domestic cultures/subcultures and their 'cultural capital' (Bourdieu and Passeron 1977; Hill 2001), educational expectations and future employment. In a heavily hierarchicalised, tiered system of schools, schools at different places on the status ladder tend to have very different versions of the National Curriculum, pedagogies and expectations. In general, working-class schools concentrate on 'the basics' whilst middle-class schools have broader curricula.

The highly prescriptive National Literacy Strategy videos on how to teach literacy have become the widely accepted model for teaching across the primary curriculum. The assault on liberal-progressive child-centred education also includes government attacks on mixed-ability teaching (for example by Education Minister Ruth Kelly calling on schools to 'group and set by ability').

New Labour made minor modifications to both the schools and the 'teacher training' curriculum, with respect to social inclusion and multi-culturalism, for example through the Multiverse programme, which provides teacher educators and student teachers/trainees with resources and materials that focus on improving the educational achievement of pupils from diverse backgrounds (Multiverse 2005). Critical pedagogy and critical reflection, for example, have been slightly facilitated through the study of 'citizenship' in the National Curriculum (see Hill and Cole 1999), and through modified requirements for student teachers (Cole 2005). To some slight extent, education theory and equal opportunities work has therefore been re-legitimated. They had been drastically restricted by the 1992/93 Conservative regulations (Hill 1997a; 1997b; 2003; 2004).

However, the teacher training curriculum is heavily prescriptive, heavily geared to skills training, and leaves very little time for the development of critical thought, or consideration of the social and political contexts of education/schooling. There is now very little space for the sociology, history, philosophy and psychology of education. There is also very little space for critical thought, for asking questions about better pasts or better futures. This is a conservative curriculum, a curriculum for conformity.

Theme 3: A neo-liberal theme: managerialism; target-setting, surveillance and punishment

The emphasis during New Labour's first term (1997–2001) was 'standards not structures'. The focus for improving standards was on 'managerialism', 'improving schools' (and LEAs) by a combination of support and pressure. The methods embraced: centralised control of the school and initial teacher education (ITE) curriculum; regular Ofsted inspections of schools and LEAs and regular Teacher Training Agency inspections of 'providers' of teacher education; performance targets; published tables of achievement; and various initiatives delegating more resources and autonomy to schools. These included the Beacon Schools initiative of rewarding selected schools financially so they could share their expertise; and the 'earned autonomy' initiative whereby high-performing schools are allowed soft-touch Ofsted inspections and greater autonomy over the curriculum.

The reverse side, the stick instead of the carrot, is 'getting tough', partly through 'naming and shaming' 'failing' schools and LEAs, closing some schools down, and various measures to enable private 'for-profit' corporations to take over 'failing' LEA services and opening up schools to takeover by 'not-for-profit' corporations. (These are often the 'not-for-profit' arms of very much for-profit corporations). The ultimate sanction of closure is designed to drive up standards in failing schools as the fear of bankruptcy drives struggling businesses (Bright 2005).

Stratifying the teaching workforce
One developing aspect of managerialism is the stratification of the workforce in schools, for example by performance-related pay (PRP) and the introduction of new 'types' and grades of teacher, on different rates of pay, such as 'superteachers' (Hill 2005). There has been a massive expansion in the number of teaching assistants, who, as part of the Workforce Remodelling Agreement, are carrying out some traditional teaching functions, at far less pay than teachers, despite being untrained as teachers.

Pay and conditions
A key element of Capital's plans for education is to cut its labour costs. For this, a deregulated labour market is essential – with schools and colleges able to set their own pay scales and sets of conditions – busting national trade union agreements, weakening union powers to protect their workforces and employing people on much lower pay scales than teachers.

In England and Wales, under the 2002 Education Act, around 1,000 schools were given the freedom to vary the curriculum and change teachers' pay and conditions. In the rapidly growing 'academies' sector of secondary schools in England and Wales, school managements can set their own pay rates and conditions of service for teachers.

These ideas have been relaunched and extended in New Labour's White Paper of October 2005 (DfES 2005) (see Rikowski 2005a, for an analysis). Paragraph 2.16 of the White Paper states that the proposed 'self-governing trust schools' could have the power and 'freedoms over pay and conditions, where the Trust can demonstrate that these will raise standards'.

These policy developments strike at the heart of professional equity, under which teachers having similar qualifications can expect the same pay and conditions at any education institution of the same level across the country'. This weakens unions.

Theme 4: A neo-liberal theme: killing off the comprehensives; market competition, new schools, and 'diversity' and selection
During New Labour's second (2001–2005) and third (2005–) terms in office, the emphasis has very much been on 'structures' as well as standards. This includes altering the structures of schooling, patterns of ownership, control, and launching different types of school.

In the 2001 Education Green Paper, New Labour called this 'modernising' comprehensive education. New Labour claims that it is encouraging 'diversity' in the types of schools to meet the needs and aspirations of all children. This supported New Labour comments, enthusiastically reported by right-wing newspapers such as the *Daily Mail*, the *Sun* and the *Telegraph* attacking 'bog standard', 'one-size-fits-all' comprehensives.

As part of this 'parental power'/diversity agenda, New Labour has allowed local parents to decide on the future of their local grammar schools, secondary schools and 11 plus system. The rules drawn up for these ballots have made it virtually impossible to get rid of local selective grammar/secondary systems in the LEAs where they still exist.

New types of school

New Labour has increased/intensified the process of diversification in types of school, by introducing new types of school – academies, specialist schools, and, in the 2005 White Paper, the proposed 'independent state schools' to be called 'trust schools'.

Academies

Academies are publicly funded independent schools with voluntary or private sector sponsors and control. The Government intends to have at least 200 academies established or in the pipeline by 2010 (Her Majesty's Government 2005, Chapter 2, Summary). Academies are outside LEA control. They can set their own pay and conditions, and 'vary' the curriculum.

Specialist schools

The Green Paper (DfES 2001) and the Education Act of 2002 promised that 'specialist' schools (in technology, languages, sports and arts, with new specialisms in business, science, engineering and enterprise) should reach nearly a half of all secondary schools by 2006 (DfEE 2001: 7). These schools are allowed to select up to 10% of their pupils 'by aptitude'. In 2003, each specialist school got a one-off grant of £100,000, plus £126 per pupil extra for four years. Those with more than 500 pupils have to raise £50,000 in sponsorship as part of their bids.

According to the *Times Educational Supplement* of 14 November 2003, over 90% of all secondary schools in England will become 'specialist schools' by 2006. This specialist schools plan, the major focus of New Labour's February 2001 plan for education for 2001–2006 was greeted by a *Daily Mail* front-page article: 'Death of the comprehensive' (Halpin 2001).

Independent trust schools

The New Labour Education White Paper of October 2005 foresees the possibility of many, or most, or all LEA controlled primary and secondary schools becoming, in effect, independent state schools, outside LEA/local democratically accountable control – with the power to 'vary' the National Curriculum – and also to 'vary' (alter) the pay and conditions of staff such as teachers, and 'vary' the 'skill mix' for example, the ratio of teachers to teaching assistants.

New Labour's policy and plans for more competitiveness and selection are a continuation, indeed an extension, of most of the structural aspects of the 1988 Conservative Education Reform Act, in terms of the macro-structure and organisation of schooling. The Radical Right neo-liberal principle of competition between schools, which results in an increasing inequality between schools (Edwards and Tomlinson 2003) and the principle of devolving more and more financial control to schools through local management of schools are all in keeping with preceding Conservative policy.

Theme 5: A neo-liberal theme: 'New Partnerships'; pre-privatisation, corporation control and schools for sale; business involvement in schools

Academies
The price of buying control of an academy, a state school (with its buildings, teachers, pupils) is between £2 million and £2.5 million. The Government/taxpayer funds the £25 million building/rebuilding costs and hands control to whichever business person, corporation or religious group has provided the £2.5 million.

In the 2005–2006 discussion on the 2005 White Paper, a number of 'Old Labour' and other Labour MPs rebelled over 'selling off state schools to assorted fringe Christian groups and second hand car salesmen'. Reg Vardy, a millionaire evangelical Christian creationist second-hand car salesman controls academies in Gateshead and Middlesbrough.

Most trade unions involved in education, such as UNISON, provide considerable data about the sponsors of academies and, more widely, those involved in 'the business of education' (see, for example, NUT 2005; UNISON 2005).

Independent trust schools
BBC education editor Mike Baker comments, 'To the cynical, the trusts look like city academies without the £25m price tag. The key to understanding the trust schools lies in the White Paper description of them as "independent state schools". This is an exact echo of the phrase used by Margaret Thatcher in the 1980s' (Baker 2005).

Privatisation
Privatisation takes many forms, different forms sometimes in different countries. In Britain, the Centre for Public Services's booklet of 2003, *Mortgaging Our Children's Future* (Hall 2003) analyses the various policies and initiatives under way in secondary schools in England and Wales (see also, Rikowski 2003; 2005a; 2005b; 2005c; Hill 2006). Hall discusses a range of initiatives including making markets, city academies and specialist schools, the Private Finance Initiative (PFI), outsourcing and restructuring of school meals and the Education Action Zones policy.

Pre-privatisation and business involvement

Currently, in Britain, there is what may be seen as the 'hidden' pre-privatisation of state schools in England by enabling schools to function as 'little businesses' through increased autonomies and business-like managements and corporate aspects, and the ability, within the 2002 Education Act, and the October 2005 Education White Paper, for schools to act as capitalist enterprises in terms of their ability to merge and engage in take-overs of other schools (Rikowski 2005a; 2005b; 2005c). Schools can enter into deals with private sector outfits. They can also sell educational services to other schools.

These measures are seen by Rikowski as means of 'softening up' the education service to business control and various forms of profit making by Capital – national and transnational corporations and those who own them, or are mega-shareholders in them. Rikowski suggests that any degree of privatisation and private involvement acts as a 'profit virus' . . . that once a public service such as education is infected ('virused') by private company involvement, then it will inevitably become liable to the regulations of the General Agreement for Trade in Services (GATS), and open up to free trade in services by national and by multinational and foreign capital (Rikowski 2003; Hill 2005). By currently encouraging private companies to bid for and own, and run and manage, state schools, New Labour is actively encouraging future privatisation and private control of state schools.

Part Three: The impacts and ideologies of New Labour's education policies

Within this section comments made throughout this chapter on the impacts and ideologies of New Labour's education policies are analysed. Here, in addition to a Marxist analysis, deliberate reference is made to writers who are not Marxist. This is to demonstrate that some of the critique and analysis, for example on the 2005 Education White Paper, is more widely shared.

Capital, corporations and education

Capital have a number of plans with respect to education.

A first plan of Capital, The Capitalist Plan For Education, is to produce and reproduce a workforce and citizenry and set of consumers fit for Capital. This has two functions, an ideological function and a labour-training function. These comprise socially producing labour-power for capitalist enterprises. This is people's capacity to labour – their skills and attitudes, together with their ideological compliance and suitability for Capital – as workers, citizens and consumers. In this analysis, Althusser's concepts of schools as ideological state apparatuses (ISA) is useful here, with schools as key elements in the ideological indoctrination of new citizens and workers into thinking 'there is no alternative' to capitalism, that capitalism, and competitive individualism with gross inequalities is 'only natural' (Althusser 1971).

A second plan of Capital, The Capitalist Plan In Education, is to smooth the way for direct profit-taking/profiteering from education. Current worldwide spending in education is 'estimated at around 2,000 billion dollars . . . more than global automotive sales' (Santos, cited in Hill 2005: 261). This plan is about how Capital wants to make direct profits from education. This centres on setting business 'free' in education for profit-making and extracting profits from privately controlled and owned schools and colleges or aspects of their functioning. Common mechanisms are for example from managing, advising, controlling and owning schools. These possibilities are widened by the New Labour Education White Paper of October 2005.

New Labour's most recent education policy moves indicate that it is the business agenda *in* schools that is becoming increasingly important as schools become sites of profit-making (see Rikowski 2005a; 2005b; 2005c), though other Marxists such as Hatcher consider the capitalist agenda *for* schools remains the dominant aim for Capital – producing tiered, skilled and ideologically supportive labourers (Hatcher 2005; 2006a; 2006b: 3).

Selection, inequality and ('raced') class

Where there is a market in schools (where high-status schools can select their intakes, whether on 'academic achievement' or other class-related criteria such as 'aptitudes'), the result is increasingly 'raced' and gendered social class differentiation (Hill and Cole 2001). The middle classes rapidly colonise the 'best' schools, pushing out the working classes. In a competitive market in schools, 'sink' schools sink further, denuded of their 'brightest' intakes. As Bright comments on the 2005 White Paper:

> With the new independent trusts, which will allow each school to set its own entrance criteria and compete openly for pupils, that pecking order will no longer be the unintended consequence of half a century of ill-judged reforms of our education system. It will be the driving principle.
>
> (2005)

Ideological analysis

New Labour has accepted and intensified Conservative education policies, though with some traditional social democratic/'Old Labour' redistributionist policies.

While there is considerable discourse and policy aimed at improving 'equality of *opportunity*' and meritocracy, greater equality of *outcome* – that is reducing the differences between rich and poor in wealth, or income, or educational attainment does not appear on the agenda. Instead, New Labour's vision is of 'meritocracy' – elitism by merit rather than elitism by birth or money.

Greater equality of opportunity (via targeted spending) is suffocated by neo-liberal and neo-conservative policies. The quiescent, non-critical neo-conservative subject curriculum and hidden or informal curriculum in schools serves to dampen – but not to destroy – resistance to an increasingly capitalised, commodified and unequal society. This increased capitalisation, commodification and ('raced' and gendered) social class inequality has been deepened by New Labour's extension of Conservative Government neo-liberal education policies such as increasing the selective hierarchical market in schooling, and imposing variable university top-up fees. This process of increasing educational inequality is reflected in and amplified by wider social, housing, and fiscal and economic policies, which have resulted in increasing inequalities in the wider society (Harvey 2005; Hill 2006).

In answer to the questions posed at the beginning of the chapter about policy, this chapter has highlighted the aims and claims of New Labour's mix of education policies, analysed the dominant ideology of neo-liberalism, and identified the winners and losers resulting from New Labour's education and wider policies. This is New Labour's 'class war from above'.

References

Althusser, L. (1971) Ideology and ideological state apparatuses, in *Lenin and Philosophy and Other Essays*. London: New Left Books.

Baker, M. (2005) Forward to the past for schools. *BBC News* 27 Oct. http://news.bbc.co.uk/1/low/education/4382220.stm (accessed 4 April 2006).

Bourdieu, R. and Passeron, J. (1977) *Reproduction in Education, Society and Culture*. London: Sage.

Bright, M. (2005) The politics column – Martin Bright revisits the great education divide, *New Statesman*, 31 October.

Cole, M. (2005) Transmodernism, Marxism and social change: some implications for teacher education, *Policy Futures in Education*. http://www.wwwords.co.uk/pdf/viewpdf.asp?j=pfie&vol=3&issue=1&year=2005&article=9_Cole_PFIE_3_1_final_web&id=212.134.24.69 (accessed 31 March 2006).

Department for Education and Employment (DfEE) (2001) *Schools: Building on Success*, Green Paper. London: DfEE.

Department for Education and Skills (DfES) (2005) *Higher Standards, Better Schools for All – More choice for parents and pupils*. White Paper, Cm6677, October. Norwich: Stationery Office. http://www.dfes.gov.uk/publications/schoolswhitepaper/ (accessed 2 April 2006).

Edwards, T. and Tomlinson, S. (2003) *Selection Isn't Working: Diversity, Standards and Inequality in Secondary Education*. London: Catalyst Publications.

Hall, D. (2003) *Public Services Work! Information, Insights and Ideas for the Future*. London: PSIRU, the Public Services International. http://www.worldpsi.org/Content/ContentGroups/English7/Publications1/En_Public_Services_Work.pdf. Also at: http://www.psiru.org/reports/2003–09–U–PSW.pdf (accessed 4 April 2006).

Halpin, T. (2001) Trash the T-shirts, tatty teachers are told, *Daily Mail* 19 February.

Harvey, D. (2005) *A Brief History of Neoliberalism*. Oxford: Oxford University Press.

Hatcher, R. (2005) Business sponsorship of schools: For-profit takeover or agents of neoliberal change? A reply to Glenn Rikowski's Habituation of the nation: school sponsors as precursors to the Big Bang? 5 November, available on Glenn Rikowski's web log: *The Volumizer*, http://journals.aol.co.uk/rikowskigr/Volumizer/entries/651 (posted 7 November).

Hatcher, R. (2006a) Privatisation and sponsorship: the re-agenting of the school system in England. *Journal of Educational Policy*.

Hatcher, R. (2006b) The White Paper: what does it intend, what would it mean, will it happen? Socialist Education Association. http://www.socialisteducation.org. uk/hatcher_jan06.htm (accessed 4 April 2006).

Her Majesty's Government (2005) *Higher Standards, Better Schools for All – More Choice for Parents and Pupils (White Paper)*, Cm 6677, October. Norwich: The Stationery Office.

Hill, D. (1997a) Reflection in teacher education, in K. Watson, S. Modgil and C. Modgil (eds) *Teacher Education and Training*, Vol. 1 of *Educational Dilemmas: Debate and Diversity*. London: Cassell.

Hill, D. (1997b) Equality and primary schooling: the policy context intentions and effects of the conservative 'reforms', in M. Cole, D. Hill and S. Shan (eds) *Promoting Equality in Primary Schools*. London: Cassell.

Hill, D. (2001) The National Curriculum, the hidden curriculum and equality, in D. Hill and M. Cole (eds) *Schooling and Equality: Fact, Concept and Policy*. London: Kogan Page.

Hill, D. (2003) Global neoliberalism, the deformation of education and resistance, *Journal for Critical Education Policy Studies* 1(1). http://www.jceps.com/ index.php?pageID=article&articleID=7 (accessed 2 April 2006).

Hill, D. (2004) Books, banks and bullets: controlling our minds – the global project of imperialistic and militaristic neo-liberalism and its effect on education policy, *Policy Futures* 2, 3–4 (Theme: Marxist Futures in Education). http://www.wwwords.co.uk/pfie/content/pdfs/2/issue2_3.asp (accessed 4 April 2006).

Hill, D. (2005) Globalisation and its educational discontents: neoliberalisation and its impacts on education workers' rights, pay, and conditions. *International Studies in Sociology of Education* 15(3): 257–288.

Hill, D. (2006) Neoliberal and neoconservative global and national capital and the class war from above. Some implications for social class analysis, *Journal for Critical Education Policy Studies* 4(1): in press.

Hill, D. and Cole, M. (1999) *Promoting Equality in Secondary Schools*. London: Cassell.

Hill, D. and Cole, M. (2001) Social Class, in D. Hill and M. Cole (eds) *Schooling and Equality: Fact, Concept and Policy*. London: Kogan Page.

Hill D. with others (2006) Education services liberalization, in E. Rosskam (ed.) *Winners or Losers? Liberalizing Public Services*. Geneva: ILO.

Institute for Public Policy Research (IPPR) (2005) Spending review will lay foundation Labour's manifesto. Press Release 29 June. http://www.ippr.org. uk/pressreleases/archive.asp?id=800&fID=61.

Labour Party (1997) *Labour Party Manifesto for the 1997 General Election*. London: The Labour Party.

Labour Party (2005) *Press Briefing on the 2005 White Paper on Education*. http://www.labour.org.uk/fileadmin/labour/user/Attachments/Labour_ Supporters_Network/schools_white_paper_05.pdf (accessed 4 April 2006).

Multiverse (2005) http://www.multiverse.ac.uk/ (4 April 2006).

National Union of Teachers (NUT) (2005) The privatisation of education – an overview. http://www.teachers.org.uk/resources/word/The_privatisation_of_education_overview_July_2004.doc (4 April 2006).

Rikowski, G. (2003) Schools and the GATS enigma, *Journal for Critical Education Policy Studies* 1 (1). http://www.jceps.com/index.php?pageID=article&articleID=8 (accessed 4 April 2006).

Rikowski, G. (2005a) The Education White Paper and the marketisation and capitalisation of the schools system in England, *The Volumizer*. http://journals.aol.co.uk/rikowskigr/volumizer (accessed 4 April 2006).

Rikowski, G. (2005b) Silence on the wolves: what is absent in New Labour's five year strategy for education. Occasional paper by the Education Research Centre, University of Brighton.

Rikowski, G. (2005c) In the dentist's chair: a response to Richard Hatcher's critique of *Habituation of the Nation*, in two parts at *The Flow of Ideas*. http://www.flowideas.co.uk, 31 Dec. 2005. Part One is available at: http://www.flowideas.co.uk/print.php?page=147 and Part Two is available at: http://www.flowideas.co.uk/print.php?page=148 (accessed 4 April 2006).

Times Educational Supplement (*TES*) (1996) 31 May 1996.

Toynbee, P. (2000) Gordon Brown speaks. And, as they say, money talks, *Guardian* 19 July.

UNISON (2005) *The Business of Education.* http://www.unison.org.uk/acrobat/B1956.pdf (accessed 4 April 2006).

7

KATE MACDONALD

England: educating for the twenty-first century

Introduction

Education reform has been a major strategic feature of Government policy over the last 25 years. This chapter will draw on theories about the nature of the State and education to examine the values of the market as a basis for meeting the challenges of the twenty-first century. It will be the argument of this chapter that the prioritisation of the market economy both as value and mechanism for the delivery of public services has redistributed opportunity within the education system and changed the way in which consensus and integration are gained rather than addressing the challenges of modernising education.

The English schooling system is provided by the partially devolved British State, which is democratic and capitalist. One of the main characteristics is stratification associated with economic inequality and access to power (Giddens 1983). It is a complex organisation dependent on legitimacy and active consent from the electorate, containing three major social forms, the cultural, the political and the economic. The political sphere in a liberal democracy confers equal rights but not economic participation and the three roles are frequently in tension (Keane 1984). In their analysis of the postwar state Clark and Dear (1984) suggested that social integration was gained through the provision of welfare; consensus in that rules of ownership, order and security were agreed and the continuation of production ensured a stable economy through national ownership of infrastructure. The welfare state was conceived as an agency, which could ameliorate the effects of economic inequality through increased provision by the state of health and education, thus acknowledging social aspirations to increased opportunity.

These three functions, analytically distinct, are interdependent in practice. Thus the policy provision of education reflects the competing values of a stratified economy, State consensus and stability. For example, education policy can potentially provide training for work, citizenship skills and equal opportunity. During the welfare period education policy took the form of opportunity to participate in and compete for enhanced provision of secondary schooling. In theory pupils of school age gained the right to achieve in a meritocracy through the benefit of secondary schooling. Criticisms of educational provision were about the failure to extend access and achieve equal opportunity.

The tension between the economic and welfare activities (Keane 1984) became the focus of New Right criticism. In particular it was argued that welfare provided limited economic growth and permitted the development of inefficient state services. Both the 1979 Conservative Government and the 1997 Labour Government were elected on manifesto promises to modernise public services, including education, and to enhance economic growth as a response to the change in the world economy. Thus, integration was no longer based around a welfare state but on an increase in freedom of choice. This chapter sets out to identify the effects of the commitment to the market and choice, and to explore whether it is compatible with the national aim of overall increase in standards designed to enhance Britain's position in the global market.

Values and the provision of education

Education policy has not only been viewed as the means to enhance opportunities for individual achievement but also as an instrument of economic and social policy. Specific reforms reflect the values and ambitions of the political group and also the contemporary social, economic and political pressures, which in the 1970s were those of economic stability and social disorder linked to youth unemployment and a claim of falling standards.

The New Right, a term used to describe the values informing the Conservative Government which came to power in 1979, drew predominately on the reassertion of economic theory (King 1987). Their views were highly critical of the welfare state as restricting both individual and economic growth. Whereas the welfare state government had been cast in the role of managing a rational bureaucracy as the best mechanism for reforming distributive justice, the New Right argued that the bureaucratic state was limiting individual freedom and was inappropriate as a means to deliver social justice. Market freedom was advocated as the only route to economic efficiency and the value of individual freedom was reasserted. While the degree of economic and political freedom was the subject of much debate, the British New Right advocated the promotion of enterprise and competition, where necessary reinforced by a strong State (Olssen et al. 2004: 136).

Edgar (1986) notes the New Right demonisation of the 1960s as a period of disorder. There was a backlash against the multicultural and gender politics of the 1960s and 70s, which were portrayed as diminishing the national consciousness and showing greater concern for equity than growth and development. The New Right built consensus around a fear of chaos and ineffective economic policy and, in the 1979 election, were successful in gaining support across the different social class groups (Levitas 1986). The political goals as measures were an application of private sector values such as accountability, efficiency and freedom applied to the public services.

In 1997, the New Labour Government took power promising a modern politics that could achieve the changes required by globalisation. They shared the New Right view that economic needs were a priority and put limits on the role of the welfare state. The values of this group are a complex blend (Paterson 2003). The term 'New' is designed to separate the group from the 'Old' Labour associated with high taxes, inefficient use of public money and a poor management of the economy (Chadwick and Heffernan 2003: 20). However they claimed to differ from the New Right in that they held a commitment to a form of social democracy, or third way, which addressed the uncertainties of the global world while sustaining the values evident in earlier forms of the welfare state such as justice and equality (Giddens 2003). Welfare remained a feature of social integration but recast in the language of partnership, participation and consumer choice (Newman 2001). While the postwar welfare state had been characterised by a commitment to social justice and to the use of the state for distributive purpose New Labour retained a commitment to welfare (Powell 1999) but broke with the monopoly state as provider. Marquand (2003) suggests that these views are characterised by the values of inclusion, individual achievement, acceptance of globalisation, decentralisation and networks. Quality standards and efficiency are associated with strong leadership along with an emphasis on the rights and responsibilities of individuals. New Labour claimed to be distinct from New Right Conservatism in its commitment to social democracy. However both prioritised the economy and individual choice, thus departing from the previous Keynesian form of welfare with its emphasis on rational State provision, not the logic of the market and consumer demand.

During the 1970s the international oil crisis and domestic high levels of unemployment brought a focus on the link between economic growth, skills and education. This is exemplified in the Ruskin speech (Tomlinson 2001: 21), which linked economic policy directly to education, and raised questions about the standards achieved by schools and the link to employer needs. New Labour was strongly influenced by the arguments of globalisation and their political solution was to promise a high skill economy achieved through better education standards. While suggesting that the capacity of the State to act was limited by globalisation, a modern social democratic state could develop a strong society that supported the individual, encouraging talent and increased opportunity of individual advancement while fostering individual responsibility within the context of social cohesion (Blair 2003: 30). Their requirement that Britain emerge as a high skill economy within a world market strengthened the value of education as an economic asset through the production of new skills and offset potential destabilisation through employment. Gordon Brown (2003) outlined his view of equality as provision for the individual of opportunity for employment, lifelong education and access to culture and power over their life decisions. The New Labour vision is one of a more inclusive society driven by individuals who are autonomous, and recognise rights and democratic authority (Giddens 2003: 37).

Underpinning the views of both New Right and New Labour is an account of the individual as a self-interested maximiser, who acts in a manner defined by narrow self-interest and social atomism (Hindess 1988). These ideas drew upon theories of rational choice, which emphasise the role of the individual acting to calculate cost and benefit. The New Right anticipated that parents would pursue higher standards and thus also provide a more qualified workforce. Within New

Labour there was commitment to modernisation and entitlement to individual choice in a diverse market. In addition the social democratic focus allowed for more explicit networks of state sponsorship, which would be used to empower individuals to join the high skill economy.

Jonathan (1997) criticises the market as a means through which to distribute education. The appeal to consumer rights emphasises the maximisation of private, and the limitation of public, benefit, and consequently removes power from the providers such as the professionals and bureaucrats. However, the provision of education is a public activity also directed to enhancement of national skills, sustenance of culture and values as well as the development of individual talent, yet the effect of aggregating individual preferences is not considered. Choice is attached to an individual and claims to give greater freedom, although within educational provision the consequences are social. For example the choices of parents impact on those of others, particularly in situations of scarcity or where parents are allowed to vote on the future of a school. Additionally, as Jonathan indicates, education is a positional good, valued because its outcomes provide differentiation for individuals. The use of the market to distribute education will thus inevitably provide competition and unequal outcomes. Markets are not natural creations but are sponsored by the State and as thus reflect specific values and policies (Woods *et al.* 1998). The transfer of rights to consumers relocates power to individuals and emphasises the significance of decision-making. While social choice theory focuses on the costs, incentives and opportunities of a decision for each individual it takes little account of the knowledge basis of choice, forms of thought and forms of power, which influence the capacity and access to decision-making in the market (Hindess 1988).

The link between education policy and economic growth is also unacknowledged. While the evidence of individual benefit from education is strong, the social rates of return are more problematic. During the 1960s policies based on human capital theory encouraged government to invest in education as a means to economic growth as well as to satisfy individual aspiration (Halsey *et al.* 1961) However, while education has a sorting and selecting process, success in education and a high income do not necessarily relate to a sound contribution to national economic growth (Wolf 2002). The changes in employment patterns during the last two decades of the twentieth century and the loss of manufacturing industry gave legitimacy to government arguments that the response to globalisation should be a high skill knowledge economy. However, as Wolf (2002) in her analysis of the labour market points out, skilled occupations have declined and managerial increased, but there has been no decline in low skill work particularly in the service sector.

Assessing the impact

When the Conservative Government took power in 1979, compulsory schooling was mainly provided by the State through local authorities. The system was one in which there was a limited degree of diversity in local education authority (LEA) provision and in the voluntary aided sector. Comprehensive schools had become the main source of secondary schooling although earlier Conservative policy at local level allowed grammar schools to remain in some areas. The Conservative Government programme was developed so that choice through competition would raise standards and poor schools would either improve or close (Whitty 2001).

The initial change to make choice and competition meaningful was a withdrawal of the requirement for local authorities to provide a comprehensive system thus securing the remaining grammar schools and diversity in the system. These goals were furthered by the introduction of the assisted places scheme, which offered access to private schooling and represented an opportunity to move out of the State system for poor but academically able children. This scheme built on a view that comprehensive schools were unable to provide anything as good as that in the private sector, thus able children needed an escape from the neighbourhood (Edwards and Whitty 1997). Evaluations indicated that it attracted a diversity of parents among which were Asian middle-class parents (Tomlinson 2001: 29). However, the parent group were not representative, were more likely to have strong educational backgrounds, and in the case of a third of participants were single parents with links to the private sector. Thus, it was parents with the capacity to understand and apply for the scheme that were most heavily represented (Walford 1996).

The market was further diversified by the development of city technology colleges. The scheme was intended to bring together employers, industry and education in joint funded projects. It was hoped that the high resource level and the modern technological profile would be attractive, particularly within inner city areas where many comprehensives were failing. This was an enhanced provision and admission was intended to identify deserving children and increase their opportunities. Early studies of the city technology colleges showed that the parents most likely to use these schools were those with a strong commitment to their child's education and, as such, supportive of the school (Edwards and Whitty 1997). It was also apparent that the parents who chose the colleges did not do so because of the link to technology but because they perceived them to be selective and a substitute for a grammar school (Whitty 2002: 54). The impact of parent choice pressured the schools toward a traditional academic status and values rather than modern technology and perceptions of national economic need.

The 1988 Education Reform Act further extended the market through allowing some schools to diversify, be independent of local planning, and through direct funding gain greater control. These grant-maintained schools were entitled to specialise, although initially there were limits on the admission process, and return to grammar school status. The Government had anticipated that this would be an attractive policy and that a large number of schools would opt for this route as a result of parent pressure. However, this was not the case and in 1993 the arrangements were simplified to encourage more applications and the Parents' Charter spelt out the entitlement. It also promised them wildly optimistic improvement in pupil achievements (Tomlinson 2001: 50). Further encourage-ment was given in 1996 when the capacity to select pupils was raised to 50% for grant-maintained schools and 30% for the technical and language colleges. Where used, parental choice continued to reflect a preference for those schools that had the characteristic of selective grammar schools (Halpin *et al*. 1997) and in response many of the schools moved to be selective both in admission of pupils and in excluding difficult pupils (Edwards and Whitty 1997).

Conservative Government policy argued that parents would measure a good school by standards and results. However, by the mid-1990s there was evidence that the market and choice were not value free and open to all. Although the access to market information was enhanced through the inspection system, publication of Key Stage and public examination results it became increasingly clear that social factors, and historical belief about a good education, influenced parents in their choices. While school outcomes, as measured by examination achievement, had risen the patterns of improvement had not been evenly distributed. Hardman and Levacic (1997) in an examination of the early impact of competition indicate that while there is some link between GCSE performance and market success this did not mean that competition would necessarily lead to high standards for all. They indicated that factors such as differences in pupil potential, parental choice and covert selection by schools, meant that choice is not a neutral mechanism and the capacity of schools to improve could be better understood in term of value added than league tables. They demonstrated that high achieving schools had lower proportions of pupils on free school meals than the middle and poor achievers (1997: 128).

In addition to results, the increased effectiveness of schools was targeted. The characterisation of the effective school was wider than the examination scores and includes features such as attendance, behaviour and attitude. Parental choice in the market depended on such issues as their own experience and expectations, which informed their priorities as well as the capacity to compete. Gewirtz *et al*. (1995) identified circuits of schooling in which parents of different socio-economic classes placed themselves. For example those in semi-skilled families were in favour of choice because it seemed to extend their opportunity when they could not afford the middle-class option of moving home. However, they were frequently unsuccessful in achieving a place in the school of choice. Their understanding of the differences between schools was not secure and they were unlikely to use the appeal system. Working-class parents brought to the market a sense of failure avoidance and anxiety contrasting with the competence and enthusiasm demonstrated by more educated and affluent parents (Reay and Ball 1997). In posing the question, 'Can effective schools compensate for society?', Mortimore (1997: 483) concluded that, while effective local schools can have an impact, social influence was strong in terms of a school's capacity to be effective and improve. Only in exceptional cases did disadvantaged students in effective schools win. The evidence at the end of the Conservative period of office was that the market in England was stratified and that the historical status of the grammar elite continued to sustain choice in favour of past ideas of a good education (Halpin *et al*. 1997).

When New Labour was elected in 1997 they claimed a new social democratic strategy for Britain, which would blend the supportive state with a successful strategy in the global economy through modernisation (Blair and Schroder 2003). This added to Conservative strategy of choice competition and quality by offering modernisation, opportunity, responsibility and inclusion. The claimed difference lay in the promise to develop inclusive strategies. All parents, as consumers, were recast as responsible individuals who would recognise the importance of educational certification in the global economy. Choice was between schools with an increasingly differentiated profile but still bound by National Curriculum and testing requirements with emphasis on raising standards for all, particularly in numeracy and literacy. An early decision was to withdraw assisted places, which were viewed as giving public funds to private schools and promoting exclusion. However, other forms of market diversity were retained and extended. Under the Conservatives nearly 1,000 schools had opted to become grant maintained and 164 grammar schools remained (Tomlinson 2001: 97). New Labour supported a strategy of further diversification (Olssen *et al.* 2004: 208). Although school titles were changed, there was no challenge to the funding and admission policies, for example grant-maintained schools were renamed foundation schools and retained privileges and resources. Subsequent initiatives have greatly extended voluntary aided faith schools while comprehensive schools have become community schools many with specialist profiles. In January 2000 there were 13 different types of school being sponsored in different ways by state funding. The strategy was contentious and was criticised by the House of Commons Education and Skills Committee (2003) on the grounds that there was little evidence that it had significant educational benefits. Evidence of the continuing commitment to the strategy is evident in the White Paper of 2005 that proposes to make academies central to educational provision and to assist their development in areas of underperformance (DfES 2005).

By the time the New Labour Government was in power there were indications that some parents were taking an increasing interest in school results (Walford 2001: 26). An account of the operation of parent choice (Ball 2003) shows that this divided groups as middle-class parents sought boundaries that cut their children off from others. The study also suggests that some parents are not satisfied with the operation of the policy, finding it difficult to judge while others were critical of the range of choice. Ball suggests that the changes in the economy provide a degree of uncertainty about middle-class employment and patterns of certification. New Labour policy was supporting the middle class by appealing to individual choice, which they could operate with a degree of competence. Power *et al.* (2003: 32) in a study of education and the middle class identify that the 'overwhelming majority believed that educational success was crucial in determining their child's prospects'. Although there was a diversity of view about what constituted a good school, particularly around the school ethos, parents viewed getting access to the right secondary school as a crucial choice.

Welsh (2004), in a study of a deprived area of Kent, shows that where there were fully subscribed popular schools, choice became very complex and parents operated a gradient of popularity to avoid their child attending the least attractive schools. She concludes that consumer choice strengthened social advantage for some but failed to meet overall educational needs or offer equitable access to schools. Parents were not making a straightforward instrumental choice, based on academic standards but balancing other values linked to the whole school experience of the child (Woods *et al.* 1998). Additionally there is evidence that the results of the most disadvantaged have not made comparable improvement. Overall school outcomes have improved but those in deprived areas are worse than those in other parts of the country. These schools were more likely to be attended by minority pupils. Despite the apparent progress of some groups (Power *et al.* 2002) it appears that the effect of the market has been at least to sustain differentials and may well have widened the gap between groups in access to educational success.

The New Labour commitment to social democracy, as a means to more inclusive success, is evident in the strategies developed for failing schools in cities. The Education Action Zones strategy was built on the recognition that multiple disadvantages could be a reason for school failure. There were some successes for the scheme but the continued success was fragile and the schemes were not retained. The evidence on school effectiveness tended to demonstrate how much harder it was for disadvantaged schools to succeed (Whitty 2002). This initiative was followed by inner city academies, publicly funded but run by private sponsors, and designed to replace failing schools. They have been the focus of much criticism as there is limited evidence that they provide increased achievement for all (Slater 2005). However, they provide another path for middle-class parents' advantage. In a report (Taylor 2005) it was shown that two-thirds of the academies, when compared with the failing schools they replaced, had a lower proportion of pupils from the poorest of families.

The proposal of a third way to ameliorate the effects of the competitive market and aid a wider dissemination of resources can be identified in the requirement that specialist schools should cooperate. For example both beacon and specialist schools are required to take a community role. This role was underlined in the House of Commons (2003) investigation into diversity of provision where a view was expressed that future funding and evaluation of specialist schools should be linked to raising pupil achievement in partner schools. Bell and West (2003) examined this strategy and concluded that the competitive market meant that cooperation was difficult particularly in relation to admissions. They also identified overlap in the policy on cooperation, and concluded that coordination, potentially by the LEA, would have improved the system, an indication that planning mechanism rather than market might be more effective.

Thus despite the claim to be inclusive, segregation of the market has remained an issue under New Labour. The data are not conclusive but where schools are able to select it would appear that there is an increase in social segregation (Taylor *et al.* 2002). Schagen and Schagen (2002) analysing which schools are best indicated that the better results of specialist and faith schools are marginal. They found that selective systems gave an overall advantage at Key Stage 3 because grammar schools were successful at enhancing the performance of least able pupils. This is not to claim that selection is the best system but that children of similar ability can obtain different results depending on the type of school they attend. The improved results are at the expense of other children who do not have a grammar school chance. Adnett and Davies (2003) reinforce this view with their evidence that choice has strengthened local hierarchies of schools and suggestion that cooperation would have provided greater dissemination of best practice.

In 2005 the Minister for Education acknowledged a decline in social mobility and that schools had failed to narrow the gap between the achievement of the rich and poor (Wilby 2005). The research evidence (Blanden *et al*. 2005) drew attention to the decline in social mobility in the United Kingdom since the 1970s. This decline has been paralleled by an increase in the relationship between family income and educational attainment. Thus the outcome of the market policies has been to sustain the advantage to middle-class parents. They conclude that while policies such as Sure Start, Excellence in Cities and Educational Maintenance Allowance could address these issues they are insufficient (2005: 14).

The operation of choice has become increasingly problematic as a means to apparently empower parents. Taylor *et al*. (2002) identify a significant increase in appeals and rise in market frustration. Parental choice amounted to an expression of preference not a choice between schools, and parents were likely to find the exercise of choice confusing (Ball 2003; Welsh 2004). There is an increasing awareness that parents were not necessarily going to achieve their preferred option with only 52% of parents getting their first choice in some London boroughs (Millar 2005) and resorting to complex strategies to avoid poor schools.

Conclusion

State intervention in schooling serves a range of competing functions in relation to the economic, cultural and political structures. Recent education policy has prioritised raising standards in pursuit of economic development and engagement with the global economy. Consensus was to be achieved through advocacy of the market mechanisms, which gave power to the parents as consumers, and would result in demand for schools that were effective and achieving high standards.

The theories focused on the individual consumer as decision maker and ignored the social context of choice in the market. However, the nature of the choice is inseparable from the social context in which it is made or from the positional nature of educational qualifications. The market mechanism offers a new way of distributing education but not a means for allowing wider availability of success. As Jonathan suggests it is an illusory freedom and increases the pressure to achieve advantage. Brown (1997) labelled the new distribution system a 'parentocracy' where power has been moved to the middle-class parents through their enhanced position in the market. Despite the claim to be more inclusive New Labour policies have strengthened stratification in the school market. Rather than offering increased standards to all it has become apparent that choice and competition have widened the gap for the disadvantaged. Despite the Government's continued assertion that 'parental choice can be a powerful driver of improved standards' (DfES 2005: 3), choice in the market is not in the public interest. Middle-class parents have been able to separate out their children leaving the less advantaged in schools with relatively poorer chances of raising standards.

Additionally this parentocracy has not been concerned with addressing issues of modernisation and globalisation but with retaining a historical pattern of elite schools. These are viewed as the route to relative advantage through traditional status and certification. As a means to modernise the skill and standards of education in all the population the operation of choice has not been effective.

References

Adnett, N. and Davies, P. (2003) Schooling reforms in England: from quasi–markets to co–opetition? *Journal of Education Policy* 18(4): 393–406.

Ball, S. (2003) *Class Strategies and the Education Market*. London: Routledge-Falmer.

Bell, K. and West, A. (2003) Specialist schools, an exploration of competition and cooperation, *Education Studies* 24(2/3): 273–289.

Blair, T. (2003) New politics for the new century, in A. Chadwick and R. Heffernan (eds) *The New Labour Reader*. Cambridge: Polity Press.

Blair, T. and Schroder, G. (2003) Europe; the third way, in A. Chadwick and R. Heffernan (eds) *The New Labour Reader*. Cambridge: Polity Press.

Blanden, J., Gregg, P. and Machin S. (2005) Intergenerational mobility in Europe and North *America*. A report supported by the Sutton Trust, Centre for Economic Performance. London: London School of Economics.

Brown, G. (2003) Equality – then and now, in A. Chadwick and R. Heffernan (eds) *The New Labour Reader*. Cambridge: Polity Press.

Brown, P. (1997) The third wave; education and the ideology of parentocracy, in A. Chadwick and R. Heffernan (eds) (2003) *The New Labour Reader*. Cambridge: Polity Press.

Chadwick, A. and Heffernan, R. (eds) (2003) *The New Labour Reader*. Cambridge: Polity Press.

Clark, G. and Dear, M. (1984) *State Apparatus*. Boston: Allen and Unwin.

Department for Education and Skills (DfES) (2005) *Higher Standards Better Schools for All: More Choice for Parents and Pupils*. London: HMSO.

Edgar, D. (1986) The free or the good, in R. Levitas (ed.) *The Ideology of the New Right*. Cambridge: Polity Press.

Edwards, T. and Whitty, G. (1997) Specialisation and selection, *Oxford Review of Education* 23(1): 5–15.

Gewirtz, S., Ball, S.J. and Bowe, R. (1995) *Markets, Choice and Equity in Education*. Buckingham: Open University Press.

Giddens, A. (1983) *Class Structures in Advanced Societies*, London: Hutchinson.

Giddens, A. (2003) The third way, in A. Chadwick and R. Heffernan (eds) *The New Labour Reader*. Cambridge: Polity Press.

Halpin, D., Power, D. and Fitz J. (1997) Opting into the past?, in R. Glatter, P.A. Woods and C. Bagley (eds) *Choice and Diversity in Schooling*. London: Routledge.

Halsey, A., Floud, J., Anderson, C.A. (eds) (1961) *Education, Economy and Society*. Toronto: Free Press Glencoe.

Hardman, J. and Levacic, R. (1997) The impact of competition on secondary schools, in R. Glatter, P.A. Woods and C. Bagley (eds) *Choice and Diversity in Schooling*. London: Routledge.

Hindess, B. (1988) *Choice Rationality and Social Theory*. London: Unwin Hyman.

House of Commons Education and Skills Committee (2003) *Secondary Education*

Diversity of Provision. At http://www.publications,parliament.uk (accessed 4 April 2006).

Jonathan, R. (1997) *Illusory Freedoms, Liberalism, Education and the Market*. Oxford: Blackwell.

Keane, J. (ed.) (1984) *Contradictions in the Welfare State*. London: Hutchinson.

King, D. (1987) *The New Right*, London: Macmillan.

Levitas, R. (ed.) (1986) *The Ideology of the New Right*. Cambridge: Polity Press.

Marquand, D. (2003) The Blair paradox, in A. Chadwick and R. Heffernan (eds) *The New Labour Reader*. Cambridge: Polity Press.

Millar, F. (2005) How to win the school-gate vote, *Guardian Education* 25 April. http://education.guardian.co.uk/egweekly/story/0,,1469788,00.html (accessed 31 March 2005).

Mortimore, P. (1997) Can Effective schools compensate for society?, in A.H. Halsey, H. Lauder, P. Brown and A.S. Wells (eds) *Education Culture Economy and Society*. Oxford: Oxford University Press.

Newman, J. (2001) *Modernising Governance*. London: Sage.

Olssen, M., Codd, J. and O'Neill, A.M. (2004) *Education Policy Globalization, Citizenship and Democracy*. London: Sage.

Paterson, L. (2003) The three educational ideologies of the British Labour Party 1997–2001, *Oxford Review of Education* 29(2): 165–185.

Powell, M. (1999) *New Labour, New Welfare State*. Bristol: Policy Press.

Power, S., Warren, S., Gillborn, D., Clark, A.S. and Coate, K. (2002) *Education in Deprived Areas: Outcomes, Inputs and Processes*. London: Institute of Education.

Power, S., Edwards, T., Whitty, G. and Wigfall, V. (2003) *Education and the Middle Class*. Buckingham: Open University Press.

Reay, D. and Ball, S. (1997) Spoilt for Choice, *Oxford Review of Education* 23(1): 89–101.

Schagen, S. and Schagen, I. (2002) *The Impact of the Structure of Secondary Education in Slough*. Slough: NFER.

Slater, J. (2005) Academies draw the better off, *Times Educational Supplement* 21 July.

Taylor, C., Gorard, S. and Fitz, J. (2002) Market frustration, *Educational Management and Administration* 30(3): 243–260.

Taylor, M. (2005) Are City Academies really helping the poorest children?, *Guardian* 3 October.

Tomlinson, S. (2001) *Education in a Post-welfare Society*, Buckingham: Open University Press.

Walford, G. (1996) School choice in England And Wales, *Oxford Studies in Comparative Education* 6(1): 49–62.

Walford, G. (2001) Does the market ensure quality? *Westminster Studies in Education* 24(1): 23–33.

Welsh, P.J. (2004) Equity, economics and educational need, some tensions between consumer and producer interests in the management of secondary school admission procedures in Thanet UK, *School Leadership and Management* 24(2): 191–203.

Whitty, G. (2001) Does the market ensure quality? *Westminster Studies in Education* 24(1): 23–32.

Whitty, G. (2002) *Making Sense of Education Policy*. London: Sage.

Wilby, P. (2005) Restore bog standards, *Guardian* 28 July.

Wolf, A. (2002) *Does Education Matter?* London: Penguin.

Woods, P.A., Bagley, C. and Glatter, R. (1998) *School Choice and Competition, Markets in the Public Interest?* London: Routledge.

8

ROBERT COE

What do we really know from school improvement and effectiveness research?

Introduction

School improvement, like motherhood and apple pie, is a *Good Thing*. Many people, including politicians, parents, teachers, and of course pupils themselves, have a strong interest in wanting schools to improve. School improvement and effectiveness have become vast areas of activity for researchers, with their own conferences, journals and methodologies. This research has had significant influence on policy and practice within education at all levels. Indeed the orthodoxy of school improvement and effectiveness research has become so dominant that it may be seen as quite heretical to question their truths. In this context, it is important to take a critical look at the findings, methods and claims of these research fields, and indeed question whether they justify that influence.

This chapter will consider some of the limitations of the methods and claims of these two research fields. In particular, we will look closely at the implications they claim to have for practice, and how far their findings can be confidently applied to the practice of improving real schools.

Limitations of school improvement research

Research into school improvement has been around for a relatively short time, especially considering its influence today. Despite this short history, some writers trace a number of stages in its development as its focus, methods and assumptions have changed (e.g. Fullan 1991). These often seem to be of the form 'school improvement research began by adopting approaches a, b, and c; when these failed it moved on to d, e and f'. The writer's assurance that past mistakes and inadequacies have now been overcome seems to be mere assertion. But just because we don't make the same mistakes again, it does not follow that we will make no mistakes at all. Moreover, there is no guarantee that we will not make exactly the same mistakes again.

Essentially, school improvement research aims to understand the processes by which schools can improve and so help to facilitate such change. The assumption that the latter follows immediately from the former is one that we need to look at carefully, however. Even if we do understand how schools change, does it follow that we can act in ways that will produce desirable changes? Schools are such complex and varied organisations that it must be very hard to predict exactly what the effects of any action will be. And if we can't say what the effect of introducing a particular approach or strategy will be in a specific situation, then how do we know whether it will in fact improve things?

School improvement research may help us to understand the nature of particular schools, their challenges and contexts, the processes of organisational change, or the various difficulties that prevent schools from improving: barriers to change, lack of capacity for managing change, 'coasting' schools, 'stuck' schools and many other types. This research often provides rich and detailed descriptions of these phenomena, to which practitioners may relate, and by which they may feel enlightened, empowered and guided. However, unless that understanding enables someone to do something better than they could have done without that knowledge, its value is academic rather than practical.

In order to have this kind of practical value, school improvement research must do two things. Firstly, it must identify clear, well-defined approaches or strategies for improvement, and specify their range of application. Secondly, it must demonstrate convincingly that these do indeed lead to improvement. Unless it can do both these things, it cannot really claim to have any practicable and trustworthy advice to offer the would-be improver. So how far can school improvement research support any claim to meet these requirements?

In relation to the first requirement, school improvement research has something of a dilemma. On the one hand, if it sets out clear, detailed, prescriptive programmes for improvement it may be accused of being overly 'technicist' and reductionist in its view of schools, of producing 'one size fits all', 'off the peg' solutions, and failing to take account of individual differences of context or to allow for improvement as a creative, interactive process. On the other hand, if it does not describe these strategies in this way, it may be criticised for having no advice to give – or at least none that could actually be followed, let alone evaluated – in other words, of being woolly, vague and unscientific.

The former criticism certainly seems to be a strong one. The need for local knowledge, appreciation of the context in which a particular school is located, and understanding of its history, capacities, resources and goals, must all be important background for anyone who would try to help a school to improve. Such a need is widely acknowledged in the school improvement literature:

> But it's really an art. That's why one can't copy successful schools. You just can't reproduce them like that, time and time again, because successful schools in difficult circumstances are *more* than the features you'd expect to see ... Which is why one can't fix a school by remote control.

> (Lodge 1998: 160)

However, the logical consequence of such a perspective is that any general advice about school improvement arising from research, or any other source, cannot really be evaluated. Any advice that is offered is sure to be well intentioned; it is likely to be plausible; it may well be supported by complex and detailed theoretical arguments. However, we really have no way of knowing whether following it is likely to help us to meet our educational aims.

On reflection, therefore, the latter criticism – that ill-defined strategies cannot be evaluated – seems to be the more serious of the two. If school improvement research has no clear advice to give, then why bother reading it? If it is so vague that we could never know whether it is right or not, then how can it be helpful?

Moreover, the former accusation, that prescriptive strategies ignore context and individuality, can be resolved empirically. For certain types of school, teacher or student, in particular circumstances, with specific characteristics, then maybe one size does fit all of this well-specified group. The problem lies in defining the limits of applicability of the solution. If we can do this, we can evaluate whether it really is a solution; if we cannot, then although a putative solution may work for some and not others, unless we know which is which, we should not waste time, energy and resources trying to implement it.

One of the problems that has been perceived with this empirical resolution is that even when school improvement strategies have been evaluated – which is surprisingly rare (Gray *et al.* 1999) – they sometimes fail to show convincingly that our most treasured improvement strategies do in fact work (e.g. Brandsma and Edelenbos 1998; Barker 2005) or if they do, the effects are disappointingly small (Borman *et al.* 2002). There may be a tendency here to blame the messenger – some school improvement researchers would argue that such rigorous evaluation is not appropriate for the kinds of work they are doing – rather than to accept the message. However, this message is an extremely important one and should not be ignored. It would be sloppy and naive to assume uncritically that just because a programme has set out to try to improve something that it has in fact done so. A more critical examination suggests that real improvement is actually quite hard to achieve, and hence unlikely.

But even if we do evaluate our most promising strategies in this stringent way and fail to show that any of them is clearly effective – perhaps because the subtleties of context are too great for us to pin down – then we are still better off than we would have been had we not even tried to evaluate them. We would simply have to concede that none of these strategies, despite their apparent attractions, can be described as evidence-based. Practitioners with real-life problems to solve can be 'advised' to get on with finding their own solutions, unencumbered by advice from researchers.

This discussion has brought us on to the second requirement, that school improvement strategies must demonstrate that they do in fact result in improvement. The main question here is about how such a claim should be properly evaluated, and relates to matters of research design and evaluation methodology. These are complex issues, about which much has been written, and space precludes any detailed discussion here. It is interesting to note, however, that there is an inverse relationship between the rigour of an evaluation and its likelihood of arriving at a positive result:

> ... empirical research over the last 15 years suggests that nothing improves the chances of apparently successful innovation as much as lack of experimental control. Marked enthusiasm for an innovation is negligible in reports on controlled trials ... Declarations that a program is successful are about four times more likely in research based on poor or questionable evaluation designs as in that based on adequate ones.
>
> (Boruch 1997: 69)

One issue we should consider, however, is the question of how 'improvement' is measured. One problem with some school improvement research is that the success or failure of the programme is judged purely by the perceptions of those (usually teachers) involved in the change. Of course these perceptions are important and one would certainly want to know how a programme of school improvement change was perceived by those whose job it was to make it work. However, there are two specific problems with using such measures as an indication of success.

The first is that such teachers' perceptions of change suffer from the problem of 'dissonance reduction' (Festinger 1957). This is the social-psychological phenomenon whereby people who believe they have freely invested effort in a particular course of action are more likely to see it as successful than those who have not invested such effort, since for the former group to see it as unsuccessful would require them to think they had acted foolishly; the alternative to the loss of self-esteem that this judgement would imply is to increase the favourability of their judgements of the success of their actions. Hence in situations where people have been persuaded, encouraged or inspired (but not forced) to put effort into making a change, they are more likely to see it as having been successful than those who did not put in effort (Brown and Peterson 1994). The fact that participants view a programme as having succeeded probably tells us more about the motivational and inspirational skills of those who recruited and persuaded them to commit to it than it does about the real impact of the programme.

The second issue with using teachers' perceptions to judge success is that, although they may be important, they are surely not the most important outcomes of change. School improvement must be about more than just keeping teachers happy: what about outcomes such as pupils' perceptions of change, attitudes towards school or academic achievement? It is extraordinary, for example, that two recent evaluations of major large-scale school improvement programmes in the US were able to say nothing about their impact on student achievement (Muijs 2004).

We may also note here that even when student achievement data are presented, it does not follow that they are well measured. For example, Government claims about the impact of their policies on attainment in English primary schools rest heavily on rising scores in national assessments. However, Tymms (2004) has shown that these apparently substantial rises greatly exaggerate the true, relatively modest, improvement.

Implications for school improvement practice

In a world where initiatives are plentiful, change is constant and advice to do things a particular way seems unending, practitioners need some help to be able to make sensible choices about what they will invest in and what they will ignore. Certainly, if you kiss enough frogs, you may eventually find a prince, but it would be nice to have some way of identifying the princes in advance – or even afterwards.

Undoubtedly, much of the effort that goes into making changes and introducing new practices into schools results in real improvements. However, it is also beyond doubt that much of it does not, and likely that some of it actually does harm. We must also remember that a similar level of effort directed into other activities might have led to even greater improvement.

In practice, decisions about what to try, or which initiative to take on, seem to be guided as much by fashion as anything. The educational world is swept by periodic trends, often returning to previously discarded ideas, investing hope in a different way of doing things; practitioners are carried along on a bandwagon of change. Unfortunately, in England official bodies such as the Department for Education and Skills or the Office for Standards in Education (Ofsted) seem to be no better than anyone else in their uncritical encouragement of such fashions. Such an unscientific approach creates fashion victims, not improving schools. School improvement research must be able to offer something better than this.

I believe it can offer something better, since there are some examples of specific improvement strategies that have been shown to work. Some of these have been widely adopted in practice, though others have not. Let us consider five particular examples.

The first is formative assessment. The evidence is strong that the use of formative assessment has the potential for substantial improvements in learning (Black and William 1998). There is also good research to show how such changes can be introduced (Black et al. 2003). In the UK and in many other countries, this approach has been supported by Governments and appears to be having a substantial impact on practice, so this is a case of policy, practice and research evidence being well aligned.

A second example is peer tutoring. The evidence here is probably just as strong (Fitz-Gibbon, this volume), and again there are some good examples of practical implementation. However, this is a strategy which has yet to receive much official support and which seems to be more the exception than the rule in practice. Policy and practice seem to be generally at odds with the evidence.

A third example is the use of performance monitoring and feedback. The evidence of benefit here is perhaps less secure than for the previous two examples, but is nevertheless quite promising. Many practical examples can be found around the world, though their implementation is not always quite in line with the best evidence (Visscher and Coe 2002). This is therefore an example of partial alignment between policy and practice and evidence.

Our fourth example is learning styles. Whereas the previous examples had well-defined strategies and good evidence of their effects, this one really has neither

(Coffield *et al.* 2004). Unfortunately, despite this lack of support from good research, the practice of adapting teaching to take account of students' supposed learning styles seems to have become widespread in England at the moment, supported by official bodies (e.g. Visscher and Coe 2002). Hence this is an example of serious misalignment between policy, practice and evidence.

A fifth and final example is academic mentoring. Once again, specific strategies and contexts for this group of interventions suffer from a fair amount of conceptual confusion, and the research evidence is far from clear that it enhances academic learning (Hall 2003). The use of mentoring to support school learning (among other things) is nevertheless a popular policy choice in many parts of the world, for example, in England as a specific part of the Key Stage 3 National Strategy (DfES 2002b). Mentoring is therefore another example of some misalignment.

These examples will no doubt be controversial and some will disagree with the rather simplistic and sweeping claims that have been made about them here. Nevertheless, they are intended merely to make the point that there are some educational interventions which meet our two requirements of being well defined and well evaluated, though others do not. In other words, school improvement research can identify some strategies that seem likely to produce benefits and others where this seems much less likely. Sadly, our examples also illustrate that policy and practice are apparently not always well informed by this knowledge.

Limitations of school effectiveness research

The research field of school effectiveness, like that of school improvement, is a relatively recent development, but one whose influence on both policy and practice is strong (Teddlie and Reynolds 2000). However, a difference may perhaps be found in the level of critique it has provoked. Opposition to the assumptions, methods, values, implications and influence of school effectiveness research has been forceful and passionate from some quarters (e.g. Elliott 1996; Hamilton 1996; Slee and Weiner 1998; Thrupp 1999; 2001; Wrigley 2004). School effectiveness research is seen by these writers as dominated by a positivist, reductionist paradigm which underestimates the importance of the social context of schooling, ignores crucial questions about values and oversimplifies educational goals. Other writers have criticised more specific aspects of the methods used and the claims made in school effectiveness research, while broadly accepting the paradigm (e.g. Coe and Fitz-Gibbon 1998; Luyten *et al.* 2005).

Many of these criticisms are sound and well made, so we will not rehearse them in detail here. However, we can illustrate the limitations of what is really known by considering a claim that is fairly typical of the field.

One of the outputs from many school effectiveness studies is a list of characteristics of effective schools. These are arrived at by first identifying schools as 'effective' or 'ineffective' and searching for other differences between them in order to explain why some should be more effective than others. One such list, in this case relating to 'effective teachers', is shown below. Effective teachers:

- set high expectations
- are good at planning
- employ a variety of teaching strategies
- have a clear strategy for pupil management
- manage time and resources wisely
- employ a range of assessment methods
- set appropriate homework
- keep pupils on task (Hay McBer 2000).

This particular list was the product of UK government sponsored research by management consultants Hay McBer (2000) and now forms the basis of the performance management system for teachers in England.

Of course, we could certainly question exactly how these schools (or teachers) are defined to be 'effective'. In practice, the definition usually relates to students' achievement in a limited range of formalised testing, adjusted to take account of (some of) their initial characteristics. Along with many of the authors cited above, we might well feel that such a definition fails to capture the full reality of what makes a good school, and conclude that the whole notion of 'effectiveness' is highly problematic (see Coe and Fitz-Gibbon 1998, for further discussion of this issue).

We might also look at the list and wonder whether it represents good value for the alleged £3m that the Department for Education and Employment paid for this research. Would we have expected that successful teachers would be more likely to keep their pupils off task? Do we habitually hear school improvement advisors suggesting that we should manage our time and resources unwisely? Is it enough to have a 'clear' strategy for pupil management, or does it actually matter what the strategy is? And how would we know whether the homework we set is 'appropriate'? In other words, most of the characteristics on this list, as with other similar lists, are either obvious, so tell us nothing that conscientious teachers were not already trying to do, or they are so vague as to be meaningless.

Of course, good research often seems obvious after it is done, so that is not necessarily an indictment of it. But it would seem more useful if it told us at least one thing that did not seem quite so obviously true. And if it also told us that some things we might have thought were obvious are in fact not true, that would be better still.

Moreover, as the list gives no indication of the relative importance of these characteristics, or even of their combined power to discriminate between 'effective' and 'ineffective' teachers, we cannot tell which of them, if any, are really important. We are perhaps reminded of the words attributed to the billionaire oil magnate, J. Paul Getty, who described the secret of his success: rise early, work late, and strike oil.

However, there is another problem which is arguably more serious than all these objections. This relates to the claim that is implicit in the list, and particularly its use in determining the pay and promotion of teachers in England. The implication is that less effective teachers who adopt these characteristics will, by doing so, become more effective. There are two major problems with this claim.

The first is that we have no way of knowing whether teachers can in fact adopt these characteristics. How should a teacher who is bad at planning become good? Should we expect that when teachers hear that employing a variety of teaching strategies is best (especially if you want to get a pay rise or promotion), they will automatically produce that variety? If a teacher has low expectations, what can we – or they themselves – do about it? In fact, on this last point there is evidence that, perhaps not surprisingly, the expectations of experienced teachers are very hard to change (Raudenbush 1984). In short, none of these characteristics provides a recipe for change.

The second problem is that even if it were possible for teachers to change in such a way as to exhibit these characteristics, it does not follow that doing so would lead to greater effectiveness. For example, as we have defined 'effective' teachers as those whose students do well and it seems reasonable to assume that realistic teachers will quite sensibly have high expectations for able students, then although it may certainly be true that effective teachers set high expectations, the direction of causality could be the opposite of what is implied in the claim; teachers have high expectations because they are effective, not the other way round. In this case, even if we could find some way to raise teachers' expectations, this might have no impact on their effectiveness – or could even reduce it. The same argument applies to all the other characteristics of effective teachers. For example, do students learn more when teachers use a variety of strategies, or are we simply likely to observe greater variety in classrooms where pupils are by nature more motivated and better behaved?

The only way to address these two problems is by conducting intervention studies, in other words, to intervene to try to change teachers' behaviour, or other aspects of schooling, and to evaluate the impact of that intervention attempt. Unfortunately, the standard methodology for school effectiveness studies is entirely descriptive, or correlational. They simply record what exists, rather than trying to change it. These studies may point out the differences between effective and ineffective schools, but they tell us nothing about how to turn the latter into the former.

Implications for schooling at local, national and international levels

We have seen that much of school improvement and school effectiveness research has limited relevance to the practical challenge of actually making schools better. School improvement research, although it is commendable for its use of intervention studies, has unfortunately often failed to specify those interventions adequately or to evaluate their impact rigorously. Although some of the strategies that are to be found in practice and promoted by policy are indeed supported by good evidence, others are not, and, moreover, there seem to be further strategies with good evidential support that are seldom seen in practice or promoted by policy. School effectiveness research, on the other hand, whilst providing us with thorough descriptions of 'effective' schools, has failed to supply any reliable strategies for improving that effectiveness.

The immediate implications of these limitations are clear: we must use our knowledge of school improvement and effectiveness research to develop specific interventions to address particular problems, and then evaluate their impact properly. However, there are also three broader implications for further research and policy. The first is that if policy is to be informed by evidence, we need enough of the right kind of evidence. In particular, evidence about 'what works' must come from high-quality evaluations of intervention studies. To claim that we cannot evaluate large-scale policies rigorously, or that we do not need to do so, is both false and dangerous (Greenberg and Morris 2005). However, on many questions of policy such evidence is simply not available, or is equivocal. Collecting more and better evidence is likely to lead to greater confidence in our knowledge about what works and how it can be implemented.

Second, as well as needing more evidence, we also need less policy. When secure knowledge about what works is lacking, it should be perfectly acceptable to operate without any specific policy. Such a policy vacuum might be abhorrent to policy-makers, but would no doubt be welcomed by many initiative-weary practitioners. Allowing practitioners to find their own local solutions to local problems is not an abdication of policy responsibility, but a sensible response to a situation in which research has no clear advice to give.

Third, we need a better match between evidence, where it exists, and policy. Much has been written about the relationship between research and policy and there is no doubt that this is a complex matter. For now, though, let us simply note that in the context of school improvement, the attractiveness to politicians of phenomena such as league tables and high-pressure accountability for schools, the potential for glory of appearing to 'drive up standards' and the 'tyranny of the international horse race' (Brown 1997) are all pathological to the important business of genuine school improvement.

References

Barker, B. (2005) Transforming schools: illusion or reality? *School Leadership and Management* 25(2): 99–116.

Black, P. and William, D. (1998) Assessment and classroom learning, *Assessment in Education* 5(1): 7–74.

Black, P., Harrison, C., Lee, C., Marshall, B. and William, D. (2003) *Assessment for Learning: Putting it into Practice.* Buckingham: Open University Press.

Borman, G.D., Hewes, G.M., Overman, L.T. and Brown, S. (2002) *Comprehensive School Reform and Student Achievement: A Meta–Analysis*, Center for Research on the Education of Students Placed at Risk (CRESPAR), Johns Hopkins University, Report No. 59. www.csos.jhu.edu/crespar/techReports/Reports59.pdf (accessed Nov. 2005).

Boruch, R.F. (1997) *Randomized Experiments for Planning and Evaluation: A Practical Guide.* London: Sage.

Brandsma, H.P. and Edelenbos, P. (1998) The effects of training programmes for principals and teachers in secondary education: a quasi-experiment based on educational effectiveness indicators. Paper presented to the International Congress of School Effectiveness and School Improvement, Manchester, January 1998.

Brown, M. (1997) The tyranny of the international horse race, in R. Slee and S. Weiner (with S. Tomlinson) *School Effectiveness for Whom?* London: Falmer Press.

Brown, S.P. and Peterson R.A. (1994) The effect of effort on sales performance and job-satisfaction, *Journal of Marketing* 58(2): 70–80.

Coe, R.J. and Fitz-Gibbon, C.T. (1998) School effectiveness research: criticisms and recommendations, *Oxford Review of Education* 24(4): 421–438.

Coffield, F., Moseley, D., Hall, E. and Ecclestone, K. (2004) Should we be using learning styles? What research has to say to practice. London: Learning and Skills Research Centre. Available at http://www.lsda.org.uk/cims/order.aspx?code=041540&src=XOWEB (accessed Nov. 2005).

Department for Education and Skills (DfES) (2002a) *Key Stage 3 National Strategy: Managing the Second Year*, ref: DfES 0143/2002. London: DfES.

Department for Education and Skills (DfES) (2002b) *Key Stage 3 National Strategy: Learning Styles and Writing in Mathematics*, ref: DfES 0381/2002. London: DfES.

Elliott, J. (1996) School effectiveness research and its critics: alternative visions of schooling, *Cambridge Journal of Education* 26: 199–223.

Festinger, L. (1957) *A Theory of Cognitive Dissonance*. Evanston, Il: Row, Peterson.

Fullan, M.G. (1991) *The New Meaning of Educational Change*. London: Cassell.

Gray, J., Hopkins, D., Reynolds, D., Wilcox, B., Farrell, S. and Jesson, D. (1999) *Improving Schools: Performance and Potential*. Buckingham: Open University Press.

Greenberg, D.H. and Morris, S. (2005) Large-scale social experimentation in Britain: what can and cannot be learnt from the Employment Retention and Advancement Demonstration, *Evaluation* 11(2): 223–242.

Hall, J.C. (2003) *Mentoring and Young People: A Literature Review*, SCRE Centre, University of Glasgow, Research report 114. Available at http://www.scre.ac.uk/resreport/pdf/114.pdf (accessed Nov. 2005).

Hamilton, D. (1996) Peddling feel-good fictions: reflections on key characteristics of effective schools, *Forum*, 38(2): 54–56.

Hay McBer (2000) Research into teacher effectiveness: a model of teacher effectiveness. Report by Hay McBer to the Department for Education and Employment. Available from http://www.teachernet.gov.uk/_doc/1487/haymcber.doc (accessed Nov. 2005).

Lodge, C. (1998) What's wrong with our schools? Understanding 'ineffective' and 'failing' schools, in L. Stoll and K. Myers (eds) *No Quick Fixes: Perspectives on Schools in Difficulty*. London: Falmer Press.

Luyten, H., Visscher, A. and Witziers, B. (2005) School effectiveness research: from a review of the criticism to recommendations for further development, *School Effectiveness and School Improvement* 16(3): 249–279.

Muijs, R.D. (2004) Tales of American comprehensive school reform: successes, failures, and reflections, *School Effectiveness and School Improvement* 15(3-4): 487–492.

Raudenbush, S. (1984). Magnitude of teacher expectancy effects of pupil IQ as a function of credibility of expectation induction. A synthesis of findings from 18 experiments, *Journal of Educational Psychology* 76(1): 85–97.

Slee, R. and Weiner, S. (with S. Tomlinson) (1998) *School Effectiveness for Whom?* London: Falmer Press.

Teddlie, C. and Reynolds, D. (2000) *The International Handbook of School Effectiveness Research*. London: RoutledgeFalmer.

Thrupp, M. (1999) *Schools Making a Difference: Let's Be Realistic!* Buckingham: Open University Press.

Thrupp, M. (2001) Sociological and political concerns about school effectiveness research: time for a new reseach agenda, *School Effectiveness and School Improvement* 12(1): 7–40.

Tymms, P. (2004) Are standards rising in English primary schools?, *British Educational Research Journal* 30(4): 477–494.

Visscher, A.J. and Coe, R. (2002) *School Improvement through Performance Feedback*. Lisse: Swets and Zeitlinger.

Wrigley, T. (2004) School effectiveness: the problem of reductionism, *British Educational Research Journal* 30(2): 227–244.

9

MICHAEL APPLE
Away with all teachers: the cultural politics of home learning

Introduction

If one of the marks of the growing acceptance of ideological changes is their positive presentation in the popular media, then home schooling has clearly found a place in our consciousness. It has been discussed in the national press, on television and radio, and in widely circulated magazines. Its usual presentation is that of a saviour, a truly compelling alternative to a public school system that is presented as a failure. While the presentation of public schools as simply failures is deeply problematic, it is the largely unqualified support of home schooling that concerns me here.

Data on home schooling are not always accurate and are often difficult to compile. However, a sense of the extent of home schooling can be found in the fact that the National Home Education Research Institute has estimated that as of the 1997/1998 school year, there were 1.5 million children being home schooled in the United States. The Institute has also suggested that there has been a growth of 15% annually in these numbers since 1990. While these data are produced by an organisation that is one of the strongest supporters of home schooling, even given the possible inflation of these figures, it is clear that this is a considerable number of students.

In a relatively short chapter, I cannot deal at length with all of the many issues that could be raised about the home schooling movement but I do want to ask a number of critical questions about the associated dangers. While it is quite probable that some specific children and families will gain from home schooling, my concerns are larger. They are connected to the more extensive restructuring of this society that I believe is quite dangerous and to the manner in which our very sense of public responsibility is withering in ways that will lead to even further social inequalities. In order to illuminate these dangers, I shall have to do a number of things: situate home schooling within the larger movement that provides much of its impetus; suggest its connections with other protectionist impulses; connect it to the history of and concerns about the growth of activist government; and, finally, point to how it may actually hurt many other students who are not home schooled.

Many home schoolers are guided by what they believe are biblical under-standings of the family, gender relationships, legitimate knowledge, the importance of tradition, the role of Government and the economy (Kintz 1997; Detwiler 1999; Apple 2006). They constitute part of what I have called 'conservative restoration' in which a tense alliance has been built among various segments of the public in favour of particular policies in education and the larger social world.

Education and conservative modernisation

Long-lasting educational transformations often come not from the work of educators and researchers, but from larger social movements which tend to push our major political, economic and cultural institutions in specific directions. Thus, it would be impossible to fully understand educational reforms over the past decades without situating them within, for example, the long struggles by multiple communities of colour and women for both cultural recognition and economic redistribution (see, e.g., Fraser 1997). Even such taken for granted things as State textbook adoption policies are the results of widespread populist and anti-northern movements and especially the class and race struggles over culture and power that organised and reorganised the polity in the United States a century ago (Apple 2000).

It should, then, come as no surprise that education is again witnessing the continued emergence and growing influence of powerful social movements. Some of these may lead to increased democratisation and greater equality, while others are based on a fundamental shift in the very meanings of democracy and equality and are more than a little retrogressive socially and culturally. Unfortunately, it is the latter that have emerged as the most powerful.

The rightward turn has been the result of years of well-funded and creative ideological efforts by the right to form a broad-based coalition. This new alliance, which is technically called a 'new hegemonic bloc', has been so successful because it has been able to make major inroads in the battle over common sense. It has creatively stitched together different social tendencies and commitments and has organised them under its own general leadership in issues dealing with welfare, culture, the economy and education. Its aim in educational and social policy might best be described as 'conservative modernisation' (Dale 1989). In the process, democracy has been reduced to consumption practices. Citizenship has been reduced to possessive individualism. And a politics based on resentment and a fear of the 'Other' has been pressed forward.

There are a number of major elements within this new alliance (see Apple 2006 for more detailed discussion). The first, *neo-liberals*, represent dominant economic and political elites who are intent on modernising the economy and the connected institutions. They are certain that markets and consumer choice will solve all of our social problems, since private is necessarily good and public is necessarily bad.

While there is clear empirical evidence about the very real inequalities that are created by such educational policies (Whitty *et al*. 1998; Lauder and Hughes 1999; Apple 2006), this group is usually in leadership of the alliance. If we think of this new bloc as an ideological umbrella, neo-liberals are holding the umbrella's handle.

The second group, *neo-conservatives*, are economic and cultural conservatives who want a return to high standards, discipline, 'real' knowledge, and what is in essence a form of Social Darwinist competition. They are fuelled by a nostalgic and quite romanticised vision of the past. It is often based on a fundamental misrecognition of the fact that what they might call the classics and 'real' knowledge gained that status as the result of intense past conflicts and often were themselves seen as equally dangerous culturally and just as morally destabilising as any of the new elements of the curriculum and culture they now castigate (Levine 1996).

The third element is made up of largely white working-class and middle-class groups who mistrust the State and are concerned with security, the family, gender and age relations within the home, sexuality, and traditional and fundamentalist religious values and knowledge. They form an increasingly active segment of *authoritarian populists* who are powerful in education and in other areas of politics and social and cultural policy. They provide much of the support from below for neo-liberal and neo-conservative positions, since they see themselves as disenfranchised by the secular humanism that supposedly now pervades public schooling. They are also often among those larger numbers of people whose very economic livelihoods are most at stake in the economic restructuring and capital flight that we are now experiencing.

Many home schoolers combine beliefs from all three of these tendencies; but it is the last one that seems to drive a large portion of the movement (Kintz 1997; Detwiler 1999; Apple 2006; Apple and Buras 2006).

Satan's threat

For many on the right, one of the key enemies is public education. Secular education is turning our children into aliens and, by teaching them to question our ideas, is turning them against us. What are often accurate concerns about public schooling that I noted earlier are here often connected to more deep-seated and intimate worries. These worries echo Elaine Pagels' argument that Christianity has historically defined its most fearful satanic threats not from distant enemies, but in relation to very intimate ones (Pagels 1995). 'The most dangerous characteristic of the satanic enemy is that though he will look just like us, he will nevertheless have changed completely' (cited in Kintz 1997: 73).

These fears about the nation, home, family, children's innocence, religious values and traditional views of gender relations are sutured together into a more general fear of the destruction of a moral compass and personal freedom. 'Our' world is disintegrating around us. Its causes are not the economically destructive policies of the globalising economy (Greider 1997), not the decisions of an economic elite, and not the ways in which, say, our kind of economy turns *all* things into commodities for sale. Rather the causes are transferred onto those institutions and people which are themselves being constantly buffeted by the same forces, public sector institutions, schooling, poor people of colour, other women who have struggled for centuries to build a society that is more responsive to the hopes and dreams of many people who have been denied participation in the public sphere, and so on.

As I noted at the beginning of this chapter, however, it is important not to stereotype individuals involved in this movement. For example, a number of men and women who are activists in rightist movements believe that some elements of feminism did improve the conditions of women overall. By focusing on equal pay for equal work and opening up job opportunities that had been traditionally denied to women who had to work for pay, women activists have benefited many people. However, for authoritarian populists, feminism and secular institutions in general still tend to break with God's law. They are much too individualistic and misinterpret the divine relationship between families and God. In so doing, many aspects of civil rights legislation, of the public schools' curricula, and so many other parts of secular society are simply wrong. Thus, for example, if one views the Constitution of the United States literally as divinely inspired, then it is not public institutions but the traditional family that is the core social unit that must be protected by the Constitution (Kintz 1997: 97). In a time of seeming cultural disintegration, when traditions are under threat and when the idealised family faces ever more externally produced dangers, protecting our families and our children are key elements in returning to God's grace.

Even without these religious elements, a defensive posture is clear in much of the movement. In many ways, the movement toward home schooling mirrors the growth of privatised consciousness in other areas of society. It is an extension of the suburbanisation of everyday life that is so evident all around us. In essence, it is the equivalent of gated communities and of the privatisation of neighbourhoods, recreation, parks and so many other things. It provides a security zone both physically and ideologically.

This cocooning is not just about seeking an escape from the problems of the city. It is a rejection of the entire *idea* of the city. Cultural and intellectual diversity, complexity, ambiguity, uncertainty and proximity to 'the Other', all these are to be shunned (Kintz 1997: 107). In place of the city is the engineered pastoral, the neat and well-planned universe where things (and people) are in their rightful place and reality is safe and predictable.

Yet in so many ways such a movement mirrors something else. It is a microcosm of the increasing segmentation of American society in general. As we move to a society segregated by residence, race, economic opportunity and income, purity is increasingly more apt to be found in the fact that upper classes send their children to elite private schools; where neighbourliness is determined by property values; where evangelical Christians, ultra-orthodox Jews and others interact only with each other and their children are schooled in private religious schools or schooled at home (Kintz 1997: 108). A world free of conflict, uncertainty and the voice and culture of the Other (in a word I used before, cocooning) is the ideal.

Even with the evident shortcomings of many public schools, at the very least they provide 'a kind of social glue, a common cultural reference point in our polyglot, increasingly multicultural society' (Shapiro 1999: 12). Yet, whether called personalising or cocooning, it is exactly this common reference point that is rejected by many within the home schooling movement's pursuit of freedom and choice.

This particular construction of the meaning of freedom is of considerable moment, since there is a curious contradiction within such conservatism's obsession with freedom. In many ways this emphasis on freedom is, paradoxically, based on a *fear* of freedom (Kintz 1997: 168). It is valued, but also loathed as a site of danger, of a world out of control. Many home schoolers reject public schooling out of concern for equal time for their beliefs. They want equality. Yet it is a specific vision of equality, because coupled with their fear of things out of control is a powerful anxiety that the nation's usual understanding of equality will produce uniformity (Kintz 1997: 186). But this feared uniformity is not seen as the same as the religious and cultural homogeneity sponsored by the conservative project. It is a very different type of uniformity, one in which the fear that we are all the same actually speaks to a loss of religious particularity. Thus, again there is another paradox at the heart of this movement: we want everyone to be like 'us' (Smith 1998); but we want the right to be different, a difference based on being God's elect group. Uniformity weakens our specialness. This tension between knowing one is a member of God's elect people and thus by definition different and also so certain that one is correct that the world needs to be changed to fit one's image is one of the central paradoxes behind authoritarian populist impulses. For some home schoolers, the paradox is solved by withdrawal of one's children from the public sphere in order to maintain their difference. For others, this allows them to prepare themselves and their children with an armour of Christian beliefs that will enable them to go forth into the world later on to bring God's word to those who are not among the elect. Once again, let us declare our particularity, our difference, in order to better prepare ourselves to bring the unanointed world to our set of uniform beliefs (Apple 2006).

Attacking the State

At the base of this fear is a sense that the State is intervening in our daily lives in quite powerful ways, ways that are causing even more losses. It is not possible to understand the growth of home schooling unless we connect it to the history of the attack on the public sphere in general and on the Government in particular. In order to better comprehend the anti-statist impulses that lie behind a good deal of the home schooling movement, I need to place these impulses in a longer historical and social context. Some history and theory is necessary here.

One of the keys to this is the development of what Clarke and Newman have called the 'managerial State' (Clarke and Newman 1997). This was an active State that combined bureaucratic administration and professionalism. The organisation of the State centred around the application of specific rules of coordination. Routinisation and predictability are among the hallmarks of such a State. This was to be coupled with a second desirable trait, that of social, political and personal neutrality, rather than nepotism and favouritism. This bureaucratic routinisation and predictability would be balanced by an emphasis on professional discretion. Here, bureaucratically regulated professionals such as teachers and administrators would still have an element of irreducible autonomy based on their training and qualifications. Yet fairness and impartiality were not enough; the professional also personalised the managerial State. Professionals such as teachers made the State approachable by not only signifying neutrality but by acting in non-anonymous ways to foster the 'public good and to help individuals and families' (Clarke and Newman 1997: 5–7).

Of course, such bureaucratic and professional norms were there not only to benefit clients. They acted to protect the State, by providing it with legitimacy. They also served to insulate professional judgements from critical scrutiny. Thus, from the end of the Second World War until approximately the mid-1970s, there was a settlement, a compromise, in which an activist welfare state was seen as legitimate. It was sustained by a triple legitimacy. There was (largely) bi-partisan support for the State to provide and manage a larger part of social life, a fact that often put it above a good deal of party politics. Bureaucratic administration promised to act impartially for the benefit of everyone. Professionals employed by the State, such as teachers and other educators, were there to apply expert knowledge to serve the public (Clarke and Newman 1997: 8). This compromise was widely accepted and provided public schools and other public institutions with a strong measure of support.

This compromise came under severe attack, as the fiscal crisis deepened and as competition over scarce economic, political and cultural resources grew more heated in the 1970s and beyond. The political forces of conservative movements used this crisis, often in quite cynical, manipulative and well-funded ways. The State was criticised for denying the opportunity for consumers to exercise choice. The welfare state was seen as swindling the taxpayer to pay for public handouts for those who ignored personal responsibility for their actions. These scroungers from the underclass were seen as sexually promiscuous, immoral and lazy as opposed to the rest of us who were hard-working, industrious and moral. They supposedly are a drain on all of us economically and state sponsored support of them leads to the collapse of the family and traditional morality (Apple 2000). These arguments may not have been totally accurate (see, for example, Fine and Weis 1998), but they were effective.

This suturing together of neo-liberal and neo-conservative attacks led to a particular set of critiques against the State. For many people, the State was no longer the legitimate and neutral upholder of the public good. Instead the welfare state was an active agent of national decline, as well as an economic drain on the country's (and the family's) resources.

These moral, political, and economic concerns were easily transferred to public schooling, since for many people the school was, and is, the public institution closest to them in their daily life. Hence, public schooling and the teaching and curricula became central targets of attack. Curricula and teachers were not impartial, but elitist. School systems were imposing the Other's morality on us. And 'real Americans' who were patriotic, religious and moral, as opposed to everyone else, were suffering and were the new oppressed (Delfattore 1992; Apple and Buras 2006). While this position fits into a long history of the paranoid style of American cultural politics and was often based on quite inaccurate stereotypes, it does point to a profound sense of alienation that many people feel.

Much of this anti-statism of course was fuelled by the constant attention given in the media and in public pronouncements to incompetent teachers who are over-paid and have short working days and long vacations. We should not minimise the effects of the conservative attacks on schools for their supposed inefficiency, wasting of financial resources, and lack of connection to the economy. After years of well-orchestrated attacks, it would be extremely odd if one did not find that the effects on popular consciousness were real. The fact that a number of these criticisms may be *partly* accurate should not be dismissed. There undoubtedly is a small group of teachers who treat teaching as simply a job that gives them many holidays and free time in the summer. Administrative costs and bureaucratic requirements in schools have risen. Parents and local communities do have a justifiable right to worry about whether their daughters and sons will have decent jobs when they leave school, especially in a time when our supposedly booming economy has left millions of people behind and many of the jobs being created are anything but fulfilling and secure (Apple 1996). (The fact that the school has very little to do with this is important.)

Yet, it is not only worries about teachers that fuel this movement. As I point out in *Educating the 'Right' Way* (Apple 2006), public schools themselves are seen as extremely dangerous places. These schools were institutions that threatened one's very soul. Temptations and Godlessness were everywhere within them. God's truths were expunged from the curriculum and God's voice could no longer be heard. Prayers were now illegal and all of the activities that bound one's life to scriptural realities were seen as deviant.

Even with the negative, powerful emotions that such senses of loss and disconnection create, an additional element has entered into the emotional economy being created here with a crushing force. For an increasingly large number of parents, public schools are now seen as threatening in an even more powerful way. They are dangerous bodily; that is, they are seen as filled with physical dangers to the very life of one's children. The spate of shootings in schools in the United States has had a major impact on the feelings of insecurity that parents have about their children. The horrors of seeing students shoot other students, and now not in those supposedly troubled urban schools but in the suburban areas that had grown after people fled the city, exacerbated the situation. If even the schools of affluent suburbia were sites of danger, then the *only* remaining safe haven was the fortress home.

Fears, no matter how powerful they are or whether they are justified or not, are not enough, however. That a person will act on her or his fears is made more or less probable by the availability of resources to support taking action. It is an almost taken for granted point, but important nonetheless, that the growth of home schooling has been stimulated by the wider accessibility to tools that make it easier for parents to engage in it. Among the most important is the internet (see Bromley and Apple 1998; Apple 2006). There are scores of websites available that give advice, that provide technical and emotional support, that tell the stories of successful home schoolers, and that are more than willing to sell material at a profit. The fact that, like the conservative evangelical movement in general (Smith 1998), a larger portion of home schoolers than before seem to have the economic resources to afford computers means that economic capital can be mobilised in anti-school strategies in more flexible and dynamic ways than in earlier periods of the home schooling movement.

Given what I have just said, we do need to recognise that there are elements of good sense in the critique of the State made by both the left and the right, such as the home schoolers I have discussed above. The Government has assumed all too often that the only true holders of expertise in education, social welfare, etc. are those in positions of formal authority. This has led to a situation of over-bureaucratisation. It has also led to the State being partly colonised by a particular faction of the new middle class that seeks to ensure its own mobility and its own positions by employing the state for its own purposes (Bourdieu 1996; Apple 2005). Some schools have become sites of danger given the levels of alienation and meaninglessness – and the dominance of violence as an imaginary solution in the popular media. However, there is a world of difference between, say, acknowledging that there are some historical tendencies within the State to become overly bureaucratic and to not listen carefully enough to the expressed needs of the people it is supposed to serve and a blanket rejection of public control and public institutions such as schools. This has not only led to cocooning, but it threatens the gains made by large groups of disadvantaged people for whom the possible destruction of public schooling is nothing short of a disaster. The final section of my analysis turns to a discussion of this.

Public and private

We need to think *relationally* when we ask who will be the major beneficiaries of the attack on the State and the movement toward home schooling. What if gains that are made by one group of people come at the expense of other, even more culturally and economically oppressed, groups? As we shall see, this is not an inconsequential worry in this instance.

A distinction that is helpful here is one between a politics of redistribution and a politics of recognition. In the first, the concern is for socio-economic injustice. Here, the political-economic system of a society creates conditions that lead to exploitation, and/or economic marginalisation (having one's paid work confined to poorly paid and undesirable jobs or having no real access to the routes to serious and better paying jobs), and/or deprivation. All of these socio-economic injustices lead to arguments about whether this is a just or fair society and whether identifiable groups of people actually have equality of resources (Fraser 1997: 13).

The second dynamic (recognition) is often related to redistribution in the real world, but it has its own specific history and differential power relations as well. It is related to the politics of culture and symbols. In this case, injustice is rooted in a society's social patterns of representation and interpretation. Examples of this include cultural domination (being constantly subjected to patterns of interpretation or cultural representation that are alien to one's own or even hostile to it), non-recognition (basically being rendered invisible in the dominant cultural forms in the society), and disrespect (having oneself routinely stereotyped or maligned in public representations in the media, schools, government policies or in everyday conduct (Fraser 1997: 14). These kinds of issues surrounding the politics of recognition are central to the identities and sense of injustice of many home schoolers. Indeed, they provide the organising framework for their critique of public schooling and their demand that they be allowed to teach their children outside of such State control.

While both forms of injustice are important, it is absolutely crucial that we recognise that an adequate response to one must not lead to the exacerbation of the other. That is, responding to the claims of injustice in recognition by one group (say religious conservatives) must not make the conditions that lead to exploitation, economic marginalisation and deprivation more likely to occur for other groups. Unfortunately, this may be the case for some of the latent effects of home schooling.

Because of this, it is vitally important not to separate out the possible effects of home schooling from what we are beginning to know about the possible consequences of neo-liberal policies in general in education. As Whitty *et al.* have shown in their review of the international research on voucher and choice plans, one of the latent effects of such policies has been the reproduction of traditional hierarchies of class and race. That is, the programmes clearly have differential benefits whereby those who already possess economic and cultural capital reap significantly more benefits than those who do not. This is patterned in very much the same ways as the stratification of economic, political and cultural power produces inequalities in nearly every socio-economic sphere (Whitty *et al.* 1998; see also Apple 2006). One of the hidden consequences that is emerging from the expanding conservative critique of public institutions, including schools, is a growing anti-tax movement in which those who have chosen to place their children in privatised, marketised and home schools do not want to pay taxes to support the schooling of 'the Other' (Apple 1996).

The wider results of this are becoming clear, a declining tax base for schooling, social services, healthcare, housing and anything public for those populations who suffer the most from the economic dislocations and inequalities that so deeply characterise this nation. Thus, a politics of recognition has begun to have extremely negative effects on the politics of redistribution. It is absolutely crucial that we recognise this. If it is the case that the emergence of educational markets has consistently benefited the most advantaged parents and students and has consistently disadvantaged both economically poor parents and students, and parents and students of colour (Whitty *et al.* 1998; Lauder and Hughes 1999; Ball 2003; Power *et al.* 2003; Apple 2006) then we need to critically examine the latent effects of the growth of home schooling in the same light. Will it be the case that social justice loses in this equation just as it did and does in many of the other highly publicised programmes of choice?

A case in point is the way in which the ongoing debate over the use of public money for religious purposes in education is often subverted through manipulation of loopholes that are only available to particular groups. Religiously motivated home schoolers are currently engaged in exploiting public funding in ways that are not only hidden, but in ways that raise serious questions about the drain on economic resources during a time of severe budget crises in all too many school districts.

Let me say more about this, since it provides an important instance of my argument that gains in recognition for some groups (say, home schools) can have decidedly negative effects in other spheres such as the politics of redistribution. In California, for example, charter schools have been used as a mechanism to gain public money for home schoolers. Charter school legislation in California has been employed in very interesting ways to accomplish this. In one recent study, for example, 50% of charter schools were serving home schoolers. Independent study charter schools (a creative pseudonym for computer-linked home schooling) have been used by both school districts and parents to gain money that otherwise might not have been available. In this and other cases, the money given to parents for enrolling in such independent study charter schools was used by the parents to purchase religious material produced and sold by Bob Jones University, one of the most conservative religious schools in the entire nation (Wells 1999; Apple 2006).

Thus, public money not legally available for overtly sectarian material is used to purchase religious curricula under the auspices of charter school legislation. Yet unlike all curricula used in public schools which *must* be publicly accountable in terms of its content and costs, the material purchased for home schooling has no public accountability whatsoever. While this does give greater choice to home schoolers and does enable them to act on a politics of recognition, it not only takes money away from other students who do not have the economic resources to afford computers in the home, but it denies them a say in what the community's children will learn about themselves and their cultures, histories, values and so on. Given the fact that a number of textbooks used in fundamentalist religious schools expressly state such things as 'Islam is a false religion' and embody similar claims that many citizens would find deeply offensive, it does raise serious questions about whether it is appropriate for public money to be used to teach such content without any public accountability.

I do not wish to be totally negative here. After all, this is a complicated issue in which there may be justifiable worries among home schoolers that their culture and values are not being listened to. But it must be openly discussed, not lost in the simple statement that we should support a politics of recognition of religiously motivated home schoolers because their culture seems to them to be not sufficiently recognised in public institutions. At the very least, the possible dangers to the public good need to be recognised.

Conclusion

I have used this essay to raise a number of critical questions about the economic, social and ideological tendencies that often stand behind significant parts of the home schooling movement. In the process, I have situated it within larger social movements that I and many others believe can have quite negative effects on our sense of community, on the health of the public sphere, and on our commitment to building a society that is less economically and racially stratified. I have suggested that issues need to be raised about the effects of its commitment to cocooning, its attack on the State, and its growing use of public funding with no public accountability. Yet, I have also argued that there are clear elements of good sense in its criticisms of the bureaucratic nature of all too many of our institutions, in its worries about the managerial State, and in its devotion to being active in the education of its children.

In my mind, the task is to disentangle the elements of good sense evident in these concerns from the selfish and anti-public agenda that has been pushing concerned parents and community members into the arms of the conservative restoration. The task of public schools is to listen much more carefully to the complaints of parents such as these and to rebuild our institutions in much more responsive ways.

We have models for doing exactly that, as the democratic schools movement demonstrates (Apple and Beane 1995; 1999; see also Apple *et al.* 2003). While I do not want to be overly romantic here, there *are* models of curricula and teaching that are related to community sentiment, that are committed to social justice and fairness, and that are based in schools where both teachers and students want to be. If schools do not do this, there may be all too many parents who are pushed in the direction of anti-school sentiment. This would be a tragedy both for the public school system and for our already withered sense of community that is increasingly under threat.

Raymond Williams may have expressed it best when, positioning himself as an optimist without any illusions, he reminded us of the importance of the *mutual* determination of the meanings and values that should guide our social life. In expressing his commitment toward the long revolution, his words are worth remembering: 'We must speak for hope, as long as it doesn't mean suppressing the nature of the danger' (Williams 1989: 322). There are identifiable dangers to identifiable groups of people in public schooling as we know it. However, the privatising alternatives may be much worse.

References

Apple, M.W. (1996) *Cultural Politics and Education*. New York: Teachers' College Press.

Apple, M.W. (1999) *Power, Meaning, and Identity*. New York: Peter Lang.

Apple, M.W. (2000) *Official Knowledge*, 2nd edn. New York: Routledge.

Apple, M.W. (2005) Education, markets, and an audit culture, *Critical Quarterly* 47(1–2): 11–29.

Apple, M.W. (2006) *Educating the 'Right' Way: Markets, Standards, God, and Inequality*, 2nd edn. New York: Routledge.

Apple, M.W. and Beane, J.A. (eds) (1995) *Democratic Schools*. Washington, DC: Association for Supervision and Curriculum Development.

Apple, M.W. and Beane, J.A. (eds) (1999) *Democratic Schools: Lessons from the Chalk Face*. Buckingham: Open University Press.

Apple, M.W. and Buras, K.L. (eds) (2006) *The Subaltern Speak: Curriculum, Power, and Educational Struggles.* New York: Routledge.

Apple, M.W., Aasen, P., Cho, M.K., Gandia, L., Oliver, A., Sung, Y-K., Tavares, H. and Wong, T-H (2003) *The State and the Politics of Knowledge.* New York: RoutledgeFalmer.

Ball, S. (2003) *Class Strategies and the Education Market.* London: RoutledgeFalmer.

Bourdieu, P. (1996) *The State Nobility.* Stanford, CA: Stanford University Press.

Bromley, H. and Apple, M.W. (eds) (1998) *Education/Technology/Power.* Albany, NY: State University of New York Press.

Clarke, J. and Newman, J. (1997) *The Managerial State.* Thousand Oaks, CA: Sage.

Dale, R. (1989) The Thatcherite project in education, *Critical Social Policy* 9(3): 4–19.

Delfattore, J. (1992) *What Johnny Shouldn't Read.* New Haven, NJ: Yale University Press.

Detwiler, F. (1999) *Standing on the Premises of God: The Christian Right's Fight to Redefine America's Public Schools.* New York: New York University Press.

Fine, M. and Weis, L. (1998) *The Unknown City: The Lives of Poor and Working-class Young Adults.* Boston, MA: Beacon Press.

Fraser, N. (1997) *Justice Interruptus.* New York: Routledge.

Greider, W. (1997) *One World, Ready or Not.* New York: Simon and Schuster.

Kintz, L. (1997) *Between Jesus and the Market.* Durham, NC: Duke University Press.

Lauder, H. and Hughes, D. (1999) *Trading in Futures: Why Markets in Education Don't Work.* Philadelphia: Open University Press.

Levine, L. (1996) *The Opening of the American Mind.* Boston, MA: Beacon Press.

Pagels, E. (1995) *The Origins of Satan.* New York: Random House.

Power, S., Edwards, T., Whitty, G. and Wigfall, V. (2003) *Education and the Middle Class.* Buckingham: Open University Press.

Shapiro, A. (1999) The net that binds, *The Nation* 21 June.

Smith, C. (1998) *American Evangelicalism.* Chicago: University of Chicago Press.

Wells, A.S. (1999) *Beyond the Rhetoric of Charter School Reform.* Los Angeles: Graduate School of Education and Information Studies, UCLA.

Whitty, G., Power, S. and Halpin, D. (1998) *Devolution and Choice in Education.* Philadelphia: Open University Press.

Williams, R. (1989) *Resources of Hope.* New York: Verso.

10

EMMANUEL MUFTI

New students: same old structures

Introduction

There is no doubt that there has been a rapid increase in the number of students attending higher education institutions in the past 40 years. Current Government figures suggest that nearly 45% of 18–30-year-olds are currently studying within higher education institutions as opposed to 6% of under-21-year-olds in 1963. It is worth noting that this figure of 45% does not solely relate to degree-level study or above but includes a range of new provision including foundation courses and other sub-degree programmes. There is also real concern that the numbers of students attending from lower socio-economic groups has not risen as rapidly as those from higher socio-economic groups. Figures available from 2003 (DfES 2003) suggest that the latter group are over five times more likely to attend higher education than the former. Additionally Galindo-Rueda *et al.* (2004) discovered that between 1994 and 2002 the increase in students from lower socio-economic groups was 0.88% compared to a 9% increase in student numbers from higher socio-economic groups over the same period. The main focus of this chapter is not primarily concerned with which students enter higher education but the provision they encounter within post-1992 institutions upon entry and their ability to engage with that provision. It is worth pointing out at this stage that I begin from the basic premise that higher education should and must be available to all students who wish to attend and that it is the institutions that must adapt rather than the student. The remainder of the chapter will focus on the needs of students entering higher education under the widening participation agenda and draw on some initial research into this student group.

Retention issues

This increase in student numbers has resulted in an expansion of provision within the institutions including the granting of university status to a range of former colleges of higher education together with an increase in the range of courses available to potential students. It is these courses, within post-1992 institutions, that have mainly benefited from the increase in student numbers. According to the DfES paper (2003) *The Future of Higher Education* this is mainly due to the lack of applications to the Russell group institutions from students who originate from lower socio-economic groups. However, current figures suggest that students entering higher education from state schools are significantly more likely to gain entry to a post-1992 institution. In addition statistical evidence from the Higher Education Statisics Agency (HESA) demonstrates that the dropout rate of students is higher amongst those institutions that primarily recruit from state schools. There is an undoubted correlation between the backgrounds of students and their likelihood of completion. For example, the national picture in 2002 suggests that 25% of the students across institutions were from social groups IIIm–V and the level of non-completers stood at 16%. However, in institutions such as Cambridge, Leeds, Durham and Bath, where the level of students from lower social economic groups is below 20%, the non-completion rate remains well below the national average. Conversely in institutions such as Liverpool Hope, Liverpool John Moores, Luton and North London, where the intake is more diverse, the non-completion rate tends to be significantly higher than the average. It is not sufficient to suggest that a more diverse intake results in a higher rate of non-completion, particularly when institutions such as Wolverhampton have a diverse intake well above the average but maintain levels of retention close to the national standard (HESA 2005). It is further worth noting that, despite suggestions to the contrary, poor levels of student retention is not a new issue. Historically non-completion rates have rarely been below 10%.

The needs of students

A range of research, for example Kerka (1995) and Moxley *et al.* (2001) have stated that whilst the reasons for student dropouts are complex, one recurring theme is where the course fails to meet students' expectations. Moxley *et al.* further state that incorrect choice of course and a growing awareness of students that their course will not enable them to fulfil their, largely career-orientated, goals results in lower levels of retention.

Tinto (1975; 1987) discusses the philosophical and theoretical approach to the issue of student retention. This primarily focuses upon the extent of social and academic integration of the student within the institution and further on their interactions with academic staff, the suggestion being that a student is more likely to drop out if, for whatever reason, they fail to fully integrate. The chapter suggests that successful integration is less likely amongst students who have entered higher education through the widening participation route. Therefore, in order to increase retention and improve the capacity of students to settle into and become a functional part of an institution, it is imperative to examine all factors that affect students' studies. Tinto's (1975) model of student retention suggests that students' decision to withdraw from a course is based upon a range of factors, not all of them within the remit of the institution. Figure 10.1 further illustrates this.

As can be seen the model suggests that in any debate concerning retention individual students and their needs must remain at its heart.

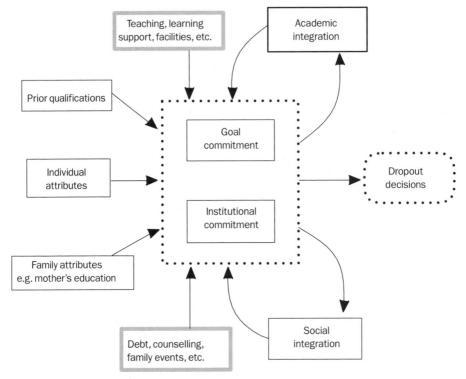

Figure 10.1   Tinto's model of student retention
Source: Draper (2003)

Cultural capital

Bourdieu and Wacquant (1992) suggests that students from higher social economic groups feel like a 'fish in water' when entering the world of higher education, that the ethos and culture of the university is an environment of which they are aware and feel a part of. This feeling of belonging can in part be attributed to prior knowledge, awareness and expectations of attending higher education institutions. Bourdieu suggests that society is made up of 'fields of power' and that within those fields individuals will dominate or be dominated dependent upon the status of their 'capital'. Bourdieu describes four main types of capital of which the most relevant to this discussion is the theoretical perspective of cultural capital. This links well to Tinto's model, drawing as it does on the 'capital invested in the individual by parents, educators and society' (Nash 1999). Effectively the suggestion is that those students who enter higher education under the widening participation agenda may have less cultural capital upon entry than students who come from families with a long history of higher level study. Perhaps more pertinently to the discussion Naidoo (2004) states that:

> 'Academic capital' is defined as an institutionalized form of cultural capital based on properties such as prior educational achievement, a 'disposition' to be

academic (seen, for example, in manner of speech and writing), and specially designated competencies.

(2004: 459)

Alternatively, Nash (1999) has referred to 'a feel for the game'. I would suggest that the 'game' and the 'academic disposition' are concepts that differ greatly between the institution, the staff and the student. Further to this Bourdieu's concept of 'habitus' suggest that choices which, on the surface level, appear to be available to students are in fact closed. Classical interpretations of habitus, as it relates to the school system, can also be examined here. Of relevance too are issues of power and knowledge outlined by, for example, Weber (1968), particularly in relation to his concept of traditional power. Weber stated that there are four main types of power; of particular interest to this chapter is his concept of traditional power. Traditional power is not exclusively based on economic power but on existing values and the preservation of social ties. I would suggest that Weber's traditional power has relevance here, not from the perspective of the students entering higher education under the widening participation agenda, but from the institutions and the staff working within them. In essence, so that our working practices in higher education remain traditional, we expect individuals to be solely devoted to their studies, to know what is expected of them and to fit into the traditional and well-established patterns of higher education. Therefore, whilst these perspectives have relevance to the debate, this chapter is not suggesting that the power relationships and cultural deprivation encountered by students in higher education is a way of preserving and protecting the status quo. Rather, that the practices relating to, and expectations of, academic achievement have become institutionalised around the perception of that 'ideal student'. Experience tells us that this can even relate to expectations of critical awareness and a general high level of reading and will almost certainly relate to reading around the subject and reading merely for interest. This links to Becker's (1963) assertion that (school) teachers have a perception of the ideal pupil/student which is not primarily based around their intake or experiences but rather on a fabricated collage of their own childhood coupled with images from the media and arts which drew them into teaching in the first instance. This concept could equally be applied to higher education and arguably is becoming more relevant as the intake continues to grow.

Naidoo refers to higher education as being a 'sorting machine' which selects students according to a 'social classification' and then moulds them towards an 'academic classification'. I suggest that our initial choice of student has altered and, therefore, it is necessary to examine the input students receive. The use of the word 'input' here relates to the experiences individual students will face within higher education.

Background to the research

The research was conducted across all three year groups in March/April 2004. A total of 243 questionnaires were returned representing 53% of the total. No sampling took place and all students from all year groups were invited to participate. The questionnaires were administered directly to students within teaching sessions. The research examines a range of issues from the viewpoint of the student. Not only did it examine their experiences within the programme and the institution, but also factors relating to their home environment, qualifications upon entry, employment whilst studying and levels of support from family and friends. It was intended to examine some of the key issues affecting retention suggested by Tinto's model.

Why Education Studies?

As the physical number of students entering higher education has increased so too has the range of pathways available to them. In addition to new avenues of progression such as foundation degrees, additional subjects following a more traditional framework have emerged. One of the more recent programmes is that of Education Studies. Education Studies is aimed primarily at students who may wish to enter educationally related careers and/or understand the impact of education upon society from a range of perspectives. The expansion of the course has been rapid and impressive with a range of institutions offering the course and Bath Spa University going as far as replacing their BA Qualified Teacher Status (QTS) courses with an Education Studies degree followed by guaranteed (if certain criteria are met) entry to the Postgraduate Certificate of Education (PGCE) programme.

Education Studies as a programme is a useful exemplar to employ when discussing issues of cultural deprivation within higher education for two main reasons. Firstly, the institutions offering the course tend to be those with higher levels of students from lower socio-economic groups. Secondly, at present, the majority of students undertaking Education Studies originally wished to enter a QTS programme and were for a variety of reasons unable to do so. This is true of the surveyed institution where the initial research demonstrates that 71% of first-year students wished to enter the teaching profession. In addition discussion with fellow institutions offering Education Studies has suggested that, as in the surveyed institution, the majority of applicants had originally selected QTS as their first choice of course. There is no doubt that Education Studies can, and is beginning to, develop an identity in its own right and institutions are working individually and collaboratively towards this aim. However, at present it is apparent that the majority of students undertaking Education Studies do so as their second choice. Throughout each year of the course, at the surveyed institution, the numbers of students wishing to enter teaching does decrease as their awareness of other careers and interest in the wider remit of education increases, with the initial research demonstrating that 57% of third-year students are still aiming towards the teaching profession. The research also demonstrates that within Education Studies at the surveyed institution 82% of students stated that they would choose the programme if they had the opportunity to re-commence their degree although it is unclear as to whether this would still be the case if QTS courses were available to them.

Initial findings

The following is a summary of research based on Education Studies students in one post-1992 institution in the north-west of England. The research is based around Tinto's model suggesting that cultural capital in terms of internal and external factors influence the success or otherwise of students enrolled in higher education.

Table 10.1 Summary of findings from initial survey

Student characteristic	%
Entering HE 1st generation	62
Living within city boundaries	44
Living within a 30-mile radius of the institution	56
Currently employed whilst studying	62
Entry to HE via 'A' levels	56
Feeling they receive good or excellent support from tutors	89
Feeling they receive good or excellent support from friends	91
Feeling they receive good or excellent support from partners	92
Feeling they receive good or excellent support from parents	86
Unable to access virtual learning environment (VLE) from home	46

First generation students

Within the Education Studies programme at the institution 62% of students are the first in their immediate family to enter higher education. For these students universities are not part of the culture of their family and as pioneers it is their responsibility to adapt to the unknown. Moxley *et al.* (2001) describe students as being faced with the 'sheer anonymity' of the institution, which can result in feelings of isolation and bewilderment in the early stages of attendance, a time that is commonly accepted as crucial in retention terms. This again links to Bourdieu's theory of cultural capital suggesting that first generation students may have less support from parents and siblings in addition to less knowledge of both the academic and practical expectations of university.

Locality of students

Within the surveyed institution, 56% of Education Studies students arrive from within a 30-mile radius with 44% living within the city itself. Forsyth and Furlong (2000) highlight issues of local students missing much of the social integration of student life, an issue that remains crucial to Tinto's model. This can result in further feelings of isolation and a sense of not truly belonging. Exploration of the reasons for remaining close to home will be developed throughout the research project. Financial considerations, at this stage, appear to have a significant impact, but issues concerning how confident students are in the choice they have made to enter higher education will be explored.

Effects of employment whilst studying

Working students can face another barrier to social integration, particularly those who work long hours while a full-time student. Sixty-two percent of Education Studies students are currently working with 8% of them in full-time jobs. Students work on average for 18 hours per week with a range of 3–50 hours. The majority of students work in order to meet everyday living costs with only small numbers working in order to gain experience in their chosen career. Callender and Wilkinson (2003) demonstrate that students from the lower social economic groups became 33% more dependent on income from part-time employment between 1995/96 and 1998/99. In the same period those from higher socio-economic groups became 2% more dependent on job-related income. Evidence from tutors and students suggests that module choices in the second and third year of study are based primarily upon a student's external, job-related commitments as opposed to academic or career-based interest. The impact of top-up fees, in whatever form, remains to be seen but it is clear that student finances are already having an impact upon academic choices made. Callender and Wilkinson further state that 80% of students believe that they spend less time studying owing to work commitments. The continuing requirement for post-1992 institutions to offer work-based placements seems misguided considering the numbers of students currently employed.

The issue of working whilst studying has a wider impact than merely high levels of academic success. Wilcox et al. (2005) discovered that the largest single reason for students leaving courses was their lack of social integration. Students who have additional responsibilities are less likely to engage in the social network that universities offer which can often lead to feelings of isolation. Wilcox et al. further discovered that a significant number of students within their small sample found independent study problematic.

Qualifications upon entry

Tinto suggests that the level of qualifications upon entry can have an impact on retention and whilst it is true that 56% of Education Studies students arrive through the traditional route of 'A' levels, the majority are at fairly low grade levels. Bekhradnia (2003) demonstrates that 'A' level results, as a predictor of degree success can be school dependent and that independent school pupils with two 'A' level grades higher than their state school counterparts will perform no better within their degree studies. The majority of students entering Education Studies at the insitution do so from state schools and degree classifications received in 2004 suggest that Education Studies students compare well to other programmes within the institution.

Ultimately, much depends on the perception of the individual student. As demonstrated earlier, the majority of Education Studies students originally wished to enter QTS courses and their results at 'A' level were the main reason for lack of acceptance; confidence in their own abilities as students can therefore, be considered low at entry. At the time of the study 71% rated themselves as being good or excellent students with 82% feeling that their studies were going well. Whilst this is initially encouraging, a significant minority have low opinions of themselves and their ability to cope with the academic demands of the programme.

Internal levels of support

Thus far, I have mainly examined issues which are outside the remit of the programme and the insitution. However, as outlined by Moxley *et al.* (2001) amongst others, one of the key components towards higher retention is the level of support students feel they receive. Eighty-nine percent of students felt that they received good or excellent support from their tutors. Whilst this figure is high, students felt they received higher levels of support from friends (91%), partners (92%) and parents (86%). As previously mentioned, whilst there has been an increase in student numbers, there has been no equivalent increase in the number of teaching staff. The level of support that tutors are required to offer can increase when students are less comfortable in the environment and less confident in their abilities. This support, be it student led or tutor led, is imperative to the continuing success of programmes and as numbers increase individual tutors and institutions need to explore a range of alternative support systems. The use of virtual learning environments (VLE) may offer a partial solution but given that 46% of students, either because of lack of resources or technical skills, are unable to access the environment from home, VLEs cannot be considered the only solution to this issue.

Changes in provision

Within this volume Dave Hill highlights the main questions to ask of any new policy and asks, 'What, if any, are the unintended consequences?' There is no doubt that increasing participation in higher education has resulted in a range of consequences. The DfES (2003) White Paper *The Future of Higher Education* highlights that Britain receives less funding for higher education than competing countries such as France, Germany, the Netherlands and even the US. Additional funding is being incorporated into the system and the increase in fees from individual students may also result in additional income for institutions. However, at present the increase in student numbers has not resulted in significant increases in funding for institutions and, as DfES figures confirm, funding fell by 36% per student between 1989 and 1997. The Association of University Tutors (AUT) in their report 'Packing them in' (2005) state that the current staff:student ratio in higher education is 1:21 which is currently higher than teacher:pupil ratios in schools of 1:18. Therefore, at a time when entrance requirements are lowering, students are offered less individual support leading to what the AUT describe as a 'production-line-based' higher education provision.

A self-selecting *Times Higher Education Supplement* internet poll in 2004 (of 400 academics) discovered that over 80% believed that standards were falling owing to pressure to fill places with institutions and that 70% of the respondents also believed that some students were given places even though they were 'not up to it'.

These findings link back to Weber's theory of traditional power that it is the academics themselves who are suggesting that students are 'not up to it'. The 'it' in this case is determined by traditional methods of operating which I would suggest do not truly reflect the 'new' student population.

Jones and Thomas (2005) describe three main approaches to access policy: the academic approach, the utilitarian approach and the transformative approach. The first two strands link to the agenda as set by the DfES whilst the final strand is their perceived way forward. The 'academic' view suggests that widening participation is about encouragement amongst those groups who have traditionally not entered higher education Therefore, it suggests a policy of promotion amongst those who are perceived as having the academic qualities necessary to achieve within higher education. Jones and Thomas criticise this approach as being simplistic and not understanding the complexity of the barriers these potential students face.

The second strand is the 'utilitarian' approach which seeks to link higher education more closely to the needs of employers, most notably amongst post-1992 institutions. This can be evidenced by new requirements such as Personal Development Planning. Jones and Thomas see both the utilitarian and academic approach as ones requiring change from the students in order to ensure that they successfully integrate into higher education.

Their third strand, that of the 'transformative' approach, links most closely to this chapter given that it suggests that 'a transformative approach to access must stress the idea that higher education should be changed to permit it to both gauge and meet the needs of under-represented groups' (2005: 5).

Effectively Jones and Thomas are arguing that it is the structure of the institutions that requires change to meet the needs of new students as opposed to a requirement that students fit into our 'traditional' power structures. Jones and Thomas suggest that these changes need to be led by the diversity of students and reflect their requirements.

Conclusion

Currently within higher education, policies are opening the doors, fairly successfully, to a much wider and more diverse group than at any other time in the history of provision in this country. Whilst research, such as that by Galindo-Rueda et al. (2004) demonstrates that far more needs to be done in this area it is of paramount importance that students who enter under the widening participation agenda, perhaps without the level of cultural capital found amongst more 'traditional' students, are given every opportunity to succeed at a high level. This does not require 'dumbing down' as suggested by the THES surveyed academics, rather it requires a full understanding of the needs, commitments and anxieties of students.

Freire (1972), Apple (2004), and Giroux (2004) have, at various times, advocated a critical pedagogical approach within schools, which effectively understands the background of the pupils and enables them to question the hegemonic structures which ensure that divisions of power remain relatively static within society. Ultimately, in order to move school and education from a legitimating tool to a tool of challenge, I would argue that a similar approach is necessary in higher education if the intention is to truly widen participation as opposed to ensuring access without equality.

Dirkx and Lavin (1995) suggest that adult learners need to understand why an issue or topic is important (for them to learn) and at times this can be a very effective question for curriculum leaders to ask of a range of topics within their programmes. For institutions there is always the fall-back of tradition but if true change is to occur then that fall-back becomes less relevant. It is crucial that institutions have a full understanding of their students and awareness that higher education may not be the main focus of their lives at present, merely one part of it.

Bowl (2003) highlights issues of 'non-traditional' students feeling isolated and unsupported throughout their studies. Effectively the environment and the expectations of them were alien resulting from a culturally deprived state. Students felt that their concerns were dismissed, that other students did not associate with them owing to issues of race and/or age and that their success was in spite of the structure rather than because of it.

If institutions are to support students then either the student needs to change or the working practices of the institution do. To force the student to change would limit the opportunity to challenge divisions in society and engage in critical pedagogy at higher education level. To force the student to change would ensure that universities seek to preserve the barriers which limit opportunity for the most under-represented groups to participate. To force the student to change would ensure that whilst policy may have allowed the back door to higher education to open the main door remains firmly closed.

References

Apple, M.W. (2004) *Ideology and Curiculum*, 3rd edn. New York: Routledge.

Association of University Teachers (2005) Packing them in – the student-to-staff ratio in UK higher education. AUT Research.

Becker, H. (1963) *Outsiders: Studies in the Sociology of Deviance*. New York: Free Press.

Bekhradnia, B. (2003) Admission of error, *Guardian* 21 January.

Bourdieu, P. and Wacquant, L. (1992) *An Invitation to Reflexive Sociology*. Chicago: Chicago University Press.

Bowl, M. (2003) *Non-traditional Entrants to Higher Education*. Stoke-on-Trent: Trentham Books.

Callender, C. and Wilkinson, D. (2003) *Student Income and Expenditure Survey: Students' Income, Expenditure and Debt in 2002/03 and Changes Since 1998/99*, Research Report No. 487. Nottingham: DfES.

Department for Education and Skills (DfES) (2003) *The Future of Higher Education*. London: HMSO.

Dirkx, R. and Lavin, J. (1995) *Assumptions about the Adult Learner*. Nebraska: Institute for the Study of Adult Literacy.

Draper, S. (2003) *Tinto's Model of Student Retention*. University of Glasgow:

Department of Psychology. http://www.psy.gla.ac.uk/~steve/localed.tinto.html (accessed 14 Dec. 2005).

Forsyth, A. and Furlong, A. (2000) *Socio-economic Disadvantage and Access to Higher Education*. Bristol: Policy Press.

Freire, P. (1972) *Pedagogy of the Oppressed*. London: Penguin Books.

Galindo-Rueda, F., Marcenaro-Gutierrez, O. and Vignoles, A. (2004) *The Widening Socio-economic Gap in UK Higher Education*. London: Centre for the Economics of Education, London School of Economics.

Giroux, H. (2004) *The Terror of Neoliberalism: Authoritarianism and the Eclipse of Democracy*. Boulder, CO: Paradigm Publishers.

Higher Education Statistics Agency (HESA) (2005) Performance indicators. http://www.hesa.ac.uk/holisdocs/pubinfo/stud.htm (accessed 14 Dec. 2005).

Jones, R. and Thomas, L. (2005) The 2003 UK Government Higher Education White Paper: a critical assessment of its implications for the access and widening participation agenda, *Journal of Education Policy* 20(5): 615–630.

Kerka, S. (1995) *Adult Learner Retention Revisited*. (ERIC Digest 166). Ohio: ERIC Clearinghouse on Adult Career and Vocational Education.

Moxley, D., Najor-Durack, A. and Dumbrigue, C. (2001) *Keeping Students in Higher Education: Successful Practices and Strategies for Retention*. London: Kogan Page.

Naidoo, R. (2004) Fields and institutional strategy: Bourdieu on the relationship between higher education, inequality and society, *British Journal of Sociology of Education* 25(4): 457.

Nash, R. (1999) Bourdieu, 'habitus', and educational research: is it all worth the candle? *British Journal of Sociology of Education* 20(2): 175–187.

Tinto, V. (1975) Dropout from higher education: a theoretical synthesis of recent research, *Review of Educational Research* 45: 89–125.

Tinto, V. (1987) *Leaving College*. Chicago: University of Chicago Press.

Weber, M. (1968) *Economy and Society: An Outline of Interpretive Sociology*. New York: Bedminster Press.

Wilcox, P., Winn, S. and Fyvie-Gauld, M. (2005) 'It was nothing to do with the university, it was just the people': The role of social support in the first-year experience of higher education, *Studies in Higher Education* 30(6): 707–722.

Section 3

Education at the margins

Section introduction

Education at the margins means those individuals and groups who are marginalised not only by society but also by the education system. They are effectively at the bottom of the socio-economic and educational ladders. The marginalised slip through political debates and educational discussions in a variety of guises: the underclass, the socially excluded and the dispossessed to name but a few.

However, they are rarely given the warm embrace of a welcome, schools do not really want those children who will not get them five A*–C grades at GCSE or Level 4 in mathematics, English and science at Key Stage 2. A provocative statement, it may be, but in these days of league tables, open enrolment and flexible entry policies it is the reality for many socially excluded groups in our society.

Social exclusion is an issue that the Government was supposed to banish as they announced that things can only get better on 1 May 1997. The newly 'reformed' Conservative Party is now engaging in the use of the appropriate language.

Yet the harsh reality of social exclusion keeps coming back, even from the strangest of places. The Sutton Trust, not a radical left-wing organisation, funded research into the socio-economic profile of the best performing comprehensive schools in the UK. They found that successful schools that were located in a poor area rarely mirrored the community that surrounded them. In effect society watches as the affluent bus into the poor community to get a good education and the children of the locality go elsewhere, to the poorly performing school down the road. The Sutton Trust (2006) research also found that the top performing comprehensive schools had much lower numbers of children who were entitled to free school meals than the average comprehensive. Free school meals are a generally accepted indicator of poverty within education.

Poverty and social class have long been with us and the socially excluded have marched through the history of our education system with the most inadequate of provision and success. As Griffiths (2003) points out, other groups have started to make claims for social justice, those who are discriminated against because of race, ethnicity, sexuality and learning difficulties to name just a few.

Social justice is more than simply providing extra resources, or for example, as suggested by Jacqui Smith, the Schools Minister (Slater and Hilborne 2006), that we send the most able, looked-after children to Eton at the cost of £20,000 per year per child. Where do you draw the line between able and not so able, as a society? Are we going to see the notion of social justice for those special lucky few who picked the correct lottery ticket? What is educational provision for those groups that are marginalised by society going to be based on – it could be you, as the National lotto suggested?

Social justice should be at the heart of education and systemic to social policy. For if not, the divisions in society will carry on, looked-after child will beget looked-after child in the process, wasting talent and ability needed by society, in addition to costing society a great deal of money in papering the cracks that inevitably occur in a society that does not provide access to education for individuals from marginalised groups. The denial of access is not a blunt no entry here, rather it is the subtle interplay of social attitudes and political policies that erect barriers to success for the marginalised, the underclass.

Through education it should be possible to change attitudes, break down barriers and provide individuals with the self-esteem that allows them to contribute to society in a positive and meaningful way. Social justice is about allowing the individuals and communities to take control of their lives in a positive and meaningful way.

This section is made up of an eclectic group of chapters but each one addresses key issues facing groups that frequently do not even get a mention in the discussions on social exclusion, or if they do, the net result is that the issues are not addressed and the problems stay the same.

Irene and John Robinson open this section with an account of the implications for teacher education of the murders of Anthony Walker and Stephen Lawrence. Before reading this chapter it might be worthwhile examining the Scarman Report (1982) on the disturbances in Brixton and other parts of the country in 1982. For the very same issues that Scarman identified as key factors are repeated in the MacPherson Report (1999) nearly 20 years later. Having read the relevant parts of the Scarman Report, the reader is then advised to have a look at the MacDonald (1989) Report on the murder of an Asian youth in a Manchester school playground. Having read the above begin the chapter and there the reader should be amazed at the lack of progress that has been made in teacher education in terms of the complete lack of commitment to anti-racism. The issues are urgent considering not only the experiences of Anthony and Stephen but also, as Jill Rutter outlines, many others in our society.

Jill Rutter provides an account of the reality that faces refugee children. In common with the other groups in the section they frequently encounter discrimination and isolation. Overlaid with quantities of poverty and fear, however, there is evidence that some children do overcome the problems that they face. Rutter also provides an account of the official policy perspectives that rarely work in favour of the refugee or refugee children. The chapter provides an account of the strength of communities to support each other in overcoming their problems. However, there are links to Kassem's chapter in that the children who arrive in this country unaccompanied end up in the care system, where they face all the problems encountered by children in care from the indigenous community.

Derek Kassem in a chapter on looked-after children provides an account of the problems faced by this group. How even over the last 20 years and the growing concern of social workers, educationalists and Government there has been no improvement in the levels of educational achievement by looked-after children. Kassem points out that, in part, the problems are due to the inability of two systems to work together, the worlds of education and social work. However, the driving force for this is the culture of targets and goal setting that informs all aspects of social provision. The targets, in effect, prevent the joined-up Government that is supposed to address the problems that the looked-after child faces and so the issues never change.

Jane Martin's chapter opens a mini-section on women. Martin's chapter describes the struggles that women faced to take a role in education. She discusses the contradiction between today's view of education, where it is seen very much as a female vocation and the past where women were excluded from the management of the education system. It might also be borne in mind that women were also excluded from education, especially higher education, until, in historical terms, quite recently. The account that Martin provides of the lives of key women in the history of education is both an inspiration from the past and an exemplar of what can be achieved. Grant's chapter carries on the story but in the present-day context.

Diane Grant examines the most invisible of all groups, older women. The chapter focuses on a group of women over 50, and argues that the barriers women face in accessing opportunities for lifelong learning are not being addressed by policy-makers. Grant goes on to explore the difficulties faced by working-class women as they negotiate the world of work, education and home. The chapter indicates that lifelong learning policies are being overshadowed by a heightened campaign for women to re-enter the workforce to meet labour shortfalls, usually semi-skilled. The approach is dominated by short-term policy needs rather than widening access to adult education that would improve both the women's lives and their community.

The section above all is concerned with addressing the educational rights of those who exist on the margin of our society in these neo-liberalist times.

References

Griffiths, M. (2003) *Action for Social Justice in Education*. London: Open University Press.

MacDonald, I. (1989) *Murder in the Playground: The Report of the MacDonald Inquiry in Racism and Racial Violence in a Manchester School*. London: Longsight Press.

Macpherson, W. (1999) *The Stephen Lawrence Inquiry* (The Macpherson Report), Cmnd. 4262-1. London: Stationery Office.

Scarman (1982) *The Scarman Report: The Brixton Disorders 10–12 April 1981*. London: Penguin Books.

Slater, J. and Hilborne, N. (2006) My confidence was destroyed. *Times Educational Supplement* 13 January. http://www.tes.co.uk/search/story/?story_id=2180675 (accessed 4 April 2006).

Sutton Trust (2006) *The Social Composition of Top Comprehensive Schools Rates of Eligibility for Free School Meals at the 200 Highest Performing Comprehensive Schools*. London: Sutton Trust. http://www.suttontrust.com/annualreports.asp (accessed 4 April 2006).

11

IRENE ROBINSON AND
JOHN ROBINSON
Stephen and Anthony: the continuing implications of the Macpherson Report for teacher education

Introduction

Although the murder of the Black teenager Stephen Lawrence in 1993 was far from being the first racially motivated murder it was undoubtedly the first murder to have so many far-reaching and impacting implications. Without the unrelenting struggle of the Lawrences to fight for justice there would have been no inquiry and ultimately no report. Discourse on race relations was now on the agenda of not only the Government but also the media and the people of Britain. Through this catalyst many members of society were forced to recognise that as they were not part of the solution they were very much part of the problem. Although they targeted the police, the Macpherson recommendations were also explicit in their implications for the education system. For teachers and teacher educators the challenges are enormous; the Citizenship Curriculum has been conceived to inform and educate children as to how to be active, informed, tolerant and responsible citizens. However, the murder of Anthony Walker in 2005, in circumstances chillingly similar to the death of Stephen Lawrence, raised the question as to whether citizenship is or can be a 'vehicle' that can have any impact on the racism that infiltrates our schools and colleges: this is discussed in this chapter and, importantly, so is the rationale that can be extended to teacher education. In the 13 years since the Lawrence murder there has been escalating racial violence: race hate crimes have doubled in London to an average of 63 a day in the 12 months to April 2005, and in the Borough of Huyton where Anthony was murdered have escalated to 53 reported racially motivated crimes in the period January to March 2005 (BBC1 News 2 August 2005). This chapter prompts the following questions: 'What kind of a future can we have if we do not collectively respond to the fact that the thrust of the Macpherson Report was about how white Britain treats Black Britain?' and 'Must we accept the complicity that has permeated the system for so long?' The chapter concludes by suggesting that teacher education and teacher educators continue to need to be much more informed about these issues.

Teacher education

Two areas, I believe, stand out, teacher training will be crucially important and I cannot emphasise enough the need for a better understanding of the factors that lead to underachievement.

A curriculum which does not acknowledge and seek to challenge manifestations of racism at individual and institutional level, through enhancing pupils' political literacy and particularly their appreciation of how power is exercised, and by whom, in this society, would, in our view, constitute a fundamental miseducation ... In order to be equipped, in professional terms, to offer their pupils a full and balanced education all teachers must be given the appropriate knowledge and skills for providing such an education.

(Swann Report 1985: 13, 551)

The TTA countered the vociferous complaints of the Commission for Racial Equality about its total dismissal of a statutory requirement for issues of race and racism to be taught to would be teachers by simply reiterating its 'wish' to see more ethnic minority students coming forward. Not the same issue at all.

(Klein 1999: 3)

The above quotations span a decade and a half and serve to illustrate the complex recent history concerning teacher education and race relations; on the one hand well-meant prescription and on the other tunnel vision and ineptitude in addressing issues concerning the training of would-be teachers in matters relating to race and cultural identity. We intend to place our argument in the context of the Stephen Lawrence Inquiry and consider evidence that suggests that current teacher trainees are frequently denied access to anti-racist education – and as a consequence denied access also to the debates that relate to the challenges of living in a pluralistic, frequently racist and class conscious society. Prior to the Swann Report, the National Union of Teachers (NUT) had conducted its own research in order to inform the Home Office for its 1981 *Report on Racial Disadvantage*. The NUT surveyed the position in all teacher training institutions in relation to teaching in a multicultural society. The report noted that:

[o]nly 15 replies out of 67 indicated that all students in training would receive some lectures or other forms of input to their course which would give them information relevant to teaching in a multicultural society and even fewer replies mentioned a compulsory element. It is therefore still possible for many teachers to emerge from their training without having covered the subject at all,

though a wide range of optional courses and lectures are provided in various Colleges and University Departments.

(NUT 1986: 27)

Is the overall situation any different two decades on? What has happened in the intervening years? Questions and concerns raised in 1981 would appear to be still unanswered; confused perceptions relating to the necessity of addressing issues concerning race in all schools and institutions in a multiracial society, not just multiracial schools, still exist. It is therefore important to acknowledge that, just as in the field of race relations, there was evidence of enormous inconsistency 20 years ago, so the likelihood of finding a measure of uniformity in the year 2000 highly improbable. 'That antiracist teaching is not specified in the Standards for Qualified Teacher Status when so many other requirements are made explicit can only serve as a disincentive to teacher educators' (Givens et al. 1999: 35). It is crucial to the debate surrounding the education of would-be teachers that we attempt to identify the nature of the input student teachers are receiving. By highlighting certain key issues and relating to these issues of 'when, how, and by whom', courses addressing racism and social justice are more likely to be given space in higher education insititutions (HEIs).

Race: the educational context

Criticisms of inconsistent and incoherent developments in teacher education have been frequently evidenced in the literature:

The disparate and optional nature of courses and procedures affecting staff development has led many teacher educators and students to argue that a comprehensive and holistic approach to equality needs to be provided.

(Siraj-Blatchford 1994: 6)

In 1985 the democratic left, as represented by the Inner London Education Authority (ILEA), had formulated equal opportunities policies as a direct response to demands from women and ethnic minority groups that any such political discourse should be informed by those groups themselves. The potential danger of resistance to 'the hegemonic power struggle' (Clay and George 1993: 127) ultimately was conceived of as an untimely threat to the Thatcher Government's concerns for policies embracing more liberal concepts of equal access, and ILEA was abolished. Although many of these equal opportunity policies were not put into practice they did inform many schools and some HEIs that the way forward, in terms of practice and policy, was to address issues of race, class, gender and other oppressions. The Swann Report (Committee of Inquiry into the Education of Children from Ethnic Minority Groups 1985) had, as previously mentioned, documented the need for concerted efforts to improve the educational experiences and achievement for ethnic minority groups. However, having been established by the then Labour Government, by the time the Committee finally reported Thatcher herself was in power and what followed was inherently a period of diffusion. The then Secretary of State for Education, Sir Keith Joseph, asked Lord Swann to write (without consultation with the rest of the committee) a short guide to the report. This guide (Swann 1985) made no reference to racism (Gillborn 1997). By the time Joseph's successor, Kenneth Baker, was in office the report was almost obsolete, made so by the huge overhauls and extensive changes to the education system that heralded the 1988 Education Reform Act.

Although the overall prescriptiveness of the Swann Report had been welcomed by some members of the teaching profession it was considered to be threatening by others, in that it curtailed personal freedom for teachers and was read as being totalitarian in seeking to control and censor people's lives. If, for example, teachers or trainees did not share the Report's multicultural views they were therefore unsuitable as a teacher or teacher trainee.

There are those who suggest that a consideration of racism on a course of professional training is at best unnecessary and at worst leads to the sick spectacle of students and teachers in institutions supposedly embodying free speech being browbeaten into false confessions of being racist for fear of failing their courses or kicked out of teaching (*Guardian* 4 July 1993: 8).

Ethnic diversity was effectively removed from the national policy agenda (Troyna 1993; Gillborn 1995; Haviland 1998) to be repackaged in a format which placed racism in a respectable and deracialised format. Concerns with colour were to be replaced with 'culture' and notions of superiority (previously a defining feature of racism) would be replaced with a focus on 'difference' (Gillborn 1997: 352). Gillborn does, however, acknowledge that, although Conservative reforms did remove race from the language of educational policy change, 'the deeper issues have remained a central and volatile presence in the debates' (1997: 352).

Further marginalisation of issues concerning race, albeit at a more grass roots level, concerned small, frequently localised, initiatives disappearing through the change in the powers of LEAs (Thatcher 1999: 597). Devolution of schools' budgeting through the introduction of local management of schools (LMS) also played a vital role in diminishing local education authorities' (LEA) ability to influence practice in schools (Gillborn 1997). Added pressure for public accountability through publication of league tables compounded a situation where, at best, permeation was considered adequate and at worst there was no evidence whatsoever of addressing matters concerning racial inequality.

In the teacher training arena the Circular 9/92 (DfEE 1992) effectively transferred the bulk of the training programmes from the universities and colleges to schools to be facilitated by partnership arrangements. This inevitably brings inconsistency of provision of would-be teachers on to the agenda (Robinson and Robinson 1999). The research of Jones (1999) looked at how beginner teachers in white areas come to understand issues of equality, particularly of race. He found in nearly all cases a refusal on the part of the students' teacher mentors to address any aspects of multiculturalism, let alone anything more contentious concerning race and social justice. These aspects were deemed the responsibility of the HEIs and to be dealt with in the safety of the lecture theatre.

It's the job of the college. They've got enough staff, it's their job. Let's be honest here, who's getting their training done on the cheap? I have never dealt with things like multicultural education with a student. It's not really an issue here anyway but it's the college who should be doing it.

(Jones 1999: 128, quoting a school-based mentor)

One response to the Macpherson Report by the present Government in the context of education has been the introduction of the statutory study of citizenship to come into place in the year 2002 for all 11–16-year-olds. Further consideration will be given to the citizenship agenda in a later point in this paper. It is interesting to note, however, that although the requirements do cover a vast range of topics they avoid mentioning racism or prejudice; furthermore no announcements have been made informing of compulsory in-service training. As Sherwood quite correctly observes: 'Given that teacher training colleges avoid ever mentioning race or racism, one can foresee that many teachers will avoid this fraught section of the subject and stick to less controversial topics' (Sherwood 2000: 25).

Figueroa suggested that teachers (among others) use a racial form of reference which 'provides those who share it with a rallying point for group loyalty and cohesion. The racial frame of reference helps to bridge the worlds of a socially divided nation and to maintain its national unity against outsiders' (1998: 20). It is also suggested that initial teacher education and training (ITET) rarely provides an appropriate context in which this racial frame can be systematically questioned (Carrington et al. 1986; Menter 1987; Cole 1989). Jones's data, a decade later, substantiate these findings and make disquieting reading regarding the attitude of some beginner teachers: 'I do not want to learn about multicultural issues because I simply do not want to teach black children' (Jones 1999: 154, quoting a student teacher).

The failure of teacher training institutions to move students beyond vague, and often ill-informed, preconceptions about issues such as social class, race and gender is self-evident and will only begin to be addressed when these same issues are identified as essential components of ITET courses.

If the reluctance on the part of the Conservative Party to prioritise race/racism in its reforms caused disenchantment, what has followed, in terms of enlightenment on the part of New Labour, has been sadly reminiscent of the lethargy of the previous years. Gillborn argued that New Labour's approach to race and education has been characterised as a form of naive multiculturalism (Gillborn 2000). Gillborn maintained that New Labour's approach accepts only limited understanding of equity, based on inadequate theory of social justice. Although the New Labour Party did inherit a multitude of problems, their initial reluctance and intransigence to address any issues other than in a superficial and ineffectual manner has been salutary. Furthermore, the language of social inclusion has contributed to a further deracialising of the discourse, whilst at the same time erasing gender, social class and other social differences from the discourse. Some would argue that the recent banning of indirect discrimination from all public places is too little too late. The Home Secretary's decision now places a legal duty on the whole public sector from primary schools to maximum security prisons to promote racial equality. Although undoubtedly a breakthrough, there does not appear to be a confirmation as to how this will be brought to pass. As reported in *The Guardian*:

> The new legal duty cannot produce results without a proper enforcement procedure. The present Act contains a vague requirement to 'consider appropriate measures' but nothing which bites. The new duty must be unambiguous and clear; its enforcement mechanism workable and effective.
>
> (*Guardian* 28 January 2000: 23)

Similarly the DfEE's response (1999a) to the Lawrence Inquiry amounted to little more than a restatement of previously announced initiatives and the 'frightening[ly] complacent conclusion that the National Curriculum already provided all necessary flexibility' (Blair and Gillborn 1999: 15). Just as considerations of the underpinnings of the political agenda were necessary to inform the context of the research so the milestone of the Stephen Lawrence Inquiry must be examined in order to proceed and further substantiate the argument which suggests that a grossly inadequate rationale is at present permeating a system that given support could be challenged and changed.

Stephen Lawrence

The unjust and untimely death of the Black teenager Stephen Lawrence murdered at a London bus stop in 1993 by a gang of white youths became not only a major police inquiry but a symbolic test for race relations in Britain. It ultimately became a historic public inquiry that many hoped would accelerate changes in society at an individual, institutional and political level that would result in 'preventing and correcting' racial injustice in Britain (Cathcart 1999). As Alibhai-Brown poignantly suggests 'Stephen Lawrence was killed by young white men for daring to wear his skin at a bus stop. Racism then interfered to prevent justice' (2000a: 28).

What was it that made the case of Stephen Lawrence so special? Why did this, rather than any other unsolved racial murder, become a test of policing, of justice and of racial attitudes? Why was this particular case seen to have implications for institutions other than the police force, who were considered to have acted in many ways inappropriately? According to Cathcart's lengthy book cataloguing in detail both the background to the Inquiry and examination of the Inquiry itself, including interviews with many participants, there are many answers. These included the impeccable character of the victim, and the judgement of Stephen's parents (who had made a shrewd and early assessment of the first investigation) and from then on were 'single minded in pursuing justice and truth, prepared to take risks and suffer setbacks so long as the objectives were clear' (1999: 417). Furthermore the character of the suspects – who generated a large degree of hatred – defined the case through the media and public opinion. The youths alleged to have murdered Stephen Lawrence went to school in the London Borough of Greenwich at a time when 'multicultural and anti-racist education' were on the classroom agenda.

Recent research (Hewitt 1994; 1996; Alibhai-Brown 2000b) has illustrated the minefield of racial disharmony among some young people and the extreme fascist and racist views held by them. As mentioned previously Cathcart's (1999) study into the Stephen Lawrence Inquiry uncovered chilling evidence relating to the culture of violence and racism which produced the five victims. The ethnic minority population in the Borough of Greenwich at the time of the murder was around 13% and demographically the conditions were 'perfect' for the growth of racism. The Asian and Black population were scattered and often isolated among the white majority. Economically the area was struggling with high unemployment; particularly the number of jobs for men had slumped disastrously. Reports of racial harassment were one of the highest in the country. In the year after the murder the research findings of Hewitt (1994) carried out in Eltham (where the murder took place) uncovered unprecedented accounts of racism in the young:

We were surprised at the level and ubiquity of the racism we encountered ... In some neighbourhoods it seemed that open and unapologetic racism was wall to wall among adolescents, with almost no gaps.

(Hewitt 1994, cited in Cathcart 1999: 23)

Hewitt concluded that these attitudes were not, in the main, learnt from parents but generated among the young people themselves:

The racism of adolescents was a world of its own, policed from within through criticism of anyone who flirted with inter-ethnic friendships, and of those 'wiggers' – 'white niggers' – who came near to embracing black youth culture.

(Hewitt 1994, cited in Cathcart 1999: 23)

This was happening in an area that was 95% white. Why this is so we can still only speculate. Hewitt (1994) suggested that white children only encountered black people in any numbers when they reached secondary school and for many the pressure to adhere to strict anti-racist policies made some feel that ethnic minority cultures were valued over their own. Importantly they felt that they had no culture as such. Howard suggests a way forward from this which involves recognising our own, ethnically located selves and 'developing a positive, non racist and authentic connection to white racial and cultural identity' (1999: 88).

Alibhai-Brown (2000b) contends such racial hatred is due in the main to bad political leadership at a time of massive social transformation without a committed national strategy. This is unarguably a major part of the story. The deep-rooted hatred felt by certain groups of society against other groups frequently, but not always based on colour (see, for example, Northern Ireland and Rwanda), has to be more than just ignorance; the ignorance that a short sharp blast of something called multicultural education could cure. Lorde (1990) stressed that the vast legacy of Western European history has conditioned us to see human difference in simplistic opposition to each other. We are therefore left with a set of oppositions: dominance/subordination, good/bad, up/down, superior/inferior. He further suggests that society sees good in terms of human need. There must, of necessity, be a group or groups that can be made to feel they are surplus by systemised oppression and who are made to occupy the space of the dehumanised inferior. This is substantiated further by O'Sullivan (1999) and serves to illustrate the desperateness of Stephen Lawence's murder. With racism hierarchical systems of power are ever present, which means that the dominant group subjugates the non-dominant group along lines of some perception of racial difference. This subjugation occurs along cultural, political, educational and economic lines. What we see in the context of racist dominant structure is a violence visited on the dominated culture that is destructive to body, mind and spirit (O'Sullivan 1999: 151). As is generally accepted, the watered down, ad hoc multicultural education of the 1980s has no place in addressing the complex reality and injustice facing many people today. (There is evidence in California that such strategies in the past have failed to address the needs of ethnic minority students (Sullivan 2000: 9) and Cullingford (2000) argues that schools are themselves often the places where racism is learned rather than overcome.) In our sheltered middle-class smug way it is easy to accept that we are part of the problem, but see only more prescriptive platitudes as part of the solution. We therefore must try to ensure the next generation are given access to education that does not strip them of identity and does ensure knowledge and understanding of social justice. Alibhai-Brown suggests that we need an education 'which can honour the truth and the diversity of black and white people and importantly bind people through a set of common values based on mutual respect and human rights' (2000a: 28). She praises the onset of the citizenship education programme due to start in 2002. Her positive feelings of 'replacing multiculturalism with modern cosmopolitanism' are laudable. The following section will consider whether the citizenship proposals will, in fact, come anywhere near enabling as a tool to promote not only racial harmony but other social justice issues.

Conclusion

Osler and Starkey's (1996) data examined teachers' and student teachers' understanding of human rights, citizenship and identities and how this prepares them for teaching. Without basic knowledge of human rights principles it is unlikely that effective teaching could take place. Inevitably the consequence will be that those who cannot or will not, will follow an alternative citizenship model (Eggleston 1999). Chillingly this consequence can be illustrated with reference to the alleged murderers of Stephen Lawrence and Anthony Walker. The former went to school in the London Borough of Greenwich at a time when multicultural and anti-racist education were on the classroom agenda. In 1991 two of the boys threatened a fellow pupil, Sean Kalitsi, in their school playground. The authority responded by mounting a study into its own approaches to anti-racism (Hewitt 1996). This found flaws in what it termed 'town hall antiracism' and indicated that pupils such as these boys who were disaffected and turned off school were going to be also turned off anti-racism (Klein 1999). This is not to suggest, however, that all disaffected youths become breeding grounds for racial bullying and abuse, rather that if the social climate and peer group pressure persuades there is a likelihood of racial disharmony, that can and does incite racial hatred within the group. Ledwith (2000) suggests that young men are both perpetrators and victims of street violence but the victims are frequently not treated by the police as having the same rights to protection in society. Suicide and unemployment is higher in this group than any other but seemingly no action is taken to alleviate this.

Ledwith's critical questioning of the overall situation has at its root the ideology that education is equal and just and that poverty can be subsumed ('poverty is no excuse', to paraphrase David Blunkett (DfEE 1999b)) and is informed by the thinking of Paulo Freire (1970) who emphasised that education is never neutral. As a teacher educator Ledwith's concerns are that the current model of teacher training does not promote an understanding or analysis of the differentials of power in society and the role of would-be teachers in reinforcing or transcending social divisions. Again this is evidenced in the research of Jones working with white beginning teachers and finding that they had no understanding of strategies for promoting equality and little commitment to issues of social justice on which the futures of some of their pupils depend (Jones 1999). Without this understanding student teachers do not have knowledge of, or even begin to question, issues concerning white privilege. They do not consider that in Western societies whiteness and white privilege bring enormous social, political and economic benefits just because of the dominance of being white (Dei 1996). Today this can be a starting point.

Without listening to the voices of the oppressed there can be no progress. O'Sullivan suggests that 'anti-racist education must define, conceptualise and perceive "difference" from the stand point of those who occupy the margins of society and continually have to resist their marginality through collective action' (O'Sullivan 1999: 162). Obviously issues concerning 'difference' must not only be concerned with racial difference but take on board the complex interweaving of other forms of difference. Consciousness must be raised about a more integrated understanding of oppressions and how they are linked.

Where then does this leave us? It is inevitable that teacher education will have to change in order to accommodate the lessons which need to be learned from the Stephen Lawrence enquiry. O'Sullivan suggests that, in order to engage with the sorts of issues outlined above, teacher education will need to allow for 'the cultivation, nourishment and development of attitudes of outrage and responsibility in the face of injustice and oppression' (1999: 272–274). Doing so will inevitably lead to struggles to change the curriculum of teacher education and the setting up of camps along ideological grounds.

With this in mind it is still of crucial importance that evidence is gathered to detail the current situation in HEIs with regard to their policies and practices specifically concerning race and human rights issues. Teacher education could and should spearhead a groundswell of awareness of what is required in schools. This could only happen with a consistency of practice that is not self-evident at present. There are no easy answers. Messages from government reiterate the platitudes and blinkered attitudes of the past. Although the literature has frequently suggested a cohesive and informed strategy none is forthcoming. It would appear that lone voices are still by and large unheard:

As teacher educators we have a dual responsibility to develop ways of confronting racism and intolerance both through an appropriate curriculum and teaching methods and through a process of awareness-raising which secures justice and the equal rights of minorities to education.

(Osler and Starkey 1996: 68)

By embedding anti-racist and multicultural elements formally into teacher education a sea change may take place which can, at this stage at least, only be considered a start in the battle to combat racism in education. However, Anthony Walker's murder in 2005, which hauntingly resembled the events surrounding the death of Stephen Lawrence, raises questions as to whether the teaching of citizenship in our schools can be a 'vehicle' that challenges the racist ideas that would seem to permeate our schools. Harker (2005) argues that the only similarity between the murders of Stephen Lawrence in April 1993 in London and Anthony Walker in July 2005 in Liverpool was the manner of their killing – at a bus stop. He argues that because in Stephen's case the police were obstructive and unresponsive to claims from the Lawrence family that the killing was racially motivated whereas in Anthony's case the police and the news media were quick to identify the killing as racially motivated 'the similarities end' (2005: 21). However, Harker is answering the wrong question. Of course it matters that policing has changed following the Macpherson Inquiry (1999) into Stephen's death, but what matters more focuses on how such an event can have taken place in the first instance. It is more a question of how strangers can be prepared to attack and kill strangers because 'they do not like the look of them' (for whatever reason).

References

Alibhai-Brown, Y. (2000a) Be at ease in your own skin, *Times Educational Supplement* 12 May.

Alibhai-Brown, Y. (2000b) *Imagining the New Britain*, London: Allen Lane, Penguin Press.

Blair, M. and Gillborn, D. (1999) Face up to racism, *Times Educational Supplement* 5 March.

Carrington, B., Millward, A. and Short, G. (1986) Schooling in multicultural society: contrasting perspectives of primary and secondary teachers in training, *Educational Studies* 12(1): 17–35.

Cathcart, B. (1999) *The Case of Stephen Lawrence*. London: Viking.

Clay, J.A. and George, R. (1993) Moving beyond permeation: courses in teacher education, in I. Siraj-Blatchford (ed.) Race, *Gender and the Education of Teachers*. Buckingham: OUP.

Cole, M. (1989) Where is this country anyway? Who was here first? Analysis of attitudes of 1st year BEd students to immigration to Britain, *Multicultural Teaching* 7(2): 15–17.

Committee of Inquiry into the Education of Children from Ethnic Minority Groups (1985) *Education for All* (The Swann Report), Cmnd. 9453. London: HMSO.

Cullingford, C. (2000) *Prejudice*. London: Kogan Page.

Dei, G. (1996) *Anti-racist Education: Theory and Practice*. Halifax, Nova Scotia: Fernwood.

Department for Education and Employment (DfEE) (1992) *Initial Teacher Training, Secondary Phase*, Circular 9/92, London: DfEE.

Department for Education and Employment (DfEE) (1999a) *The Stephen Lawrence Inquiry Report: Action Plan*. London: DfEE.

Department for Education and Employment (DfEE) (1999b) *Ethnic Minority Pupils Must have Opportunity to Fulfil their Potential*. David Blunkett Press release 90/99. London: DfEE.

Eggleston, J. (1999) Learning to be a citizen in the global age, *Multicultural Teaching* 18(1): 8–11.

Figueroa, P.M.E. (1998) Race relations and cultural difference: some ideas on a racial frame of reference, in G.K. Verma and C. Bagley (eds) *Race Relations and Cultural Difference*. London: Croom Helm.

Freire, P. (1970) *The Pedagogy of the Oppressed*. London: Penguin.

Gillborn, D. (1995) *Racism and Antiracism in Real Schools: Theory, Policy, Practice*. London: Unwin Hyman.

Gillborn, D. (1997) Racism and reform: new ethnicities, old inequalities, *British Educational Research Journal* 23(3): 345–360.

Gillborn, D. (2000) 50 years of failure: race and educational policy in Britain, in R. Majors (ed.) *The British Education Revolution: The Status and Politics of Educating Afro-Caribbean Children*. London: Falmer Press.

Givens, N., Almeida, D., Holden, C. and Taylor, B. (1999) Swimming with the tide: ethnic minority experiences in ITE, *Multicultural Teaching* 17(2): 30–36.

Harker, J. (2005) Stephen and Anthony, *Guardian* 3 August.

Haviland, J. (1998) *Take Care Mr Baker*. London: Fourth Estate.

Hewitt, R. (1994) *Routes of Racism*. London: London University Institute of Education.

Hewitt, R. (1996) *Routes of Racism*. Stoke-on-Trent: Trentham Books.

Howard, G.R. (1999) *We can't Teach What we don't Know: White Teachers in Multicultural Schools*. New York: Teachers' College Press.

Jones, R. (1999) *Teaching Racism or Tackling it: Multicultural Stories from White Beginning Teachers*. Stoke-on-Trent: Trentham Books.

Klein, G. (1999) Editorial, *Multicultural Teaching* 17(2): 2–4.

Ledwith, M. (2000) Some thoughts on social justice in relation to the lives of young people, Personal communication.

Lorde, A. (1990) Age, race, class and sex: women redefining difference in R. Ferguson, M. Gever and C. West (eds) *Out there: Marginalization and Contemporary Culture*. Cambridge, MA: MIT Press.

Macpherson, W. (1999) *The Stephen Lawrence Inquiry* (The Macpherson Report), Cmnd. 4262-1. London: Stationery Office.

Menter, I. (1987) Evaluating teacher education: some notes on anti-racist programmes for BEd students, *Multicultural Teaching* 5(3): 39–41.

National Union of Teachers (NUT) (1986) *Education for Equality: The National Union of Teachers Response to the Swann Report*. London: NUT.

Osler, A. and Starky, H. (1996) *Teacher Education and Human Rights*. London: David Fulton.

O'Sullivan, E. (1999) *Transformative Learning: Educational Vision for the 21st Century*. London and New York: Zed Books; Toronto: OISE/UT published in association with University of Toronto Press.

Robinson, I. and Robinson, J. (1999) Learning to live with inconsistency in student entitlement and partnership provision, *Mentoring & Tutoring* 7(3): 223–239.

Sherwood, M. (2000) Education and the Lawrence Inquiry, *Multicultural Teaching* 18(2): 25–26.

Siraj-Blatchford, I. (1994) *The Early Years: Laying the Foundation for Racial Equality*. Stoke-on-Trent: Trentham Books.

Sullivan, A. (2000) United Colours of America, *Sunday Times News Review* (Section 5) 15 October.

Swann (1985) *Education for All: A Brief Guide to the Main Issues of the Report*. London: HMSO.

Thatcher, M. (1999) *The Downing Street Years*. New York and London: HarperCollins.

Troyna, B. (1993) *Racism and Education: Research Perspectives*. London: Routledge.

12

JILL RUTTER
Meeting the educational
needs of forced migrants

Since 1989 increasing numbers of refugees have migrated to the UK, including many children of school age. This chapter examines debates about their educational and psychosocial needs. It argues that notions of resilience should be used as a framework for developing holistic support for refugee children.

Who are refugee children?

The word 'refugee' was introduced into the English language by Huguenots who sought sanctuary in the UK in the late seventeenth century. At this time, the status of being a refugee had no basis in law and there was no immigration control in England. It was not until 1951 that the term refugee became a legal construct, with the UK's accession to the 1951 UN Convention Relating to the Status of Refugees. Passed in the aftermath of the mass displacements of the Second World War, the 1951 UN Convention and its 1967 Protocol define a refugee as someone who has fled a country of origin, or is unable to return to it

> owing to a well-founded fear of being persecuted for reasons of race, religion, nationality, membership of a particular group or political opinion.
> (From the 1951 UN Convention Relating to the Status of Refugees)

The 1951 UN Convention Relating to the Status of Refugees and its 1967 Protocol provide the legal basis for refugee protection. The US Committee for Refugees estimated that by the end of 2003 there were some 11.9 million asylum-seekers, refugees and those living in refugee-like situations outside their home country (US Committee for Refugees 2004).

In the UK, families of most children described as refugees have usually sought to regularise their immigration status by applying for political asylum. The asylum determination process is managed by the Immigration and Nationality Directorate (IND) of the Home Office. An application for asylum can be made at the port of entry, or 'in-country' after an asylum-seeker has passed through UK immigration control. The application involves the asylum-seeker presenting oral and written evidence to the IND which is then used to determine the asylum claim. At present there are four possible outcomes of an asylum claim: refugee status, humanitarian protection, discretionary leave or a refusal of asylum.

When a person is granted refugee status s/he receives a UN Refugee Document. Those with refugee status are also granted other entitlements, such as the right to work. Recently the right of a person with Convention refugee status to remain in the UK indefinitely has been curtailed and today refugees receive five years' right of residency in the UK, revocable at any time.

Humanitarian protection is granted to asylum-seekers who have been refused refugee status, and whose lives would be at risk if they were repatriated. Those who receive humanitarian protection are usually granted it for a period of three years, although shorter periods can be granted. They have full rights to benefits and employment, but no automatic right to family reunion. The Home Office also grants some people discretionary leave to remain in the UK. This is a time-limited status often granted to:

- those refused asylum, but who cannot be returned to their home country or a safe third country
- unaccompanied children who have been refused asylum or humanitarian protection, who cannot be legally returned until they are 18 other cases where individual circumstances are so compelling that it is considered appropriate to let that person stay, for example a person with a life-threatening illness.

Table 12.1   Asylum applications and decisions 1999–2004

Year	Asylum applications	Refugee status %	Leave to remain %	Refusal %
1999	71,160	42	12	46
2000	80,315	10	12	78
2001	71,700	9	17	74
2002	85,865	10	24	66
2003	49,370	6	11*	83
2004	33,930	3	8†	88

* Figures for 2003 include those granted ELR, hHumanitarian protection (0%) and discretionary leave. Source: Home Office (2004). Figures exclude dependants.

† In 2004 no applicants were granted humanitarian protection when an initial decision was made, while 8% of decisions were that of discretionary leave to remain.

As Table 12.1 indicates, the majority of asylum-seekers have their cases refused in the UK, an issue that concerns refugee advocacy organisations. Some asylum-seekers who are initially refused asylum in the UK go on to appeal against a negative decision and in 2004 some 19% of all asylum appeals were successful (Home Office 2004). Others may be removed from the UK, leave voluntarily or become irregular migrants.

Asylum-seekers, those granted refugee status and forms of temporary protection such as humanitarian protection and discretionary leave, as well as those in the asylum appeals process or awaiting removal from the UK are the target groups of refugee advocacy groups such as the Refugee Council. Two further target groups of the Refugee Council are:

- those granted refugee status overseas and admitted to the UK as part of a settlement programme – programme refugees such as the Chileans and Vietnamese, as well as those arriving on the new refugee resettlement programmes
- those fleeing persecution or armed conflict overseas and granted temporary protection while overseas such as Bosnians (1992–1995) and Kosovars evacuated on the 1999 Humanitarian Evacuation Programme.

The implication of refugee advocacy groups and much refugee educational literature is that refugee children are a clearly demarcated group. But consider the cases of the children below:

'Emiliano' is 12 years old and was previously internally displaced in Colombia. He arrived in the UK with his uncle and aunt in 2002, entering with a visitor's visa. Emiliano has remained in the UK, overstaying his visa.

'Zizi' is the daughter of a Zimbabwean nurse. Her family is Ndebele and from Bulawayo. Zizi's mother has secured a work permit and is working as a nurse in London.

'Anna' is a Czech Roma. She and her family sought asylum in the UK. On 1 May 2004 Anna ceased to be an asylum-seeker when the Czech Republic joined the European Union.

All of these children have experiences of forced migration, although they have not used the asylum determination system. There is much evidence to suggest that migratory movements to the UK are becoming more complex and involve endangered peoples using other means to enter and remain in the UK (Castles and Loughna 2002). That so many asylum applications are refused appears to act as a disincentive to apply for asylum. Instead work permits and student visas can be used to enter the UK, or a person may enter as an irregular migrant. For this reason, migration theorists distinguish between forced and voluntary migration, rather than discussing specific immigration status.

In the education world an acknowledgment that asylum-seeker and refugee are externally ascribed legal and bureaucratic identities is long overdue, as is recognition that refugee children are not a clearly demarcated group. Support systems in local authorities and schools, therefore, should not be determined by immigration status.

Asylum legislation and its impact on children

That proportionally fewer asylum-seekers are granted refugee status or temporary forms of protection in the UK is a recent policy change. Since the mid-1980s, throughout Western Europe asylum-seekers are now seen as a challenge to the State's control over its borders, and a population whose entry to the EU must be tightly controlled. Legislative and policy changes have been enacted that are designed to keep asylum-seekers out of 'fortress Europe', with these changes comprising:

- Barriers that prevent asylum-seekers entering the UK, for example visa requirements, carrier sanctions and immigration checks at overseas airports.
- Processes to ensure the rapid determination and removal of asylum applicants judged to have unfounded cases.
- Restrictions on asylum-seekers' social and economic citizenship rights, used as a deterrent measure. Such deterrents include the use of detention, the restriction of welfare benefits, housing, work and education. This is an EU-wide trend, with constantly shifting boundaries between citizen, denizen and outsider (Levy 1999; Minderhoud 1999).
- Tightening the criteria by which the Home Office judges an asylum application, so that in 2004 some 88% of initial asylum applications resulted in refusal.

Since 1987 there have been five Acts of Parliament targeted at asylum-seekers: The Immigration (Carriers' Liability) Act 1987, the Asylum and Immigration (Appeals) Act 1993, the Asylum and Immigration Act 1996, the Immigration and Asylum Act 1999, the Nationality, Immigration and Asylum Act 2002 and the Immigration and Asylum (Treatment of Claimants, etc.) Act 2004. At the time of writing further legislation – the Immigration, Asylum and Nationality Bill 2005 – is being debated in Parliament.

All of these changes impact on the welfare of asylum-seeking children as members of asylum-seeking families. Some of these legislative changes have a specific impact on asylum-seeking children as learners at school, most significantly the Asylum and Immigration Act 1996 and the Immigration and Asylum Act 1999. The former removed benefits from some groups of asylum-seekers, making them the responsibility of local authorities. What resulted was a chaotic system detrimental to both the asylum-seekers and local government.

The Immigration and Asylum Act 1999 introduced a new support system for asylum-seekers administered by the National Asylum Support Service (NASS), part of the Immigration and Nationality Department of the Home Office. Asylum-seekers presently have the option of applying to NASS for support and accommodation or a 'support-only' package. Today, support means a cash allowance, amounting to about 70% of income support. People with nowhere to stay are usually dispersed out of Greater London, to NASS-commissioned housing in the new regional asylum consortia areas. Within each consortium some accommodation is provided by local authorities and some by private landlords.

Children's rights and refugee agencies have described many concerns about the NASS support scheme, highlighting the following issues that may impact on children's education:

Poverty: The NASS scheme is meant to provide essential living needs only, at a level of 70% of income support for adults and 100% for children. Any parent who needs to travel by bus to accompany a young child to school will find this journey, made 20 times a week, impossible to make on such a low income.

Isolation: Many asylum-seekers are being sent to areas that have no existing refugee communities and report loneliness and isolation, rendering them far more psychologically vulnerable.

Vulnerability to racial attack: Despite the Home Office guidance on the choice of accommodation, many asylum-seekers will end up being housed in areas where there are few other people from visible ethnic minorities. Some areas will inevitably be places of existing tension and high unemployment. Given the hostile attitudes of much local and national print media towards asylum-seekers, the Refugee Council believes that some groups will be very vulnerable to racial abuse and racial attack (Rutter 2003).

Reception centres and large hotels: Large hostels/hotels may be particularly unsuitable for asylum-seeking children. They are institutional and no substitute for family housing. Yet some of the accommodation for NASS is in hostels and hotels, particularly that offered by the private sector.

Social exclusion in London: In late 2001 an estimated 70% of single adults and 30% of families opted not to be dispersed in the interim support system, or left their areas of dispersal within a few weeks of arrival. It is presumed that these families moved back to join compatriots in London and are likely to be living in overcrowded and often temporary accommodation in the capital. This trend will continue.

Mobility: Asylum-seekers who do opt for NASS support may well choose to move on after receiving positive decisions. Schools who receive large numbers of asylum-seeking children may experience high levels of pupil mobility and this affects all children in the school, not just asylum-seekers.

As a result of the NASS-led dispersal of asylum-seekers, as well as labour migration of other forced migrants, almost all local authorities in the UK have resident refugee populations, small or large. However there is a lack of demographic data about refugee populations in the UK, both nationally and locally (Stewart 2004). Population data that are available include Home Office Asylum Statistics, NASS Statistics, Census data and school language surveys. A few local authorities have also conducted refugee surveys in schools, although it can be intrusive to ask direct questions about children's immigration status. The indistinct boundary between forced and voluntary migrant also means that collecting demographic data on refugee children is very challenging, but existing statistics do reveal important trends, discussed below.

Data suggest about 60,000 school-age children with likely experiences of forced migration were living in the UK in 2005. Their main countries of origin are Somalia (largest community), Sri Lanka (2nd largest), Turkey (3rd), Zimbabwe (4th), Iraq (5th), Afghanistan (6th), Iran (7th).

In 2003 the local authority with the largest population of refugee children was the London Borough of Newham, with 7,128 refugee children, followed by Haringey (2nd) and the City of Manchester (3rd). The London borough of Haringey has the highest proportion of forced migrants – 19.4% of the school population. By 2003, some 39 local authorities were educating more than 500 children, including most London local authorities. However, the proportions of refugee children resident in Greater London has fallen, from 85% in 1994, to 65% today, partly as a result of the dispersal of asylum-seekers out of London by local authorities and NASS.

Within most local authorities there is also a very inequitable distribution of refugee children in schools. (Refugee children tend to be very over-represented in schools that are judged to be 'underachieving' or 'unpopular' by sectors of the population that experience less housing mobility).

Refugee children – what research tells us

Research literature about refugee children is dominated by studies that examine the traumatic experiences of refugee children and their psychological adaptation in exile. A trauma or traumatic stressor might be defined as 'an overwhelming event, resulting in helplessness in the face of intolerable danger, anxiety and instinctual arousal' (Eth and Pynoos 1985). Until the late nineteenth century, trauma was understood as a physical reaction to injury, but as the psychiatric and psychotherapeutic professions began to emerge, the notion of trauma was extended to include the psychological sequelae of distressing events (Young 1995). During the 1970s, epidemiological and psychometric studies, mostly conducted in the USA, generated a new condition: posttraumatic stress disorder (PTSD). This condition was given full recognition in the *Diagnostic and Statistical Manual – Version Three* (DSM-III) of the American Psychiatric Association. It is diagnosed if a patient exhibits a range of symptoms, including:

- symptoms of intrusion, such as nightmares, flashbacks and intrusive thoughts
- symptoms of constriction and avoidance, such as efforts to avoid places or activities that are reminiscent of the trauma
- symptoms of increased arousal such as poor concentration or insomnia (American Psychiatric Association 1994; Bracken 1998).

Most of the research on the psychological sequelae of war and persecution conclude that refugee children manifest high levels of mental illness, meaning their ability to function in normal social settings is severely and adversely affected (Hodes 2000; Fazel and Stein 2002). Hodes suggests that 40% of refugee children in the UK manifest psychiatric disorder. Another study, conducted among unaccompanied refugee children in London concluded that 23% of the sampled group manifest severe psychological distress (Hollins *et al.* 2003). Both research studies were undertaken through questionnaires delivered in clinics. None of the children was observed in social settings such as schools or their homes. Nor was there a control group in either study. This is an important consideration in the UK where refugees usually reside in areas of high deprivation. My own research suggests that in many schools attended by refugee children, it is the non-refugee population who manifest greatest psycho-social dysfunction (Rutter 2006).

There are also a small number of studies that suggest that refugee children *do not* experience increased long-term psychiatric morbidity compared with other urban child populations (Allodi 1989; Munroe-Blum *et al.* 1989; Rousseau and Drapeau 2003). Munroe-Blum *et al.* looked at the strength of association between child immigrant status and child psychiatric disorder, poor school performance and use of mental health and social services. The cohort studied included many refugees (1989: 510–519). It concluded that immigrant children in Ontario, Canada, were not at increased risk of psychiatric disorder or poor school performance. The authors attributed this to the selective nature of migration – it is the most innovative and resourceful families that are the first migrants. Rousseau and Drapeau interviewed 57 young Cambodian refugees, then conducted a follow-up interview after four years. Data were compared with a control group of 45 young people born in Quebec. Rousseau and Drapeau noted the large discrepancy between intense psychiatric symptoms at the first interview and the good social adjustment of this group after four years. The authors suggest that the young Cambodians exhibit a high degree of resilience, enabling them to 'recover'.

Increasingly, however, psychological treatments for PTSD, as well as the construction of PTSD itself, have become contested (see, for example, Young 1995; Bracken 1998; Richman 1998; Summerfield 1998; Summerfield 2000; Chatty and Hundt 2004). Concerns about PTSD are numerous. Loughrey suggests that PTSD is a construct of psychiatry and clinical psychology and asserts there is no evidence of increased PTSD symptomology after the Second World War or at the height of the Troubles in Northern Ireland (Loughrey 1997). Summerfield discounts the assumption that PTSD arises from a failure to process traumatic memories, disputing that traumatic memory exists in isolation from social memory (Summerfield 1998; 2000). Other writers present critiques of psychological and psychotherapeutic interventions, questioning the relevance of Western psychotherapy to non-Western societies (Bracken 1998).

In *Refugee Children in the UK* I argue that the research literature about the traumatic experience of refugee children has had a major impact on how they are viewed by their teachers (Rutter 2006). The adjective 'traumatised' is widely used when talking about refugee children. Refugee advocacy groups are complicit in this process; such organisations have had to mobilise discourses of trauma in order to argue for asylum-seekers to be granted sanctuary. Additionally, the language of trauma has been invoked to argue for greater healthcare and welfare resources.

As a consequence of the language of trauma entering the vernacular, refugee children's background and needs are framed by educationalists largely in terms of trauma. An understanding of pre-exile experiences, other than the 'trauma', is neglected. The post-exile experiences of refugees in the UK, which may include material deprivation, loss of social status, as well as racist attack, are deemed less significant. In exile, refugee children are constructed in an homogeneous manner – and labelled as universally traumatised. Refugee children's problems in schools are viewed as mental health problems that require a medicalised response, most usually provided by the health service.

Resilience and vulnerability

As a result of critiques of PTSD, in particular its sidelining of the social worlds of refugees, some recent psychological literature on refugee children has suggested a new framework for understanding their adaptation: that of resilience or vulnerability.

The concept of resilience draws on Michael Rutter's work with physically and sexually abused children and the observation that some children survive abuse without manifesting severe psychological distress while others do not (Rutter 1985). Rutter and others outline protective factors (sometimes called mediating factors) and resilience on one hand, and risk factors (adverse factors) and vulnerability in children's lives. Protective factors are attributes or conditions that make it more likely that a child will achieve some degree of resilience as an outcome and less likely that a child will manifest distress severe enough to render them dysfunctional. Risk factors are attributes or conditions that make it less likely children will achieve some degree of resilience (Elbedour et al. 1993). Notions of resilience draw on ecological models of children's development (see Bronfenbrenner 1992; Brooks-Gunn 2001).

For refugees, risk and protective factors can be divided into:

- those related to personal characteristics and the personal world of the child, for example being able to talk about stressful events and thus gain mastery over them
- those particular to the home country and flight, such as repeated exposure to stressors
- those due to the immediate milieu in exile, such as quality of parenting, secure housing, access to the language and cultural forms of the home country
- those which are part of the external environment, including school, for example academic progress (Bolloten and Spafford 1998; Elbedour et al. 1993: 805–819; Witmer and Culver 2001).

Despite the paucity of the literature, the concept of resilience is very relevant for educationalists. I believe that resilience, rather than trauma offers a model for developing support systems for refugee children. A key question for schools is what makes some refugee children resilient and others not. From this, schools and educational support workers can consider interventions to minimise vulnerability and maximise resilience. Indeed many interventions to support refugee children in less economically developed countries use resilience as their conceptual framework and focus on rebuilding refugee children's social support systems. Such interventions might focus on supporting refugee parents as primary carers for very young children and ensuring children had access to schooling (for a discussion of such projects see Tolfree 1996).

A resilience-based framework for supporting refugee children

There is a growing consensus about what comprises good practice at a school and local authority level, with a number of local authorities using resilience as their framework for developing support services (see, for example, Camden 1996; Bolloten and Spafford 1998; Enfield 1999; Refugee Council 2000; Rutter 2003).

At local authority level good practice for refugee children is likely to include:

- multi-agency planning, involving education, housing, other statutory services such as further education colleges, the police and the health service, as well as non-governmental organisations
- ensuring that the Education Development Plan (EDP) and their Welsh and Scottish equivalents target refugee children and involve schools, as well as community stakeholders in drafting
- access to good-quality interpreting and translation services
- ethnic monitoring, including monitoring of the uptake of non-compulsory educational services such as early years and youth work provision, as well as educational achievement and school exclusions
- admissions practices that facilitate the early admission of refugee children to school
- the active involvement of educational psychology teams in assessment of refugee children, therapeutic work with them, advice for teachers and other professionals as well as in-service training for teachers
- programmes to support refugee community schools which may teach the home language, as well as supplementing the mainstream curriculum; a number of London LEAs that fund and support such schools
- work by the youth service to ensure that refugee children have full access to youth clubs, leisure, mentoring, after-school and holiday projects and that refugee community organisations be supported in their development of youth services
- the active involvement of early years providers for services for refugee children
- work by libraries and leisure services to meet the particular needs of refugee communities, for example ensuring that refugees have access to books in their home languages.

A number of local authorities employed specialist refugee support teachers or teams. Job descriptions and working practices differ across local authorities, but refugee support teachers may:

- admit and settle asylum-seeking and refugee children into school before handing over responsibility for their education to mainstream and English as an additional language (EAL) teachers

- provide a total package of support, including EAL support for refugee children
- support refugee children whose needs go beyond that of learning English: for example a child who is not coping as a result of an overwhelmingly traumatic past
- act as a contact point within the local authority and representing education on multi-agency working parties
- act in an advisory capacity – organising in-service training and helping schools develop practices.

Present provision – schools

Here too there is also growing consensus about good practice for refugee children at school level, again based on the notion of developing resilience. Such school-based practice may comprise:

- reflexivity – an analysis of past experiences of working with bilingual children, promoting anti-racist and multicultural education and working with children in temporary accommodation
- access points for information about refugee children
- an examination of school admission and induction practices, to ensure that refugee children are made to feel welcome
- specialist help and strategies for refugee children who are not coping as a result of their pre-migration and present experiences
- adequate support for children with English as an additional language, including support for more advanced learners of English
- encouragement to maintain and develop the home language(s)
- action to counter hostility and the racist bullying of refugees. This may compromise links with other organisations such as race equality councils and community groups. Schools also need effective sanctions against racist bullying and should use the curriculum to promote ethnic diversity as positive
- good home–school liaison (Rutter 2003).

The way forward

Despite a growing consensus about good practice, there remain many concerns about the education of children who are forced migrants. Refugee children have very mixed experiences of the UK education system. In the world's fifth richest nation, many refugee children have great difficulty finding a school place. Education is a basic human right, yet schools, local authorities and central government invoke procedural and bureaucratic arguments to try to escape fulfilling a legal and moral duty.

The last fifteen years have seen an increase in the numbers of forced migrants in UK schools. From 1989 until very recently, most of these children entered the asylum determination system. Today increasing numbers of children whose families have experiences of forced migration are remaining in the UK as children of work permit holders, overseas students or as irregular migrants. This trend is likely to continue. Policy interventions targeted at children who are forced migrants should not exclude a group purely on the basis of immigration status.

Racist bullying of refugees is an all too common occurrence in schools. Many factors contribute to this, including unbalanced and inaccurate media reporting. Sadly, schools are rarely successful in challenging commonly held beliefs about refugees.

Some refugee children are enjoying a measure of success at school. Others are not, including many Congolese, Somali, Turkish and Kurdish children (Jones and Ali 2000; Mehmet Ali 2001; Rutter 2006). In 2003, just 30% of Turkish-speaking children and 22% of Somali-speaking children gained five grade A*–C in GCSE examinations, with the causes of this underachievement being complex and often localised. Many factors contribute to the lack of progress of refugee children. Some relate to their pre-migration experiences. Others are associated with post-migration conditions – within the child's inner micro-system as well as the school, community and nation. Interventions to support refugee children's achievement need to be ecological in their approach, and promote resilience.

There are other specific interventions that would make a difference to the lives of refugee children. Debate about the real costs of providing English as an additional language support is needed. This would enable assistance to new groups of migrants whose arrival may be sudden and unplanned. Targeted funding for refugee children should also enable more schools and local authorities to employ home–school support workers who would offer parents casework support.

Many refugees have organised their own community schools. These institutions offer a key role in providing peer support for young people. Community schools can also help in the transmission of educational cultural capital – values that support learning. Yet many community schools are under-funded and operate in isolation from mainstream education. Central government and a greater number of local authorities need to see community schools as partners.

Two policy initiatives offer real opportunities to support refugee children. The development of extended schools in England, and their equivalents in Scotland and Wales, may enable schools to offer broad-ranging support for refugee children and their carers. By 2010 all schools in England will be expected to offer a range of activities that might include additional schooling, homework clubs, arts and leisure activities for pupils, community learning opportunities for parents, childcare and welfare support for children and their parents and carers.

The reform of 14–19 education as envisaged by Mike Tomlinson is also essential (DfES 2004). The proposed 14–19 diploma offered real opportunities for refugee children. The original proposals would let young people progress through education at their own rate; mixed-age classes would be an outcome of this reform. Refugee children would be afforded the chance to catch up with new curricular concepts, as well as develop language fluency in mixed-aged classes. They would also be able to study different subjects at different levels. Children who arrived in the UK with little or no prior education would be more likely to leave school with a qualification. The requirement for a single piece of coursework would also benefit refugee children. For many children who arrive in the UK mid-way through a GCSE course, the demands of completing multiple pieces of coursework prevent good GCSE grades.

Finally, if refugee children are to make progress, inequalities associated with social class, migration and ethnicity must be tackled by holistic Government interventions. In the early twenty-first century, the arrival of new immigrants in UK schools is inevitable and unstoppable. Faced with this reality, we need new educational visions, based on justice and equality.

References

Allodi, F. (1989) The children of victims of political persecution and torture: psychological study of a Latin American community, *International Journal of Mental Health* 18(2): 3–15.

American Psychiatric Association (1994) *Diagnostic and Statistical Manual of Mental Disorders,* 4th edn. Washington, DC: APA.

Bolloten, B. and Spafford, T. (1998) Supporting refugee children in east London primary schools, in J. Rutter and C. Jones (eds) *Refugee Education: Mapping the Field.* Stoke-on-Trent: Trentham Books.

Bracken, P. (1998) Hidden agendas: deconstructing post traumatic stress disorder, in P. Bracken and C. Petty (eds) *Rethinking the Trauma of War.* London: Save the Children.

Bronfenbrenner, U. (1992) Ecological systems theory, in R. Vasta (ed.) *Six Theories of Child Development: Revised Formulations and Current Issues.* London: Jessica Kingsley.

Brooks-Gunn, J. (2001) Children in families in communities: risk and intervention in the Bronfenbrenner tradition, in P. Moen, G. Elder and K. Lusher (eds) *Examining Lives in Context: Perspectives on the Ecology of Human Development.* Washington, DC: American Psychological Association.

Camden, London Borough of (1996) Refugee educational policy. Unpublished policy document.

Castles, S. and Loughna, S. (2002) Trends in asylum migration to industrialised countries 1990-2001. Unpublished paper for UN University, World Institute for Development Economic Research.

Chatty, D. and Hundt, G. (2004) Advocating multidisciplinarity in studying complex emergencies: the limitations of a psychological approach to understanding how young people cope with prolonged conflict in Gaza, *Journal of Biosocial Science* 36(4): 417–31.

Department for Education and Skills (DfES) (2004) *14–19 Curriculum and Qualifications Reform: Final Report of the Working Group on 14–19 Reform.* London: DfES.

Elbedour, S., ten Bensel, R. and Bastien, D. (1993) Ecological integrated model of children of war, *Child Abuse and Neglect* 17: 805–819.

Enfield, London Borough of (1999) *Refugee Education Handbook.* London: London Borough of Enfield.

Eth, S. and Pynoos, R. (eds) (1985) *Post Traumatic Stress Disorder in Children.* Washington: American Psychiatric Press.

Fazel, M. and Stein. A. (2002) Mental health of refugee children, *Archives of Disease in Childhood* 87(5): 366–370.

Hodes, M. (2000) Psychologically distressed refugee children in the United Kingdom, *Child Psychology and Psychiatry Review* 5(2): 57–68.

Hollins, K., Heydari, H. and Leavey, G. (2003) *Refugee Adolescents without Parents*. London: Barnet, Enfield and Haringey Mental Health Trust.

Home Office (2004) *Asylum Statistics 2003*. London: Home Office.

Jones, C. and Ali, E. (2000) *Meeting the Educational Needs of Somali Pupils in Camden Schools*. London: London Borough of Camden.

Levy, C. (1999) Asylum-seekers, refugees and the future of citizenship in Europe, in A. Bloch and C. Levy (eds) *Refugees, Citizenship and Social Policy in Europe*. Basingstoke: Macmillan.

Loughrey, G. (1997) Civil violence, in D. Black, N. Newman, J. Harris-Hendricks and G. Mezey (eds) *Psychological Trauma: A Developmental Approach*. London: Gaskell.

Mehmet Ali, A. (2001) *No Delight*. London: Fatal Books.

Minderhoud, P. (1999) Asylum-seekers and access to social security: recent patterns and contemporary realities, in A. Bloch and C. Levy (eds) *Refugees, Citizenship and Social Policy in Europe*. Basingstoke: Macmillan.

Munroe-Blum H., Boyle, M., Offord, D. and Kates, N. (1989) Immigrant children: psychiatric disorder, school performance and service utilization, *American Journal of Orthopsychiatry*, 59(4): 510–519.

Refugee Council (2000) *Helping Refugee Children in Schools*. London: Refugee Council.

Richman, N. (1998) Looking before and after: refugees and asylum-seekers in the West, in P. Bracken and C. Petty (eds) *Rethinking the Trauma of War*. London: Save the Children.

Rousseau, C. and Drapeau, A. (2003) Are refugee children an at-risk group: a longitudinal study of Cambodian adolescents, *Journal of Refugee Studies* 16(1)67–81.

Rutter, J. (2003) *Supporting Refugee Children in 21st Century Britain*. Stoke-on-Trent: Trentham Books.

Rutter, J. (2006) *Refugee Children in the UK*. London: Open University Press.

Rutter, M. (1985) Resilience in the face of adversity – protective factors and resistance to psychiatric disorder, *British Journal of Psychiatry* 147: 598–611.

Stewart, E. (2004) Deficiencies in UK asylum data: practical and theoretical challenges, *Journal of Refugee Studies* 17(1): 29–49.

Summerfield, D. (1998) The social experience of war, in P. Bracken and C. Petty (eds) *Rethinking the Trauma of War*. London: Save the Children.

Summerfield, D. (2000) Childhood, war, refugeedom and trauma, *Transcultural Psychiatry* 37(3): 417–433.

Tolfree, D. (1996) *Restoring Playfulness: Different Approaches to Assisting Children who are Psychologically Affected by War or Displacement*. Stockholm: Radda.

US Committee for Refugees (2004) *Refugee Report 2003*. Washington, DC: US Committee for Refugees.

Witmer, T. and Culver, S. (2001) Trauma and resilience among Bosnian refugee families: a critical review of the literature, *Journal of Social Work Research and Evaluation* 2: 173–187.

Young, A. (1995) *The Harmony of Illusions: Inventing Post Traumatic Stress Disorder*. Princeton: Princeton University Press.

13

DEREK KASSEM
Education of looked-after
children: who cares?

Introduction

Social inclusion is now, at least in terms of rhetoric, a universally accepted political intent. However, the actual practicality of addressing social inclusion is a very different matter. A number of identifiable groups in society, including ethnic minorities and those from poor socio-economic backgrounds, have suffered a social disadvantage that has not changed a great deal in the last twenty years. This is particularly true of looked-after children, even though they have been the focus of a great deal of government policy. The national data on looked-after children demonstrates that they suffer from extremely high levels of social exclusion and deprivation before they enter the care system (Statham *et al.* 2002). Unfortunately for a large number of children, their situation does not improve much once they have entered the care system.

Going into care

Looked-after children is the term used to describe those children who are cared for by the state; in the UK this means the local authority, in one form or another. This may mean care in a local authority children's home, foster care or in secure accommodation. This list does not really do justice to the varied forms that these placements actually take, for instance foster care may mean a child is looked-after by a family unit in which the foster child is the only child in care. Equally foster care may mean the child is one of many 'foster children' looked-after in a community run on a private basis funded by the local authority.

The reasons for a child entering care are as varied as the forms of care. One important point is that fewer than 10% of the children that are in the care of the state are there because of their own behaviour (SEU 2003) or because they will not attend school. It is worth noting that since the passing of the Children Act 1989, education departments have lost their right to start care proceedings for lack of school attendance. Most children end up in care because they are in need of care and protection for one reason or another, family breakdown, abuse both sexual and physical, neglect and emotional abuse, death of parents, or for social reasons within the family that result in the child entering the care system on a voluntary basis. What is known is that children are more likely to enter the care system if they come from one-parent families, a poor household, live in overcrowded accommodation or are from a mixed heritage background (Statham *et al.* 2002). However, what must be remembered is that, no matter the background or the reason, a child who has entered care suffers a double disadvantage. Firstly, the actual process of going into care is frequently a harrowing experience for the child because of family breakdown or abuse. Secondly, being in care is in itself a disadvantage as shown below. It is the child's own personal 'double whammy' to borrow a well-used election slogan.

Indicators of educational achievement

The numbers of looked-after children are comparatively small compared with the child population as a whole. The latest available figures put the number of children looked-after at 60,900 children (DfES 2005) in England or approximately 0.5% of the child population. The difficulties they face in terms of their education effectively put them at the bottom of society's education achievement stakes. For example, only one in 100 looked-after children enters university compared with 43% of all children; 8% of the looked-after children obtained five GCSE A*–C grades compared with over half the whole population in 2005 (Jackson *et al.* 2005). In 2004/2005 43% of children aged 16 leaving care had only one GCSE or GNVQ (DfES 2005); this means that 57% of those leaving care that year had no qualifications. This should also be contrasted with the population as a whole where 95% of the 16-year-olds achieve one or more GCSE or GNVQ.

Looked-after children are also less likely to be entered for formal assessments of any kind at the age of 16. One recent study (Fletcher-Campbell and Archer 2003) found that 26% of their sample were not entered for any GCSEs and for a further 31% there were no data. They also found that the greater the number of placements, that is where a child lives, increases the instability in the child's life and the number of schools they attend. Children who change schools frequently not only repeat a lot of their learning but also are less likely to be entered for formal academic assessments. Quite simply, the school may not have the information about the child to make an informed judgement as to which examination a child may possibly be entered for, so frequently they are not entered for any. The logic from the school's point of view is hard to fault, in these days of league tables, which represent high stakes for schools in terms of funding and status. It might be noted that children who are labelled as educational failures by the system, which looked-after children are often perceived to be, are not considered as assets to their school.

It is possible to argue that for a child who is looked after, just to stay in school represents a considerable achievement, as they are ten times more likely to be excluded from school than the school population as a whole. One recent study indicated 32% of children in care were reported as being excluded from school (Armstrong *et al.* 2005).

Younger children who are looked after fare no better, as their level of achievement is substantially lower than their peers at both Key Stages 2 and 3. However, the extent of the educational difficulties that younger children face is very difficult to quantify, as there are very few data available on the success rates or otherwise of looked-after children. This in itself is a cause for concern as there is evidence that the number of younger children going into care is the fastest growing group (Statham *et al.* 2002).

Life chances

The poor levels of academic achievement by children in care do not diminish once they leave care. Research into the outcomes for children who have left the care system has constantly produced findings which show that they remain educationally disadvantaged and that this, in turn, leads to disadvantage in other areas of their lives (Hayden *et al.* 1999). The life chances of those who have been in care present a frequently gloomy reality, for example, between 25% and a third of rough sleepers were in care (SEU 2003). This figure is similar to the one identified by the *Big Issue* who found around 18% of their vendors had been in care at some point in their lives (*Big Issue* 2001). Around a quarter of adults in prison have spent some of their childhood in care (SEU 2002) and children in care are 2.5 times more likely to become teenage parents (SEU 1999). Furthermore, in one study by the Home Office into vulnerable people (Cusick *et al.* 2003), it was found that 42% of the sex workers interviewed had spent some period of their childhood in care. The same study also found similar rates for drug users. This is not to say that all children who have been through the care system have unsuccessful lives, quite the contrary, but a great many do have problems in later life due in part to poor education.

The experiences of looked-after children represent a major challenge for the government agenda of combating social exclusion. As they encompass a range of key initiatives, such as Every Child Matters, the social exclusion agenda, including child poverty targets, must be seen alongside specific educational targets for looked-after children. The effectiveness of the implementation of the strategies to address the needs of looked-after children therefore acts as a litmus test for all the initiatives mentioned above. Failure to improve the situation for this group raises questions as to the effectiveness of these initiatives both in terms of improved life chances for looked-after children and their cost-effectiveness. However, if they are not working for looked-after children, to what extent are they working for the other socially excluded groups that the policies are aimed at?

Being in care – the educational experience

Currently 68% of looked-after children have placements in foster care (DfES 2005); this is an increase of 9% over the previous year. Of those children in care for periods of more than 2.5 years, the majority, 65%, have lived in the same place for at least two years. This is important as stability of placement has a major impact on children's lives and their educational experiences. However, this still means that a substantial number of children who have been in care for just over two years have had more than one placement in that period. Change of placements also, frequently, mean a change of school; inevitably this means that the child's education is disrupted. For instance one child commented, 'I missed a lot of school and that, moving about a lot . . . doing different topics and that at different schools' (Jackson and Sachdev 2001: 66).

The movement of children and the subsequent disruption of their education is, in part, due to education not being the main concern of social workers. The evidence (Morris 2000) suggests that it is, firstly, finding somewhere for the child to stay, which is not always an easy task. Secondly, the general care and wellbeing of the child takes priority over everything else, and education is the least of their concerns:

> We just get children dumped on us, usually at very short notice. It's very difficult to see how we can be part of a service 'targeted on the need of the individual child', which is what they say we're supposed to be. Basically, children end up with us because there's nowhere else for them to go.
> (residential care manager, Morris 2000: 11)

Education of looked-after children is not just a low priority in terms of placements but there is generally a lack of support and monitoring of children's educational progress. For example, on entering the care system each child should have a personal education plan (PEP). This planning and monitoring form should be started within twenty school days by a social worker and a designated teacher. However, they have a very low priority and are not adequately planned for (Jackson and Sachdev 2001). In part, 'planning was hampered by the reality of placement availability. The ability to plan care placements is crucial in planning a child's education' (Hayden 2005). One research project found there were difficulties ensuring that all children had a PEP (Fletcher-Cambell and Archer 2003). This is especially significant because the PEPs represent one of the new approaches that the Government has introduced in order to address high levels of underachievement by looked-after children. The consequence of the lack of planning and monitoring of looked-after children's education is that education authorities and social services fail to set targets and monitor the progress of a number of children in their care (Jackson and Sachdev 2001).

It is suggested that the difficulties in planning for looked-after children's education are due to the increasing complexity of the monitoring and planning that both education and social services are expected to keep. The overlapping nature of the records that are required to be kept (Hayden 2005), PEPs (social services) or individual behaviour plans (IBPs) and National Curriculum test results in schools conflict with each other and do not provide a complete picture of the child's needs. Looked-after children would benefit from a simplification of the record-keeping process that focuses on them and their placements should always be planned with education as a key target.

Looked-after children are provided with a degree of extra support in their education. However, the support that is offered is frequently inadequate in one way or another and this is true of the experiences of children no matter what part of the British Isles they live in:

[a volunteer worker sent by social services to provide educational support] didn't know Welsh and French, you know, she didn't know at all. She didn't know much mathematics ... But they said they'd get me another one. I have got another volunteer worker and she said she'd come and see me a month ago, but she hasn't come.

(a looked-after child in Wales, Jackson and Sachdev 2001: 61)

Another child commented:

... support with revision, they were trying to get to know me, sort everything out so it was just like I've got my GCSEs next week and then I can't ... just made sure I settled down and was happy and then just got me through to start college and resitting but I didn't do resits.

(Jackson and Sachdev 2001: 61)

It is important to note that not all children have these negative experiences with support services; some, in fact, have very positive experiences. However, a great many children do suffer from an approach that effectively puts educational attainment at the bottom of the ladder, in terms of immediate concerns when addressing children's needs. What is also clearly signalled by these realities is the main concern of social and residential workers, the placement of a child followed by their general wellbeing but not their education.

The majority of looked-after children do not have a special need but there are a significant number who do. Of those children who were continuously in care for a year 27% held statements of special educational needs. This is compared with a general population figure of 3% (DfES 2005). The NCH (2005) estimates the number of children with a statement of special needs at 36% with a further 14% having some learning difficulties, usually literacy. According to the DfES figures, this means that a looked-after child is nine times more likely to have a statement of special needs than a child not in care. The statement of need that most often occurs relates to behaviour. This should not really be that surprising, as the process of going into care is usually paved with experiences of abuse, neglect and powerful feelings of rejection that are not easily overcome. The child, once in care, must come to terms with a very new situation with different adults who will move in and out of their lives, each adult bringing with them different sets of attitudes and expectations. Yet research indicates that the educational needs of looked-after children with a special need are ignored (NCH 2005) or they are labelled, boxed off and institutionally dealt with. This is especially true if they exhibit difficult behaviour and they are either excluded from school or sent to a special school. One particular author describes the consequences in a very powerful way:

The social consequences of being assessed and placed in a specialised category, particularly one with the historical stigmatic connotation of EBD, are long term and potentially harmful to the individual. Despite good intentions they become marginalised as members of society. Then stigmatic social identity becomes a means by which they can be segregated from their peer group, friends, home and local community, denied access to the educational experiences offered to normal children and offered a curriculum which may subsequently deny them access to further education, training or most types of employment.

(Galloway *et al.* 1994: 117, cited in Jackson and Sachdev 2001: 109)

The point here is that some children in public care not only suffer from the double whammy of going into and being in care, but once there, their emotional and mental wellbeing is often not dealt with appropriately. A triple whammy. In terms of school exclusion looked-after children are given very little support to challenge an exclusion order by a school. Unlike most children who have a parent who will support their child, the local authority, the corporate parent, does not rise to the defence of their children. There is an acceptance by the very institutions that are supposed to support looked-after children that the child is guilty as charged. Therefore why appeal on their behalf or raise awkward questions in respect of the implementation of school procedures and the equity of decisions? The process is in effect a confirmation of the labelling of looked-after children as a problem. They are to blame for all their problems. As one child explains:

I was fighting ... They straightaway suspended me ... She [the other person in the fight] stayed in school.

(Jackson and Sachdev 2001: 117)

Another pupil comments:

I went to school with this girl. She kept talking to me. She'd ask all these questions and I'd just say back off, mind your own business, keep your nose out of my life. She said did I want a fight. And no, [I said] I don't want to fight I just want you out of my face ... and then she started to fight me. I got chucked out of school, not that girl.

(Jackson and Sachdev 2001: 117)

While the vignettes above do not prove the case, they do provide an insight into the school environment that a lot of looked-after children experience. One has to remember that a looked-after child is ten times more likely to be excluded from school than a child who has a parent. One study found that 43% of their sample had at least once, since entering care, being excluded from school (Harker *et al.* 2003).

Looked-after children are often the victims of bullying due to the attitudes of adults and consequently children in schools and the wider society (Morris 2000). It is the very notion of difference that the bullying is centred on, as one child points out:

I know it's said a lot but it's true, everyone hates difference. A lot of people hate difference and in a school it's a very small minority who are in care. So we're different from the majority.

(Morris 2000: 56)

Within the teaching environment the evidence suggests that teachers often have low expectations of looked-after children: an account of the experience and effect of low teacher expectations was recounted in the *Times Educational Supplement*:

Seven years and several menial jobs after leaving care with just a single GCSE, Alex Sykes was finally diagnosed with dyslexia. The former children's home resident blames teachers at his secondary school in Halifax for failing to spot his condition because of low expectations they had of children in local authority care. He said: 'If someone had given me help with dyslexia earlier, it could have changed my life. Instead my self-confidence was destroyed. People presumed that because I was in care I was going to have a problem.'

(*TES* 13 January 2005: 3)

Another former looked-after child stated that:

Some teachers don't like you or they're more strict with you than anyone else because you're in care. And then some teachers don't really care if you don't do nothing, they say, 'Oh, you've got problems, don't worry.' And that's what annoys you, you just want to be treated like everyone else. You don't want to be treated different.

(Morris 2000: 22)

The evidence suggests that it is not only low expectations of pupils by teachers. Rather it is a general labelling of looked-after children, often by school and society, that they are for some reason bad boys and girls. They are almost criminalised by the very institutions that should be providing support. 'As soon as you say you are in care, people stigmatise you. Some people seem to think that a child is in care because they have done something wrong' (Katie Morris in care since the age of 9, just graduated, *TES* 23 December 2005).

It would seem that schools do not always offer the refuge that looked-after children might expect. Although, as with every situation there are teachers and schools that are effective and provide good quality experiences for looked-after children. There is also good-quality provision made by local authorities, for example, just as with ethnic minority children there is a vast discrepancy in the rate of school exclusions from one authority to the next. This same pattern is reproduced for looked-after children. In essence, some local authorities do support and have good-quality systems for looked-after children in place (Jackson and Sachdev 2001).

The policies and targets

The education of looked-after children, whilst not at the forefront of this Government's political agenda, is at least in the background. This is a major improvement on the past, and has seen an improvement, at least in terms of the general awareness of the issues. One only has to read Jackson's (1987) seminal report on the state of education of looked-after children to see the improvement.

The Government has produced targets for the education of children in public care, for example:

> local authorities to improve the educational record of the children they look after so that the proportion of children leaving care aged 16 or above who have gained at least one GCSE or GNVQ qualification increases to 50% by 2001, and to 75% by 2003.
>
> (Archive of Official Documents 2005)

However they failed to meet this target. The logical step for the Government was to revise the target so it would seem a challenge, but also achievable. The Government has set a target for this year 2006, to improve the life chances of looked-after children:

In 2002, the Government promised to substantially narrow the gap between the attainment of those in care and their peers by 2006. Targets included:

- raising the achievement of 11-year-olds in care to at least 60% of that of their peers
- ensuring no more than 10% reach 16 without having sat one GCSE or equivalent
- raising the percentage who get five Cs or better at GCSE by four points each year ensuring at least 15% can reach this level in every council (*TES* 13 January 2006: 3).

Added to this list of targets, the Government recognised that one of the key factors in the poor levels of educational attainment of children in public care was the instability of their living arrangements or, as it is known, placements. They set a target that the proportion of looked-after children under 16 who have been in care for 2.5 years or more will have lived at the same place for at least two years to 80% of the cohort. This is a very bold target given the difficulties of finding placements for children that are long term and of a satisfactory nature. There is of course no indication that the child's education should be paramount in the planning of their placements. The Government has admitted they will not meet these targets, though they do suggest that they might reach their target for younger children at Key Stage 2. The proportion of children in public care who leave care with a single GCSE has not improved since 2003 and they have not met their 2001 target for the number of children gaining one GCSE (*TES* 13 January 2006).

The failure is not because the Government has not focused on the needs of looked-after children; quite the contrary, they have set targets as indicated above. They have also discussed sending the brighter looked-after children to public schools at the cost of £20,000 a year per child, and looked-after children are clearly a focus for the Every Child Matters agenda. Looked-after children are provided with a mention in the Government's White Paper on secondary education and although specific targets are not mentioned, they are clearly an issue the Government wishes to address along with others such as the achievement levels of ethnic minority children. However, the Government's failure to meet its own targets is more to do with the contradictions within the system it is creating.

If the proposed secondary school reforms are taken as an example, it is possible to see how the conflicts within the policies are working against the groups they are supposed to be helping. On one hand the secondary reforms are supposed to be aimed at improving the educational lot of those in most need. However, in allowing schools to develop independently, with admission policies not enshrined in law, there is a real possibility that those groups in greatest need will not be admitted to the school of their choice. Evidence for this is to be found in the study carried out by the Sutton Trust (2006) on the proportion of children in receipt of free school meals at the 200 top performing comprehensive schools. They found that they had a much smaller proportion of children with free school meals than schools as a whole and that if they were located in poorer districts they were not representative of the socio-economic profile of the locality. Given that, what chance does a looked-after child have? The contradiction between aim, stated target and implementation of policy also occurs in other aspects of the world inhabited by looked-after children.

The educational attainment of looked-after children is determined in most respects by two very different worlds. Firstly social services and social workers, and secondly education and teachers have different professional cultures, and in today's world, separate targets and goals that must be met and are set by the Government. The target-driven culture we exist in is part of the process of ensuring value for money and for effective public services. As Harker *et al.* (2004) point out:

> the pre-care experiences and characteristics of looked-after children cannot fully explain the underachievement of this group. Additional explanations highlight certain structural features of the care and education systems which can prevent the education of looked-after children being prioritised. Key departments involved in looking after children are not always successful in adopting a corporate parenting approach and consequently fail to communicate effectively to share relevant information and coordinate services.
>
> (2004: 179)

While it is recognised that there are many issues encountered in inter-professional working, not least language and professional culture, the key issue for looked-after children is, as Harker *et al.* (2004) point out:

> the lack of inter-professional practice at operational levels was conflicting priorities within the workload of teachers and social workers . . . it was felt that the workload of social workers could prevent them from viewing educational issues as a priority over urgent placement issues and dealing with emotional and/or physical needs.
>
> (2004: 182)

This conflict of priorities between social workers and the educational aims for looked-after children is not a one-way street. Teachers equally have their priorities and workload commitments that act as barriers in dealing with the needs of looked-after children. In part, these conflicts are the product of a system that sets targets and policy initiatives that send mixed messages to the very people that are required to implement them (see Anning in this volume for further discussion on this issue). For example, the Every Child Matters agenda includes looked-after children, but is it as a vulnerable child with a focus on child protection or is it the whole child including their education? The response depends on whether the professional involved is a social worker or teacher. For example:

> pressure on teaching staff to meet performance targets for whole school populations was not viewed as conducive to establishing and maintaining communication with social workers where looked-after children were concerned.
>
> (Harker *et al.* 2004: 179)

Various organisations, pressure groups and the media, including the *TES*, NCH and Barnardo's are campaigning to raise the issues of the poor levels of educational attainment of looked-after children and they point to lists of what should be done by individuals or organisations such as schools and local authorities. All these are very positive and will show, no doubt, some improvement for looked-after children. The progress made so far is due in part to the changes in the legislation, starting with the Children Act 1989 and subsequently the Children Act 2004 and the Children Leaving Care Act 2001. The real problems they do not address are:

- the mixed messages enshrined in the policy initiatives by the Government
- the overuse of target setting
- the structural problem of inter-professional working between social workers and teachers that have to implement the above two points.

Conclusion

The key issues are that too many professionals, teachers and social workers locate the blame in the low educational achievement of looked-after children within the experiences the child went through before coming into care. That is in effect locating the problem within the child. The real issue is located within the system and attitudes of many of the people who work with looked-after children. One has only to read the work by Jackson and Sachdev (2001) where children talk for themselves to see how important it is to instigate a change in attitudes of professionals. The leader responsible for changing the perception of looked-after children must be the Government, not least because they set the targets that the system must implement. A key change would be to have the same targets for looked-after children as those for the population as a whole. It should be remembered that most looked-after children do not have a special need, they have the same talents and abilities as the general population, so why do they have to have lesser goals? By having lower targets the Government reinforces the lower expectations of teachers, social workers and possibly the children themselves of what they can achieve.

The failure to meet the needs of looked-after children is an institutional and governmental failure that society cannot afford, neither in terms of the wasted lives and potential nor also in the cost in economic terms. How much does it cost society in taxes to keep former looked-after children who are now in prison? In terms of policy and the social inclusion agenda it would seem that the continued failure to address the needs of looked-after children by the Government is an example of the failure of joined-up government at the operational level. This must be changed.

References

Archive of Official Documents (2005) http://www.archive.officialdocuments.co.uk/document/cm41/4105/chap-02.htm (accessed 30 Dec. 2005).

Armstrong, D., Hine, J., Armaos, R., Jones, R., Klessinger, N. and France, A. (2005) *Children, Risk and Crime: The On Track Youth Lifestyles Surveys* London: Home Office.

Big Issue (2001) 10th birthday survey, *Big Issue*, September edition.

Cusik, L., Martin, A. and May, T. (2003) *Vulnerability and Involvement in Drug Use and Sex Work*. London: Home Office.

Department for Education and Skills (DfES) (2005) *National Statistics: Children Looked After in England (Including Adoptions and Care Leavers)*. London: DfES.

Fletcher-Cambell, F. and Archer, T. (2003) *Achievement at Key Stage 4 of Young Children in Public Care*. London: DfES.

Galloway, D., Armstrong, D. and Tomlinson, S. (1994) *The Assessment of Special Educational Needs – Whose Problem?* London: Longman.

Harker, R., Dobel-Ober, D., Lawrence, J., Berridge, D. and Sinclair, R. (2003) Who takes care of education? Looked after children's perceptions of support for educational progress, *Child and Family Social Work* 8: 89–100.

Harker, R., Dobel-Ober, D., Berridge, D. and Sinclair, R. (2004) More than the sum of its parts? Inter-professional working in the education of looked after children, *Children and Society* 18: 179–193.

Hayden, C. (2005) More than a piece of paper? Personal education plans and 'looked after' children in England, *Child and Family Social Work* 10: 343–352.

Hayden, C., Goddard, J., Gorrin, S. and Van Der Spek, N. (1999) *State Child Care Looking After Children?* London: Jessica Kingsley.

Jackson, S. (1987) *The Education of Children in Care*. Bristol: University of Bristol.

Jackson, S. and Sachdev, D. (2001) *Better Education, Better Futures: Research, Practice and the Views of Young People in Public Care*. London: Barnado's.

Jackson, S., Ajayi, S. and Quigley, M. (2005) *Going to University from Care*. London: University of London Institute of Education.

Morris, J. (2000) *Having Someone Who Cares? Barriers to Change in the Public Care of Children*. London: National Children's Bureau.

NCH (2005) *Close the Gap for Children in Care*. London: NCH the Children's Charity.

Social Exclusion Unit (SEU) (1999) *Teenage Pregnancy*. London: SEU.

Social Exclusion Unit (SEU) (2002) *Reducing Re-offending by Ex-prisoners*. London: SEU.

Social Exclusion Unit (SEU) (2003) *A Better Education for Children in Care*. London: SEU.

Statham, J., Candappa, M., Simon, A. and Owen, C. (2002) *Trends in Care: Exploring Reasons for the Increase in Children Looked After by Local Authorities*. London: University of London Institute of Education.

Sutton Trust (2006) *The Social Composition of Top Comprehensive Schools: Rates of Eligibility for Free School Dinners at 200 Highest Performing Comprehensive Schools*. London: Sutton Trust.

14

JANE MARTIN
Women and state schools: Britain 1870 to present day

Introduction

The standard way of writing about the making of educational policy has been to foreground the ideas and activities of men. However, revisionist thinking has challenged historians to shift the emphases of the 'master' narrative both to include women and to use gender as a lens through which to examine the past. This chapter forms part of a recent trend, which aims to take account of the motives for and outcomes of female involvement at various levels of education policy-making and administration. A collective biographical approach is used to rediscover the voices and achievements of women who became educational policy-makers within the sphere of local government and State activity. Taking London as a case study, I examine the careers of a group of women whose participation in English educational policy-making has only recently been recovered from historical obscurity: the women members of the London School Board and the Education Committee of the London County Council. London was chosen because of the conspicuous strength of women in metropolitan politics, both in terms of the numbers involved and the scope and power accorded them. Turning to central government, I explore the political journeys of women appointed to the education portfolio between 1945 and the present day.

Women and educational policy

British politics has evolved in conjunction with masculinity, masculinism and patriarchy and women's mass mobilisation has often been viewed as something of an anomaly. Historical analyses of policy imperatives, power structures and political discourse show the legacy of deeply held beliefs that politics was men's business although it should be acknowledged that the structure of the British State provided limited space for women's participation even when women were excluded from Parliamentary politics. Set up to administer the 1870 Education Act, the eligibility of women to be elected to the newly created school boards was of great importance. Directly elected and independent of existing forms of local government, these bodies were responsible for the creation of something resembling a system of State-maintained elementary schools for working-class children. By the end of the nineteenth century women also served as members of local technical instruction committees, educational commissions and central government committees. Nonetheless, the controversial 1902 Education Act, which replaced the school boards with the education committees of local authorities, dealt a severe blow to women's political progress since they were no longer able to vote or participate as elected representatives. Yet the campaign and pressure exerted by the women's movement was influential in securing the restoration of these rights in 1907.

At the national level, women did not obtain the vote in general elections until 1918 and even then only at the age of 30. Women finally achieved suffrage on the same terms as men in 1928, when the age limit was lowered to 21. In the competition for political office, education was a likely portfolio, suggesting that prime ministers subscribed to conventional ideas about women's domestic skills and interests. The implication of this valorisation of essentialist views of sexual difference is evidenced in the fact that in the 1920s, two of the four female office-holders in the House of Commons were Parliamentary secretary at Education and the only two women who reached the Cabinet between 1945 and 1959 were also at Education. For Margaret Thatcher (born 1925) Conservative Prime Minister from 1979 to 1990, Secretary of State for Education and Science in Edward Heath's 1970 Government, the post was part of her route to the top. But Thatcher's precursors in local government had already made their mark in the years before the national suffrage grant in 1928.

Women, work and public life

In the analysis that follows, the sentimentalisation of family life is considered a crucial aspect of the links between gendered practice and discourse. Campaigners for women's rights reconfigured the idea that a woman's place was in the home, to argue that just as the ideal family needed the active cooperation of feminine with masculine brains and hands, so the voices of women should be heard in every area of life. The concept of social motherhood, based on so-called female attributes, enabled a minority of women to operate in ways considered appropriate and respectable in the public sphere. Women's self-organisation in clubs and social movements provided a focus for political mobilisation: widening opportunities for action, for developing and expressing opinions of their own, as well as building lifelong friendships. Simultaneously, the spread of state education offered new opportunities and possibilities for working class children to get an education and become teachers. In her overview of the history of women teachers from the 1850s to the mid-1990s, Jane Miller (1996) documents the growth of teaching as a female-dominated profession in a context of contradictions embedded in gendered notions of the caring self drawing on discourses of motherhood, femininity and familialism.

Feminist critics of contemporary British politics argue that the distribution of political power reflects a social bias that makes it easier for some individuals and groups to see their objectives come to fruition than others. Exploring how gender has influenced and continues to influence the political process, Joni Lovenduski (1996) points to the existence of positional, policy and organisational bias in favour of men. When considering the factors which have helped, or hindered, women's public participation one has to take account of the gendered production of direct political power and leadership. Here I engage critically with Pierre Bourdieu's concepts of capitals, habitus and field to interrogate women's biographies and political journeys.

Bourdieu understands society as made up of 'fields of power'. A field is a social arena which functions according to its own tacit logic or set of rules. Acceptance as a legitimate player of the game is achieved by access to specific goods/resources or stakes. A central aim in Bourdieu's sociology is to develop an understanding of how forms of division, domination and exclusion are historically based and maintained. In this he identifies four main types of capital. These are economic, cultural, social and symbolic. Economic capital refers to income, wealth, financial inheritances and monetary assets. Cultural capital, defined as high culture, can exist in three forms: embodied cultural capital, objectified cultural capital and institutional cultural capital. The last is the product of investment in formal education. Social capital is the product of sociability, which speaks of investment in culturally, economically, or politically useful networks and connections. These economic metaphors can be used to examine the different forms of power and relationships that help the prospects of women in politics. For instance, to achieve political success, the different forms of capital need to be recognised as legitimate, whereupon they take the form of symbolic capital. It follows that while in most contexts the social effects of femaleness may make the possession of direct political power problematic for women, the power mechanisms of masculine domination can be compensated for by the possession of other forms of capital, notably that of social capital. Legitimation is the key mechanism in the conversion to power and Bourdieu provides an 'equation' to show the relationality of all three concepts:

'(Habitus × Capital) + Field = Practice'

(Reay 2004: 435)

This model relies on an understanding of people and the relations between them as distributed in metaphorical social space depending on the exchange-value of a particular form of self. Positions in the social space are constituted in social relations and through social practice, while the habitus is formed through the process of internalisation of capitals. Habitus is defined as systems of durable, transposable dispositions that predispose individuals to do certain things: it explains how behaviour can be regulated without being the product of obedience to rules. Learned more by experience than by teaching, habitus relates to a way of seeing and being within the world. Bourdieu is talking about social practice linked to, for example, linguistic competence, lifestyle, politics and prestige, combined with particular dispositions, attitudes and tastes. Biographical approaches can be used to reconstruct the acquisition of the activist habitus historically to the extent that it inscribes the individual with a repertoire of practices, with a history, that facilitate or otherwise the taste for contention. For Ellen Wilkinson, who had a long career as a Labour MP, the pioneer socialist Katherine Bruce Glasier (1867–1950) was tremendously influential: 'to be able to sway a great crowd as she swayed it, to be able to make people work to make life better, to remove slums and underfeeding and misery just because one came and spoke to them about it . . . that seemed the highest destiny any woman could ever hope for' (Wilkinson 1938: 414). Wilkinson's experience suggests that exposure to and accrual of the activist habitus predisposes certain individuals to enter the political field. Here this heuristic model of social topography is used to show the conversion process which provides particular conditions and possibilities for a successful engagement in the political field, based on the attribution of value, in local symbolic forms of exchange. Atypical members, such as women, will need more exceptional qualities because of the need to compensate for the gender bias in the political field. We turn now to a collective biography of women and educational policy-making at local and national level.

A biographical approach to women's role in the development of state schools

Created under the terms of the 1870 Education Act, the London School Board (LSB) was the world's largest educational parliament and Britain's most influential school board. Soon it had 55 members and controlled nearly 400 schools. The creation of the London County Council (LCC) in 1888 inspired prospects and hopes for popular political programmes and their extensions in policy by the world's largest municipal authority in the world's largest city. The absorption of the LSB in 1904 forced the largest rate rises of the period of Progressive rule and this helped turn the tide in favour of the Conservative Party who would hold office from 1907 until Labour won control in 1934. Led by Herbert Morrison (1888–1965) the London Labour Party grew in strength throughout the 1930s but we need to recognise that Morrison addressed well-educated women as part of his strategy for Labour in London: encouraging them to contest metropolitan elections. In consequence 1934 saw the return of a record number of women: some 23% of the victorious councillors were women, compared with 8% of their Conservative opponents (Clifton 1989: 9). But Labour's triumph caused problems for central government, particularly when the central authority was Conservative controlled and in 1965 the LCC suffered the same fate as its predecessor, the LSB. Education in London was put under the control of a new body, the Inner London Education Authority (ILEA), a quasi-autonomous committee of the newly created Greater London Council. Subsequently the Labour Party once again took control of the capital's business and the break-up of the ILEA as part of the Conservative Government's 1988 Education Reform Act marked the end of London-wide government of education in the capital city. But what was the impact of women's presence in the field of education politics? We turn first to the 29 women members of the LSB who, along with their male counterparts, laid the foundations in the areas they served.

In terms of female representation, the breakthrough came in 1879 when women made up 18% of LSB members (Martin 1999). Not until the Labour Party introduced all-women shortlists for the 1997 general election did Parliamentary representation match this. Most LSB women were from middle-class backgrounds although their financial circumstances could vary considerably. The exception was Mary Bridges Adams (1855–1939) who came from a Welsh working-class background and had to train through the pupil teacher system. In her case educational success and social capital accrued through the British Labour movement, provided her with habitus that was operating in an unfamiliar field. All but three of the women members represented London Progressivism, a broadly based constituency comprised of Liberal Association members, trade unionists, Nonconformists, social reformers and the rank and file of the working men's clubs. Clearly they all participated in a rich metropolitan political life and most were active in the women's suffrage movement. It is a significant fact that female networks worked as social capital for women candidates, especially in the West End division of Marylebone which had a 21-year record of continuous female representation starting with the pioneer doctor Elizabeth Garrett (1836–1917) who finished top of the poll in 1870. Florence Fenwick Miller (1854–1934) was the youngest woman member, just 22 years old when she took her seat in 1876. Like Garrett before her, she married while serving but was exceptional in going through pregnancy and childbirth as an elected representative. Prevailing conventions have some bearing on the fact that Annie Besant (1847–1933) was the only divorcee and of the remaining 28, two were widowed when they first took office, ten were married and sixteen were single. I have been able to establish that eight of the married women were mothers. However, Besant lost custody of her daughter over her initiatives on the question of birth control.

The Board held open meetings every Wednesday, beginning at 3 pm and usually continuing until 6.30 pm, although it was often much later. Their main purpose was to hear the recommendations set out in reports from the various committees that conducted the work of the Board; these were accepted, amended or referred back. Members had a right to propose alternative motions of policy, and debate them, before an open vote was taken, with each individual answering 'yes' or 'no' at the division. An accent on parliamentary tradition meant the male organisational bias was very apparent, so was a culture of male fraternity. Although the presence of women members complicated struggles over power and advantage, male and female territories and responsibilities show the impact of gender differentiation on political careers. For instance, whereas women dominated the Cookery, Laundry and Needlework Sub-Committee, they rarely served on the Finance Committee or the Works Committee responsible for the school building programme and the general care of Board properties. Members often regarded their service on the Boards as important social work and the unpublished autobiography of Florence Fenwick Miller indicates the scale of their commitment (Martin 2000). In the 1870s and 1880s she spent two or three days at the Board offices, while the rest of the week was taken up with constituency work. Miller was not a wealthy woman and she often went without food on Board days, thinking it a wild extravagance to lunch out, on top of the money spent on bus fares and a cup of tea at the Board's tearoom.

Women's claims to political power were based on the distinctive character of the female contribution. In particular, they were contingent upon a classed and gendered construction of special needs. Girls were regarded as having different requirements to boys (either physical, emotional or intellectual) and women candidates found it advantageous to campaign as being ready to champion the interests of girls and women teachers. A brief look at debate on the elementary schoolgirls' curriculum and the interests of women teachers makes it possible to assess whether these female politicians made a distinctive stand on the interests of girls and women. The issue of school attendance will be used to assess the policy gender bias in the politics of schooling.

From 1862 onwards, failing to teach working-class girls needlework was one of the few offences for which a school could lose its Government grant. By the 1890s there was a complete division of the sexes in practical subjects, though boys did not receive practical instruction equivalent to the girls' sewing, cooking and cleaning. Nonetheless, the voting record of the thirteen women elected in the 1870s and 1880s shows not all women supported these developments. Florence Fenwick Miller, Henrietta Muller (1845/6–1906), Helen Taylor (1831–1907) and Elizabeth Surr (born 1825/6) were the most vocal opponents, supported by the two working-class members – Benjamin Lucraft (1808–97) and George Potter (1832–93). Happy to work with men who were sympathetic to their arguments, these four women were always in a minority but managed to score some victories. For example, Muller secured a reduction in the number of stitches to the inch required in the needlework regulations, after women teachers reported that it was damaging the girls' eyesight. When they took up the cudgels on behalf of women teachers they overturned proposals to exclude women from headships and bar the employment of mothers of infants under two years old. In contrast, more socially conservative women like Rosamond Davenport Hill (1825–1902) accepted the assumptions of the domestic ideal. Hill promoted practical training in domesticity in the belief that domestic work and love of the home should be the focus of working class girls' lives: both in their own households and in the homes of others (as domestic servants). Born into a leading social reform family of the day (her father helped draft the first bill to attempt to win property rights for married women in 1854), for Hill, middle-class moral femininity was both a resource and a symbolically legitimate form of cultural capital.

Irrespective of ideological differences, women members were active in shaping the embryonic reform school system, developing alongside the board schools. Then, as now, school attendance was an issue and although girls were the more irregular attenders, there was a tendency for the system of rewards and punishment to focus on boys. The ultimate sanction was committal to a single-sex residential truant or industrial school, or a co-educational day industrial school. Early opponents of a separate curriculum for girls also took up the issue of child welfare in these institutions: exposing the cruel use of punishment not always officially sanctioned. They also addressed the issue of female exclusion by pressing for early years' provision so schoolgirls would not be kept home to 'mind baby'. In the 1890s, elected women tried to ban the use of public floggings meted out to boys re-admitted to a truant or industrial school. They wanted alternative sanctions to those they saw as dehumanising.

Overall, school board politics provided some white, educated, mainly middle-class women with a position of authority and a position of fulfilment. These women were a powerful force in their local communities and the preceding discussion highlights a distinct and vocal minority who resented party discipline and rigid allegiance to party. This form of women's politics became less viable on the LCC as the party machines steadily increased their grip. As Council leader from 1934 to 1940 Herbert Morrison appointed a number of Labour women to committee chairmanships including Eveline Lowe (1869–1956) to Education.

The daughter of a Congregational minister, Lowe was educated in fee-paying religious institutions that enabled the further acquisition of social and cultural capital. After a spell of teaching she returned to her alma mater, Homerton College, as lecturer; eventually becoming vice-principal, a position she held until she left to marry George Lowe, a veterinary surgeon who qualified as a doctor in 1911. He lived and worked in Bermondsey and the Lowes participated in charitable activity directed towards the local poor. This exposure to the activist habitus played a crucial role in propelling her toward municipal politics. She spent several years as a Poor Law Guardian and helped found the Bermondsey Independent Labour Party in 1908. Widowed in 1919, Lowe became even more committed to public life. The Labour group co-opted her to the LCC education committee and in 1922 she gained one of the two West Bermondsey seats at County Hall. In 1934 she became chair of the Education Committee having established herself as London Labour's expert in this field.

Local authorities had been forced to make cuts in the economic crisis of the early 1930s and Labour's three-year programme for London education had two priorities. These were to increase the level of secondary school provision and secure improvements in the standard of elementary schooling, while demonstrating to the electorate Labour's care with public spending. Emphasis was also put on child welfare and the need to improve working-class access to secondary education by increasing the number of scholarships. Within days of Lowe taking office, Empire Day in the schools was renamed Commonwealth Day. Within weeks, the Council pressed national government to restore a 10% cut in teachers' salaries and raise the school leaving age to 15. Within months, the Education Committee was asked to report on all aspects of post-primary education. It recommended the abolition of selection and a common schooling for each child up to the age of fourteen. Generally, Lowe was considered to have done a good job although she did not go far enough for some.

Helen Bentwich (1892–1972) was the next woman chair of the LCC Education Committee. For Bentwich, it is possible to see her London childhood as pivotal to the formation of an activist habitus. She grew up in one of the interrelated banking and broking families who comprised the Anglo-Jewish elite. Both her parents were notable for their participation in charitable activity directed towards the capital's poor and her mother, Caroline Franklin (1863–1935) also served on Buckinghamshire Education Committee. Her uncle Herbert Samuel (1870–1963) was the first practising Jew appointed to the British Cabinet. Bentwich had a good education but was not expected to take up paid employment. She spent the 1920s in Palestine where her husband was Attorney General, one of the most powerful posts in the

British Mandated Territory. Here she combined voluntary work with a political hostess role and became involved in the feminist-inclined Palestine Council of Jewish Women. This positioning and engagement in public activity demonstrates a very particular gendered habitus underpinned by high levels of economic, social and cultural capital. Soon after her return to London she joined the Labour Party and twice stood unsuccessfully for Parliament. However, in the spring of 1934 she received a late night phone call from Eveline Lowe, inviting her to become a co-opted member of the LCC Education Committee (Martin 2005).

In various speeches reported in the 1930s and 1940s, Bentwich condemned the class inequalities in education, advocated the abolition of private education and called for equality of opportunity. In these years she was part of the Labour leadership that produced educational plans and policies in accord with the comprehensive ideal. Hence when the 1944 Education Act introduced free secondary education for all and each authority was asked to make a school development plan the LCC already had its preparations in hand. Bentwich became chair of the Education Committee in 1947 and that same year the Labour Minister of Education accepted the London school plan for reorganising secondary education, which was drawn up on comprehensive principles. In 1949 the Minister approved a proposal to build the capital's first purpose-built comprehensive, Kidbrooke School, described as London's pride when it opened in 1954. By the 1950s Bentwich was among those identified as part of an inner cabinet on the Council: a time when it was seen as prestigious to teach in LCC schools (Jones 1989: 87).

Besides party women like Lowe and Bentwich, it remained possible for feminists like Agnes Dawson (1873–1953) to make their mark within the field of local education politics. The daughter of a journeyman carpenter who was often out of work, Dawson followed the pupil-teacher route into a teaching career. In 1925 the past president of the National Federation of Women Teachers resigned her headship of Crawford Street Infants' School to stand for the LCC as a Labour member in the safe seat of Camberwell (Kean 1990). Fittingly it was Dawson who, having kept the question alive, moved the successful resolution whereby London's women teachers and women doctors were allowed to retain their posts on marriage after August 1 1935, a right they had lost in March 1923.

Just before the outbreak of the Second World War Eveline Lowe made history when she became the first woman chairman [sic] of the LCC. When the fighting had finished, after the Labour landslide in the 1945 general election, Ellen Wilkinson became the first Labour Minister of Education. 'Red Ellen' (also known as the 'fiery particle') was educated in elementary schools in Manchester, won a pupil teaching bursary in 1906, and a further scholarship enabling her to enter Manchester University in 1910. In 1924 she became the youngest woman to enter Parliament as Labour MP for Middlesbrough but was defeated in the 1931 general election. Four years later she won Jarrow, a seat she held until her death in February 1947. In 1936 she supported the hunger march from Jarrow to London, walking with the men for long stretches and addressing meetings organised each night en route. As a backbencher, she took little part in the Labour Party's development of educational policy in the 1920s and 1930s. In office, she prioritised her first public pledge to raise the school-leaving age to 15, even though this exacerbated the teacher shortage brought about by the war and necessitated the introduction of an Emergency Training Scheme. Like Barbara Drake (1876–1963) of the LCC Education Committee, she expanded the provision of free milk and meals for schoolchildren. Unlike Drake she did not actively promote 'the common school principle' later called comprehensive. Wilkinson was criticised for this, though it should be noted that the postwar Labour Party was itself divided on the issue of selection, reflecting an earlier tendency to focus on the question of access for working-class children, to be achieved via the abolition of secondary school fees, and neglecting the question of what they were getting access to. Neither should it be forgotten that this woman from a northern working-class background headed a ministry that was dominated at every level by men with very different social and cultural capital. Their background had been the major public schools and Oxbridge.

Florence Horsbrugh (1889–1969) was the next woman Minister of Education and the Conservative Party's first woman minister in charge of a department. A second choice for the Prime Minister, Winston Churchill, when he appointed her in the autumn of 1951, Churchill excluded her from the Cabinet (until September 1953) and downgraded both education and the principle of women's access to a Cabinet seat in the process (Betts 2000). Besides dutifully implementing education economies her period in office had a direct impact on London's plans since she refused to allow the incorporation of Eltham Hill School, a girls' grammar school, in the capital's first purpose-built comprehensive. Months later, in the autumn of 1954, Horsbrugh was relieved of her post.

The creation of the Department of Education and Science in 1964 has been seen as evidence of the Conservative Government's determination to put education on a par with the Foreign Office, the Home Office, the Treasury, the Department of Trade and Industry, and (formed at the same time) the Defence Department. Not only was Margaret Thatcher the first woman minister of the new department, she was also the first mother. Despite a tenacious defence of the Tory pledge to raise the school leaving age, the incident that made her a truly famous politician was a row over school milk. The chant 'Thatcher the Milk Snatcher' resonates with the workings of gender: 'For a woman to have taken the milk from the mouths of needy innocents was somehow especially wicked' (Young 1991: 73).

There have been four other women at education since Margaret Thatcher. Taken chronologically they are: Labour's Shirley Williams (born 1930) appointed in 1976, the Conservative's Gillian Shephard (born 1940) appointed in 1994, New Labour's Estelle Morris (born 1952) and Ruth Kelly (born 1968), chosen by Tony Blair in 2001 and 2004 respectively. Like Thatcher, three of the four were graduates of Oxford University. The exception was Morris: raised on a Manchester council estate, she attended state schools, failed her 'A' levels and completed teacher training at Coventry College of Education and a BEd at Warwick University. However, Shephard was also a school teacher and like Morris had a background in local government before moving into the national political field. Kelly holds a number of records: as the youngest female cabinet member in history and by giving birth to four children while an MP. Her appointment increased the overall number of women in the cabinet to a record six; less distinctive is the fact that like the majority of the politicians who have held the education portfolio, she was privately educated.

For this is not an argument for alternative heroines. It is, rather, an argument for new ways of seeing the same historical space. A majority of all teachers in Britain are women and yet there is a continuing tendency to overlook this significant fact and women's presence in educational debates and decision-making. This is as true of the history as current public discussions of education (Miller 1996). In her resignation letter Morris said she had come to see herself as ineffective, or not as effective as the Prime Minister needed. This was an extraordinary confession. Born into a strongly political family (her father and uncle were both Labour MPs) we can speculate about the acquisition of the activist habitus through a disposition toward the taste for contention. And yet, in saying 'sorry' she demonstrated her refusal to play the political game. What does this say about the gender/power relations in social life when a society is prepared to hand over the running of its education system to politicians who fall if they show themselves as 'caring' ministers? Historically, investment in caring discourses created empowering social identities for political women who can never quite be one of us, if one of us is defined as a middle-class, professionally educated, white man. But as a counter-discourse it remains problematic. It does not challenge the way in which women are positioned through symbolic masculine domination, neither does it challenge what may be seen as the negative aspects of a particular form of hegemonic masculinity that has been a pervasive influence in the development of state schools in England from the 1870s to the present day.

As the story of Estelle Morris tells us, it is hard to struggle for alternative spaces. A female politician needs to have access to specific goods/resources or stakes to be able to challenge the gendered power deficits embedded in her femininity. For councillors like Eveline Lowe and Helen Bentwich their social practice demonstrates a particular middle-class gendered habitus born out of high social capital and sufficient cultural capital to develop, albeit slowly, symbolic capital within the political field. This is in stark contrast to the experience of Ellen Wilkinson, who was catapulted into Westminster. Her political trajectory was of its historical moment. She developed her political skills, first in the suffrage movement, and then in the trade union movement and local politics. This investment gave her the necessary social capital to convert in the field of national Labour politics. What it did not give her, perhaps, was resources with which to counter prejudice on the grounds of class and gender, both in Parliament and in Whitehall.

This is not true of Ruth Kelly living in a very different historical moment: in what we are told is a classless, post-feminist society. If we are to speculate intelligently about her political trajectory it is here that historians can make a serious contribution to our understanding. At the time of writing (autumn 2005) it is too early to assess the impact of an education White Paper Kelly has just set out. The main thrust of the proposals was toward offering parents more choice over their children's education by bringing new providers into the system: business, the voluntary sector, philanthropy. After reading this chapter the reader might come away with a sense of déjà vu. History repeats itself with a striking circularity between our starting point and the vision of self-governing trust schools out of local authority control. Indeed the proposals are strangely reminiscent of the laissez-faire voluntarism of the era before the creation of the school boards. Between that time and this, English women established a base in local government where many, Helen Bentwich included, felt they could play a more constructive and satisfying role.

References

Betts, R. (2000) Parliamentary women: women ministers of education 1924–1974, in J. Goodman and S. Harrop (eds) *Women, Educational Policy-making and Administration in England*. London: Routledge.

Clifton, G. (1989) Members and Officers of the LCC 1889-1965, in A. Saint (ed.) *Politics and the People of London. The London County Council 1889–1965*. London: Hambledon Press.

Jones, C. (1989) The Break-up of the Inner London Education Authority, in L. Bash and D. Coulby (eds) *The Education Reform Act. Competition and Control*. London: Cassell, 85–99.

Kean, H. (1990) *Deeds Not Words: The Lives of Suffragette Teachers*. London: Pluto Press.

Lovenduski, J. (1996) Sex, gender and British politics, in J. Lovenduski P. and Norris (eds) *Women in Politics*. Oxford: Oxford University Press.

Martin, J. (1999) *Women and the Politics of Schooling in Victorian and Edwardian England*. Leicester: Leicester University Press.

Martin, J. (2000) To 'blaise the trail for women to follow along': sex, gender and the politics of education on the London School Board 1870–1904, *Gender and Education* 12(2): 165–181.

Martin, J. (2005) The London Labour Party, 'the shrieking sisterhood' and city schooling, from the later 1930s to the early 1960s: transforming education and politics? Paper presented to the American Educational Research Association Annual Meeting, Montreal, 11–15 April.

Miller, J. (1996) *School for Women*. London: Virago.

Reay, D. (2004) It's all becoming a habitus: beyond the habitual use of habitus in educational research, *British Journal of Sociology of Education* 25(4): 431–444.

Wilkinson, E. (1938) Ellen Wilkinson, in Countess of Oxford and Asquith (ed.) *Myself When Young*. Plymouth: Frederick Muller.

Young, H. (1991) *One of Us*. London: Macmillan.

15

DIANE GRANT
Lifelong learning: just a slogan? The reality for working-class women

Introduction

Education was heralded as New Labour's flagship policy to effect a transformation away from the traditional notions of education, towards a vision where education for all would be a lifelong process, accessed at any time during the life course. The National Advisory Group for Continuing Education and Lifelong Learning (NAGCELL) was established by the then Secretary of State, David Blunkett, shortly after the election. Their report 'Learning in the Twenty-first Century' laid out how the Government would approach the concept of lifelong learning (1997). The previous interpretations of learning opportunities in their wider context were sketchily outlined in this document and then organised around several core values: coherence; equity; people before structures; quality and flexibility; effective partnership; and shared responsibility for ensuring the success of lifelong learning (NAGCELL 1997).

The concept of lifelong learning as a means to ensure equality of opportunity for all is both admirable and timely; many in today's society do lack many of the skills and educational qualifications required to be able to compete in the modern technological world of today. The importance of lifelong learning is highlighted by recent reports which suggest that 12 million adults have a reading ability similar to that of primary school age children (*Guardian* 24 January 2006). Purportedly the opening up of new learning initiatives for such groups will help to mitigate some lost opportunities in the past, when, for instance, many of today's older people were denied the learning options that were taken for granted by the more affluent and articulate classes. Yet for many socially excluded people in Britain the possibility of taking up educational opportunities remains influenced by their socio-economic position, the environment in which they live and their family responsibilities, as well as the internal barriers people construct often based upon past failures and subsequent disillusionment with the education system.

This chapter will focus on one group of people, women over 50, and will argue that the barriers women face in accessing opportunities for lifelong learning are not being fully addressed by policy-makers. The chapter will determine the difficulties faced by working-class women as they negotiate the world of work, education and home. It will show that lifelong learning policies are being overshadowed through a heightened campaign to facilitate re-entry into the workforce to meet labour shortfalls. Furthermore, the failure to adopt a longer term view on widening access to adult education will miss out on a valuable and mutually beneficial opportunity for the economy, the individual and the communities in which they live.

Social inclusion policies

Political measures which claim to tackle social exclusion such as New Deal 50 Plus (ND50+), Pathways to Work, the New Deal for Lone Parents (NDLP) and other inducements to improve the employability of people only partly address the factors which contribute to the exclusionary status of certain groups in society. Lack of labour market attachment as a result of low educational attainment, redundant skills and family caring roles, which are then compounded by disability, race, gender and more increasingly age, pose serious threats to an individual's future economic stability and increase the risk of poverty and poor health in later life.

The principles that underpinned the New Deal and related programmes have not been without contention. Levitas (1998) argued that the central characteristic of the generic New Deal programme was based, not upon addressing the structural dynamics of inequality, but instead on the personal characteristics of the excluded. This is exemplified by comments made by Alistair Darling in 1999, then Secretary of State for Social Security, who stated: 'Poverty today is complex. It's not just a simple problem about money, to be solved through cash alone.' An integral part of the problem remains a poverty of expectation. The current welfare relationship with lone parents which highlights that the past neutrality of the State towards them being either stay-at-home parents or working, has now clearly been replaced by a strong commitment to facilitate a return to the workplace for as many as possible (DSS 1999; Meadows and Grant 2005).

For the growing number of economically inactive older people in society the shortfalls in the labour force, coupled with the future cost of pensions, has opened up the debate on the value of the older worker. This has been underpinned by the ND50+ and the Pathways to Work programmes designed to get people back into work. The impetus for such measures is due to dramatic declines in the labour force participation of men and women aged 50–64 which has been described as 'one of the most remarkable labour market transformations in modern times' (Duncan and Loretto 2004: 101). This is taking place in conjunction with policies to engage people in lifelong learning, but as Withnall comments, 'Older people are still marginalised in education policy circles ... by continued emphasis on economic competitiveness' (2000). Yet the importance of lifelong learning offers a valuable opportunity to improve qualifications and training for marginalised groups thus providing the potential to lift people out of lower status employment and into meaningful career pathways.

An emerging concern is that opportunities for retraining for new careers have clearly been prioritised in favour of the younger elements of society (see Anning in this volume for examples). The 50% aspiration for 18–30-year-olds entering higher education and the arbitrary age ceilings on skills-based learning, such as modern apprenticeships, mean that people in their 30s and upwards face considerable difficulties in trying to update their education and skills in order to enter new professions (Frost 2005). This sends out a clear message to older people that study for these age groups will find little support from the public purse, meaning those who can afford to pay are those most likely to benefit and those who cannot pay will remain in their current situation. Equity of opportunity, one of the key principles of lifelong learning, is called into question when age restrictions and income limitations reduce learning opportunities and prevent engagement with those people most in need of such opportunities.

The number of people who lack qualifications in today's society partly reflects an historical lack of opportunities and also how the constraints of gender roles have impacted upon opportunities, with older age groups having the least qualifications, and higher percentages of women, especially in the 35 and over age categories, having no qualifications compared with similar aged men (Table 15.1). For women over 50 the picture is bleak with one-third having no qualifications (ONS 2002).

Table 15.1   Proportion with no qualifications by gender and age

Proportion of age group who have no qualifications (thousands)				
	16–59/ 64 years	16–24 years	25–34 years	35–49 years	50–59/ 64 years
All people of working age	5,944 (16%)	890 (14%)	815 (10%)	1,925 (15%)	2,314 (27%)
Women	3,159 (18%)	415 (13%)	428 (10%)	1,117 (18%)	1,199 (33%)
Men	2,785 (15%)	475 (15%)	387 (9%)	808 (13%)	1,115 (22%)

Base: All people of working age (men 16–64, women 16–59).
Source: Labour Force Survey (Spring 2001 – United Kingdom)

The predominance of women undertaking caring responsibilities has helped to facilitate a withdrawal from economic activity as well as increasing older women's participation in part-time work. For some women moving from full-time work creates the opportunity to combine caring with part-time work. One in five people between the ages of 50 and 59 regularly provides both informal and unpaid care. In terms of who provides that care we know that women provide more care than men and more intensive care (Arber and Ginn 1991; Mooney *et al*. 2002).

In addition to the provision of care for older people, women also support the needs of their offspring to provide care for grandchildren. Currently there are approximately 6 million carers in the UK, 60% of whom are women between the ages of 45 and 64 (Stationery Office 2004). According to the British Social Attitudes survey they found that three-quarters of grandparents have had to 'put themselves out' to look after grandchildren and 34% of children under 15 whose mothers are in paid work are looked after by their grandparents (Dench *et al*. 2002; Stationery Office 2004).

Older women in the workforce

In a similar vein to lone parents, older women now find themselves becoming marginalised in the workforce due to their lack of skills, lower educational qualifications and lack of access. Economic activity rates for older women have decreased quite markedly over the last 30 years. In 1971 data suggest a gradual withdrawal from work for women during their 50s. By 1996 whilst more women had entered the workforce generally, the withdrawal rate began from around age 45 (Collis *et al*. 2000). According to the Third Age Employment Network 30% (2.7 million) people between the ages of 50 to state pension age are economically inactive, with just one in three women over 50 being economically active.

More recently researchers have identified not only gender discrimination but also ageism within the workplace creating a double jeopardy for women of gendered ageism. As Redman and Snape (2002) note, the 'glass ceiling' has been replaced by a stronger and more resilient 'silver ceiling'. Duncan and Loretto (2004) argues that the incremental nature of female employment forces women today to work beyond pension age or risk living in poverty in later life. Viewed in this way, the phenomenon of early exit has had more negative repercussions for women than men, yet female ageing in employment and education remains under-researched.

Training and educational opportunities for older people viewed alongside the experiences of being both an employee and an adult learner within employment or education, raises questions on equality of access and perceptions of ageism within both the workplace and the academy. A study by Taylor and Urwin (2001) found that older workers were less likely to be offered or take up offers of training in comparison with younger workers. Similarly the Labour Force Survey (May 2005) found that when employees were asked whether they had undergone any kind of training in the last four weeks 40% of women aged 35–49 had, compared to only 16% of 50+ women. It is unclear whether it is due to lack of opportunity given to the older workers or a reluctance to train from this group.

Working within the education sector Meg Maguire argues that 'specific discourses and discursive practices of ageism are deeply sedimented into the educational system of the United Kingdom'. She asks the question, who defines at what stage a women is 'older'? The 'invisible barrier of ageism' means that 'women will be displaced and replaced' within the education sector (1995). If this is the case for women in education are similar assumptions operating on perceived ageist competencies when considering older women learners? Women, in this study, felt that their age and sex had restricted their employment prospects within the sector and that women were more likely to experience ageist attitudes concerning their appearance or sexuality than men.

Reay (2003) looked at the experiences of learning from the perspective of older working-class women undertaking an Access course. She charts the complexities they faced when juggling caring, work and study, which often resulted in time poverty for the women. She suggests that universities need to change how they accommodate older learners, to provide positive experiences for the non-traditional entrant.

In a study looking at the value of community interventions and lone parents the authors found that there were clear differences in the self-efficacy of those parents who had become involved in any kind of small-scale community initiatives or drop-in centre. Their self-esteem had been markedly higher than those who had no involvement with external agencies or groups (Meadows and Grant 2005).

Some of the genuine apprehensions women experience when attempting to change directions and combine previous roles with new identities may prevent engagement of the potential older learner with education. The fear of straddling two identities, according to Barnett, whereby the adult who chooses to leave one life world to enter the intellectual world of learning, faces the 'existential anxiety', of 'inhabiting two discourses at once' (Barnett 1999: 38). Furthermore, on a more practical level the admission of being in a state of learning can amount to an unsettling disclosure of lack of knowledge to their employers and colleagues, for those undertaking learning whilst in paid work. In such circumstances, learning opportunities can be perceived by the individual to be threatening. The renegotiation of identities is complex especially when coming from working-class roots. Being a woman presents further hurdles such as having to renegotiate some of their previously held roles and responsibilities within the family.

Such evidence calls into question the equality of opportunity for older women and when taken as a whole points to an emerging issue of unequal access in employment, education and training.

Social exclusion can mean many things. The Government defines it as 'what can happen when people or areas suffer from a combination of linked problems such as unemployment, poor skills, low incomes, poor housing, high crime, bad health and family breakdown' (SEU 1997) or 'the dynamic process of being shut out … from any of the social, economic, political and cultural systems which determine the social integration of a person in society' (Walker and Walker 1997: 8). Being excluded from opportunities to work, networks of support, groups and institutions will impact upon a person's outlook and perception of themselves as confident and competent individuals.

However the Government's target to create fairer access to education through an Office of Fair Access and increase the opportunities for education to all is evidenced through the HEFCE widening participation strategic plan:

> We aim to ensure that all those with the potential to benefit from higher education have the opportunity to do so, whatever their background and whenever they need it. *This means providing for the needs of a growing number of students with a broad variety of previous life and educational experiences* [emphasis added].
>
> (House of Commons Library 2004)

Implicit in this statement is the increased acknowledgement of the need to develop support mechanisms for the older learner. The economic policy objectives to facilitate re-entry, retention or access into work have clearly been given more impetus and support than those concerned with expanding provision and access to learning. Primarily the policy aim is to both provide the capability to remain longer in employment or help people back into employment or voluntary roles.

In an effort to gain a greater understanding of the difficulties women face in taking up lifelong learning research data were extracted from a project investigating ageist perceptions and gender discrimination funded by the European Union. The results highlight how experiences, perceptions and beliefs of women over 50 impact upon their ability, willingness and motivation to participate in education and training.

The following section presents some findings from a study into older people (93 women, 137 men) on their history, experiences and perceptions of education in their lifetime.

In this survey almost half of all women had undertaken education (post-school) either full time, part time or both at some stage, with only just over one-third of men doing the same. When asked what the main motivations were for study almost half said there was a clear relationship between gaining qualifications as a means to increase employability or improve job prospects; however, almost one-third undertook study for non-job related reasons. The economically inactive tended to cite non-job related reasons whilst the employed cited career opportunities (Grant et al. 2005).

One third of the sample said they would welcome the opportunity to enter higher education, with slightly more in work than out expressing this desire. This clearly indicates the potential interest and possible demand for higher qualifications from both working and economically inactive people over 50.

Explorations of work histories provided interesting information on experience both pre- and post-equal opportunities legislation. Over one-third of women cited older age as being a factor in their discrimination. One in three women had experienced gender discrimination as opposed to only one in five men. Just under one in four men and women had experienced other forms of discrimination which included bullying and sexual harassment.

Interestingly just under half the sample felt that age would not be perceived as a barrier within higher education. This was despite their experiences of such in their previous work. In general the main barriers to entering higher education were cited as:

- high cost of higher education (and the impact this would have on their incomes)
- feeling too old
- lacking the necessary qualifications.

The following extracts from interviews with women over 50 highlight how financial concerns were often cited as barriers to participation:

> Yes, I've thought about it, but what's holding me back is the funding side of it ... But looking at courses, like at night school ... it's so much a course and I just can't afford, you know, so it's the funding.

I've got a pension with X, but I'm not eligible for that until I'm 60 so it is a bit of a catch 22 situation . . . you'd like to get higher education, but you've got to pay for it.

. . . it's always the money isn't it . . . the dole is not enough. This big £10 wouldn't even get you out of bed. They need to give you a lot more to retrain, especially when you've got people like me on their own, you've got to pay rent, gas and whatever, it's a big 'no no' for us otherwise I would have gone back.

The cost of entering education was perceived by the women as being the prime factor in the decision whether or not to engage with learning. This was expressed by those in work and those who had reached retirement age. Income, or lack of it, coupled with the perceived cost of education created a barrier of access for many in the sample.

The responses from women on their caring roles ranged from the lack of acknowledgement by the education gatekeepers of the skills required to be a parent, to the difficulties of trying to combine caring and nurturing support for family members whilst undertaking study.

. . . you can start a job and do these NVQs, but nobody gives you an NVQ for being a mother . . . I mean, you know, a housewife, a manager, you're budgeting for a things or when a problem comes up, or you've got sickness in the house, your children are ill, or you're off to hospital or whatever . . . you've got to think on your feet a lot of the time.

Juggling home and study for some proved to be difficult, as family members still expected the woman to continue providing the usual measure of attention and support.

Pressure – it's there, yes. You don't know it. I think what happens is, especially if there's family still at home, and especially if they've got a man, the old fashioned ideas come back in again . . . I should be there to put the tea on, I should make sure the washing is done.

You've got to sit down and got this homework, that's where the problems come in for a lot of people, it's the homework. You're all right in college, but once you step back into your own home, that's where the pressure comes back, the family come, the phone will go and you really don't get much peace. If you're not used to doing homework, it creates a big problem.

Experiences of past discrimination were considered a factor on future decisions to return to education with some women citing lack of confidence in their ability to study.

I think they [college tutors] also understand that our brain doesn't work as fast and we do get self-conscious, and a lot of it, I think is lack of confidence with older people.

Whilst not specifically viewing these experiences as evidence of discrimination the effects nevertheless were damaging and long term.

The confidence [my mentor] had built up in me, plummeted. I stopped, feeling ... I wasn't worth it. Then a course came up in X [FE college] so I thought, I'll try there, so I rang up and by then I think I was 49 or 50 and he said, 'How old ... can I ask you how old you are?' I said, 'I'm 50.' He said, 'Won't you feel stupid in a class of 16–19-year-olds? ... And I went [shrugs shoulders]. But again my confidence ...

Educational experiences

Once the women had entered higher education their experiences of stepping outside their normal environment created some difficulties:

I just got overwhelmed by it, at that time, I just think I wasn't able to do it. It was when I went to have a look round, it just seemed ... you were left on your own and I didn't think I'd be able to do it. Yet, I did get some good grades in my A levels so ... I just, I was a bit weak ... I should have done it but I didn't ...

It was sort of, everybody was enrolling that day and it was, you know, the first day there. Yes, I mean they were OK. You were treated the same way as everybody else, you know.

One returnee to education pondered on how her previous accomplishments may have been a factor in her success when compared to the difficulties faced by her fellow students:

I think a lot of the women that were there [didn't have confidence] ... I mean at least, I had a bit of an academic background, I'd done 'O'levels, I'd done 'A'levels, I'd gone to a grammar school, and a lot of the women there hadn't, you know. They'd left to work at 15 16 and were now doing exams. They hadn't done anything since leaving either. Whereas I'd done little bits at least ... it sounds stupid, but I'd always written letters, you know, I'd always corresponded so I'd always been used to the flow of writing and I think a lot of them hadn't and I think they might of [sic] found it a bit off putting.

For some the acquisition of basic qualifications did not necessarily hinder their ability to find work, but not the work desired. This was coupled with the realisation that without further qualifications their horizons were limited:

I've got 'O' levels, that's it and I mean that's nothing. But I never got the chance to take 'A' levels or to go to sixth form and ... from school ... there were jobs available, so ... no-one ... push[ed] the higher education route. It was sort of come and get a job and so I started work ... I often look in the paper and I get really disillusioned, you've got all these job applications, you know, and ... think, I'm not qualified for any of that.

When asked whether they felt higher education institutions did enough to attract or encourage older people into learning:

No, none whatsoever. The impression is, 'young' ... you don't see anything where it say's it's for older people ... If they have got anything different, they should advertise it and tell people, let people know about it.

The extracts above highlight how the barriers faced by women are both internally generated and external reinforced. Such barriers range from ageist perceptions, financial difficulties, feelings of inability, lack of confidence, having the stamina to see it through; whilst trying to provide social support to the family and run the home. These are hurdles that many women will identify with and are major obstacles preventing engagement with lifelong learning. The evidence also provides an insight into the thoughts and perceptions on educational institutions as well as raising questions as to how such barriers can be removed.

Conclusion

The aim of creating 'a learning society' formed an important part of New Labour's manifesto, designed to 'break down barriers' and widen participation. The Government's aim of changing attitudes towards older people are clear and focused, but when viewed in the context of the actual experiences of these women it becomes much less obvious how the older learner is included in this vision of a learning society, with their opportunities for furthering their learning being supplanted by the emphasis of policy on economic competitiveness.

The reality of educational opportunities for older women paints a dismal picture, with a clear focus on education up to age 19 coupled with a 50% target of participation of 18–30-year-olds in higher education, little seems to be emanating from policy-makers as to how increased participation of the older learner can be achieved (DfEE 1999). Walker argues, 'Despite the vogue for lifelong learning initiatives, older learners are still perceived as largely missing from both policy and practice in educational provision' (Walker 2000).

Apart from the obvious competitive benefits to the economy of an educated, skilled workforce we can safely say that the wider benefits of learning contribute to the physical, mental and emotional health of the older learner and enable them to be active within their communities for longer (Summers, cited in Tuckett and McAuley 2005).

The arguments in favour of rolling out educational opportunities for all are strong. Some groups may not have aspirations to re-enter education or paid work for a variety of reasons and especially so at crucial stages of their caring responsibilities. But for those who do, the benefits to the economy are secondary to the positive benefits reaped by recipients leading to increased autonomy and self-esteem, creating positive role models and decreasing periods of poor health in later life.

The notion that people have equal choices in life is challenged in this chapter. Lifelong learning policies as a means to improve and enhance both the material and cultural wellbeing of society are admirable ideals. However, it is argued that access to lifelong learning for working-class women is at present little more than a myth and that the internal and external barriers identified and the constraints of gendered roles, coupled with drive for re-entry into the workplace, for the majority of working class women continues to perpetuate their social disadvantage.

References

Arber, S. and Ginn, J. (1991) *Gender and Later Life: A Sociological Analysis of Resources and Constraints*. London: Sage.

Barnett, R. (1999) cited in D. Boud, and J. Garrick (eds). *Understanding Learning at Work*. London: Routledge.

Collis, C., Green, A., and Mallier, T. (2000) Older female workers in Britain and its regions: millennium prospects, *Local Economy* 15(1): 1 May 1.

Dench, S., Aston, J., Evans, C., Meager, N., Williams, M., and Willison, R. (2002) *Key Indicators of Women's Position in Britain*. Women and Equality Unit: London.

Department for Education and Employment (DfEE) (1999) *Age Diversity in Employment – Code of Practice*. London: DfEE.

Department for Education and Skills (DfES) (2002) *Birth to Three Matters: A Framework for Supporting Children in their Earliest Years*. London: DfES.

Department of Social Security (DSS) (1999) *Opportunity for All: Tackling Poverty and Social Exclusion*. London: HMSO.

Duncan, C. and Loretto, W. (2004) Never the right age? Gender and age based discrimination in employment, *Gender, Work and Organisation* 11: 95–114.

Frost, K., (2005) *Third Age Network*. http://www.taen.org.uk/news/pressreleases. htm (accessed 4 April 2006).

Grant, D., Walker, H., Meadows, M. and Cook, I. (2005) Too old to study? Paper presented to the European Conference on Gender, Equality and Higher Education at Oxford Brookes University, 31 August–3 September.

House of Commons Library (2004) The Higher Education Bill. Research Paper 04/08. http://www.parliament.uk/commons/lib/research/rp2004/rp04-008.pdf (accessed 11 April 2006).

Labour Force Survey (2005) http://www.data-archive.ac.uk/-findingData/ sndescription.asp?sn = 5259#doc (accessed 11 April 2006).

Levitas, R. (1998) *The Inclusive Society: Social Exclusion and New Labour*. Basingstoke: Macmillan.

Maguire, M., (1995) Women, age and education in the United Kingdom, *Womens Studies International Forum* 18(5/6): 559–571.

Meadows, M., Grant, D. (2005) Social and psychological exclusion: the value of community interventions for lone mothers, *Community, Work and Family*, 8 (1): 5–21.

Mooney, A. and Statham, J. with Simon, A. (2002) *The Pivot Generation. Informal Care and Work After Fifty*. Bristol: Policy Press.

NAGCELL (1997) Learning for the Twenty-First Century. First report of the National Advisory Group for Continuing Education and Lifelong Learning.

Office of National Statistics (ONS) (2002) *Labour Force Survey*. http://www.statistics.gov.uk/STATBASE/Source.asp?vlnk=358 (accessed 31 March 2006.

Reay, D. (2003) A risky business? Mature working-class women students and access to higher education, *Gender and Education* 15(3): 301–318.

Redman, T. and Snape, E. (2002) Ageism in teaching: stereotypical beliefs and discriminatory attitudes towards the over-50s, *Work, Employment and Society* 16(2): 355–371.

Social Exclusion Unit (SEU) (1997) *Social Exclusion Unit: Purpose, Work Priorities and Working Methods*. London: Stationery Office.

Stationery Office (2004) *Social Trends 34*. http://www.statistics.gov.uk/downloads theme_social trends34.pdf (accessed 24 August 2005).

Taylor, P. and Urwin, P. (2001) 'Age and participation in vocational education and training', *Work, Employment and Society*, 15 (4): 763–779.

Tuckett, A. and McAulay A. (2005) *Demography and Older Learners: Approaches to New Policy Challenge*. London: NIACE.

Walker, A. and Walker, C. (eds) (1997) *Britain Divided: The Growth of Social Exclusion in the 1980s and 1990s*. London: Child Poverty Action Group.

Walker, J. (2000) Fifty plus learning: A consultation exercise, *Education and Ageing* 15(3): 297–313.

Withnall, A. (2000) Older learner – issues and perspectives. Paper given at Global Online Colloquium, University of East London, Festival of Lifelong Learning, June–October.

Section 4

Global education: global issues

Section introduction

There can be no doubt that *globalisation* is a process and a product that affects all our lives in some way, whether it be through the consequences of what happened on 9/11 or whether it concerns the products we consume at home. For some, globalisation is about the emergence of supranational institutions whose decisions shape and constrain policy options for any particular nation state. For others, it means the overwhelming impact of global economic processes of production, consumption, trade, capital flow and monetary independence. For others still, it signals the rise of economic liberalism as a dominant policy discourse. For some, it is about changing cultural forms, communications technologies, the shaping and reshaping of identities, and interactions within and between cultures. For others globalisation is a product, the construction of policy-makers responding to the demands of organisations such as the World Bank (WB), the International Monetary Fund (IMF) and the World Trade Organization (WTO) which leave governments with 'no choice' but to play by a complex set of global rules, rules not of their making. Whether one adopts a process or a product philosophy regarding globalisation it is possible to see globalisation as having a dark side or a light side – like fire – which has both its supporters and its detractors. In this section we are going to explore some of these issues in relation to internationalising education and globalisation, to examine the light and the shade of this relationship and to focus on the nature of the impact of globalisation on the central issues of sustainability.

Globalisation, in some shape or form, has been a fact of human exchange for a significant part of our histories. What we are concerned with here, though, is what might be referred to as *contemporary globalisation* that some commentators place as having its origins in the world petroleum crisis between 1971 and 1973. These changes went hand in hand with the adoption of neo-liberal economic policies by many nation states. At the same time global economic downturns have put increasing pressure on the financial demands of the welfare state in many nations, with the funding of social services, health services, housing and education all being affected, one of the consequences of which was an increasing privatisation of these welfare services. Thus the relationship between the State and its workers changes – probably irrevocably. Two types of citizens were created – those protected or included by the State who have access to jobs and enhanced life chances, and those unprotected or excluded from employment with reduced life chances, with the latter group being the larger group, often comprising of women living in poverty in both advanced industrial nations and less developed countries (Offe 1985; Harvey 1989). The consequences of these changes have been a unification of capital on a global scale, under the ownership of the TNCs, with workers and other subordinate groups being fragmented, divided and deskilled.

A further consequence of these changes has been an increasing reliance on the market to solve the problems which the unification of capital has brought about – a lessening of environmental quality and a decrease in social justice. In education the privatisation of parts of the service has been sold as an increase in consumer choice, with the market forcing up standards as 'consumers' become more choosy about the products that they wish to 'purchase'. It is argued that the WB, the IMF and the WTO had contributed to a decline in the power of national governments. National governments are largely concerned with national issues and many have shown a lack of political will to deal with the negative consequences of globalisation. Global businesses have a global constituency. Consequently global businesses are well placed to fill the vacuum left by this apparent lack of political will to deal with the negative consequences of globalisation (Mary Robinson, UN High Commissioner for Human Rights 2002). This development gives capital (and capitalists) considerable leverage over nation states, although this leverage is often exercised indirectly. Intellectual leaders, that is leaders of large corporations who have become established as business gurus, set the limits of policy options for nation states (Korten 1995), allowing the AINs to 'control' the LDCs under the banner of contemporary globalisation, which as we shall see later, can be regarded as a contemporary form of imperialism or colonialism. An increasingly borderless world limits and delimits the powers of nation states to control their own economies. Globalisation, then, or contemporary globalisation, refers to a set of technological, economic and cultural changes. Globalisation has become a regime of truth of the 1990s, 'imbued with its own rationality and self-fulfilling logic' (Blackmore 2000: 131).

Equally important for our consideration are issues to do with the internationalising of education. These manifest themselves in several ways. One important concern is the way in which European Union education policy can be seen to have supranational political goals such as combating xenophobia and enhancing democracy (see Robinson 2003). A second important issue here is what Phillips and Ochs (2004) identify as the process of policy borrowing. Policy borrowing is seen as one of the purposes of international education. Borrowing conveys deliberate and purposeful transfer in which an innovation in one context can be traced to an existing model elsewhere. However this transfer has to be selected by the host country, not imposed, as the American system was on Japan after the Second World War or the English system on many former British colonies. Policy borrowing, according to Phillips and Ochs takes place through four stages – attraction, decision-making, implementation and internalisation.

The four chapters in this section pick up on this range of issues in different ways. Mike Cole draws upon Marxist theories to examine whether, as suggested above, globalisation can be seen as a force for good. In a carefully constructed argument about the close relationship between capitalism, neo-liberalist economics and globalisation Cole rejects such arguments in favour of globalisation. In the context of this book, however, it is important to apply this analysis to educational policy and practice. Drawing on the work of Hatcher (2001), Cole identifies a significant neo-liberalist agenda within New Labour's education policy programme, and this raises questions about whether, given such an analysis, education can contribute to the achievement of the goals of social and environmental justice, or whether it perpetuates inequalities. Anil Khamis turns the spotlight on Pakistan. As an emergent, Islamic nation, Pakistan provides an interesting example of a crucible where the coming together of the forces of democratisation through capitalistic globalisation and the resilience of traditional values can be examined. An important question that is raised here concerns the extent to which, through educational reform involving policy borrowing, Pakistan should become Western-focused. Susan Robertson and Roger Dale, in the third chapter in this section, take up these arguments in the context of a case study of the governance of education in the European Union. Like Cole, Robertson and Dale focus on developments of the neo-liberal market, which as a manifestation of globalisation has enabled politicians to construct education as a good or a product to be traded for profit. Their case study shows that the creation of a supranational (European) education space, which subsumes national educational systems, creates openings and contradictions. They identify five key contradictions within the rescaled European education space, which are the consequences of the globalising and internationalising of education. These contradictions, echoing Cole, might be seen to be restricting the role of education in terms of its nation-building role in favour of its economy-building role, which, within the context of a capitalistic European economic space, further constrains social justice rather than enhancing it. In the final chapter in this section John Robinson and Tony Shallcross consider the implications of these arguments for the nature of the futures which might be constructed. In the context of debates about sustainable futures, they suggest that education could become a transforming, leading apparatus of the State, rather than a responding, following enterprise. This transformative role allows education to take on the agenda of creating a discourse about the trajectory which societies choose in relation to the consumption or reduction of consumption of resources. This final chapter of this book provides a different story for education's future. Like any story, it may come true or it may not.

References

Blackmore, J. (2000) Globalisation: A useful concept for feminists rethinking theory and strategies in education?, in N.C. Burbules and C.A. Torres (eds) *Globalisation and Education: Critical Perspectives*. New York: Routledge.

Harvey, D. (1989) *The Conditions of Postmodernity*. Oxford: Blackwell.

Hatcher, R. (2001) *The Business of Education: How Business Agendas Drive Labour's Policies for Schools*. Stafford: Socialist Education Association.

Korten, D.C. (1995) *When Corporations Rule the World*. West Hartford, CN: Berret-Koehler.

Offe, C. (1985) *Disorganized Capitalism*. London: Hutchinson.

Phillips, D. and Ochs, K. (2004) Researching policy borrowing: some methodological challenges in comparative education, *British Educational Research Journal* 30(6): 773–782.

Robinson, J. (2002) Contemporary globalization and education, in S. Bartlett and D. Burton (eds) *Education Studies: Essential Issues*. London: Sage.

Robinson, M. (2002) Globalization and human rights. 21st Century Trust Seminar on Globalization: Rhetoric, reality and international politics. Congress, Washington, DC, 31 October 2003. http://www.21stcenturytrust.org/Robinson.pdf (accessed 4 April 2006).

16

MIKE COLE

New Labour, globalisation and social justice: the role of teacher education

Introduction

> The next stage for New Labour is not backwards. It is renewing ourselves again. Just after the election, an old colleague of mine said: 'Come on, Tony, now we've won again, can't we drop all this New Labour and do what we believe in?' I said: 'It's worse than you think. I really do believe in it.'
>
> Tony Blair, speech to the British Labour Party Conference 2 October 2001
> (*Guardian*, 3 October 2001)

In this chapter, I begin by evaluating claims made by Tony Blair that globalisation can be put in the hands of the many and, if combined with justice, can be a force for good. Referring to Marxist theory, I find reason to reject this vision. I then go on to examine the capitalist agenda for education in Britain before looking at the potential role of teacher education in enabling citizens to make informed choices about major international and national processes such as globalisation, as well as more national and local ones. I argue that, currently, much of what goes on in schools in Britain (and elsewhere) amounts to miseducation and that there is an urgent need for education to be critical and emancipatory.

The snippet, above, from Tony Blair's speech to the Labour Party Conference is informative about what the British Prime Minister really believes in and the ideology of New Labour and this revelation is important on at least two levels. First, following the terrorist attacks on the United States on 11 September 2001, Tony Blair has become second only to George W. Bush as a representative of world capitalist political power. Second, Blair, described by the *Wall Street Journal* as 'America's chief foreign ambassador' (Rawnsley 2001: 29), appears to have the ear of the President of the world's only superpower and bastion of capitalist hegemony and may thus influence major US policy decisions.

'Renewing ourselves again', rather than going 'backwards', means, for Blair, continuing 'the modernisation programme'. Modernisation, a key component in

Blairite rhetoric, is the conduit through which New Labour justifies ideologically the policy of continuing alignment to the needs of the global market (Cole 1998: 323; 2005). Modernisation means embracing global neo-liberal capitalism. Modernisation means a final break with 'Old Labour' and an end to any speculation that the Blair Government might recommit to social democratic, let alone socialist values as New Labour's core guiding ideology. Blair is, in fact, quite open about this break. The problem is not that trade has become too global, but that 'there's too little of it' (*Guardian* 3 October 2001). At the TUC Conference in 2005, Blair effectively told trade union leaders to get real and face globalisation or cease to exist. He urged them to find solutions 'based on reality' and stressed the necessity for 'fundamental modernisation' (Carlin and Hope 2005). In a pre-2005 Labour Party Conference speech to the Cabinet, he stated: 'We have to secure Britain's future in a world ... driven by globalisation ... We have to change and modernise ... to equip everyone for this changing world' (*The Argus* 22 September 2005).

Blair's stated vision for the future is globalisation with 'power, wealth, and opportunity' in 'the hands of the many, not the few', a globalisation combined with justice; globalisation as 'a force for good'. For Blair, this 'commitment to the poor and weak ... not the contentment of the wealthy and strong' is to be achieved by the vacuous concepts of 'the power of community' and 'the moral power of a world acting as a community' (*Guardian* 3 October 2001).

Blair's vision of benign globalisation needs to be seen in the light of the events of 9/11. Among other things, these events increased awareness in 'the developed world' that 'we' cannot just forget about more than half of humanity. In Blair's words: '[o]ne illusion has been shattered on September 11: that we can have the good life of the West, irrespective of the state of the world' (*Guardian* 13 November 2001). So, is his vision of remedying global inequalities within the context of world capitalism a viable one? I want to argue that globalisation with power, wealth and opportunity in the hands of many, not the few is an oxymoron and that globalisation is, in fact, antithetical to social justice.

Globalisation and neo-liberalism

Globalisation

First, I would argue that, rather than view the current orthodoxy of globalisation as a new epoch, the global movement of capital might more accurately be seen as a cumulative process and one that has been going on for a long time; in fact, since capitalism first began four or five centuries ago.

Second, one of the central features of capitalism is that, once rooted, it grows and spreads. This double movement is thoroughly explored by Marx (1965 [1886]) in *Capital* and elsewhere (for a summary, see Sweezy 1997). For example, as Marx and Engels put it in *The Communist Manifesto*, when describing the development of capitalism:

[t]he markets kept ever growing, the demand ever rising ... The place of manufacture was taken by the giant, Modern Industry, the place of the industrial middle class, by industrial millionaires ... Modern industry has established the world-market. The need of a constantly expanding market for its products chases the bourgeoisie over the whole surface of the globe. It must nestle everywhere, settle everywhere, establish connexions everywhere ... In one word, it creates a world after its own image.

(Marx and Engels 1977 [1888])

Third, this expansion takes three main forms: first, spatially (globalisation), as capital occupies all known socio-physical space (including outside the planet) – this is *extension*; second, capital expands as the differentiated form of the commodity, creating new commodities – this is *differentiation*; third, it expands through *intensification* of its own production processes (Rikowski 2001a: 14). Capitalism is thus a thoroughly dynamic system.

Capital is also out of control, as Rikowski has argued:

[c]apital moves, but not of its own accord: the mental and physical capabilities of workers (labour-power) enable these movements through their expression in labour. Our labour enables the movements of capital and its transformations (e.g., surplus value into various forms of capital). The social universe of capital then is a universe of constant movement; it incorporates and generates a restlessness unparalleled in human history ... It is set on a trajectory, the 'trajectory of production' ... powered not simply by value but by the 'constant *expansion* of surplus value'. [It is a movement] 'independent of human control' ... It is a movement out of control.

(2001a: 10)

Any idea of putting the control of globalised capital into the hands of the many is therefore not viable. Furthermore, for those planning our schools system, the demands of globalised capital can never be satisfied once and for all. As the New Labour White Paper on education argues: '[s]tandards must keep rising in the globalised world in which we now live' (Her Majesty's Government 2005: 7). The capitalist state in England demands ever more from teachers, pupils and increasingly parents (see Her Majesty's Government 2005: Chapter 5) regarding raising educational standards.

Neo-liberalism

Martinez and García (2000) have identified five defining features of the global phenomenon of neo-liberalism:

(1) The rule of the market

- the liberation of 'free' or private enterprise from any bonds imposed by the state no matter how much social damage this causes

- greater openness to international trade and investment
- the reduction of wages by de-unionising workers and eliminating workers' rights
- an end to price controls
- total freedom of movement for capital, goods and services

(2) Cutting public expenditure

- less spending on social services such as education and healthcare
- reducing the safety-net for the poor
- reducing expenditure on maintenance of, for example, roads, bridges and water supply

(3) Deregulation: reducing government regulation of everything that could diminish profits

- less protection of the environment
- lesser concerns with job safety

(4) Privatisation: selling state-owned enterprises, goods and services to private investors, for example banks, key industries, railroads, toll highways, electricity, schools, hospitals and fresh water

(5) Eliminating the concept of 'the public good' or 'community'

- replacing it with 'individual responsibility'
- pressurising the poorest people in a society to by themselves find solutions to their lack of healthcare, education and social security.

Clearly, the driving force of neo-liberalism is more and more profit for capital *at the expense of* human welfare and the environment. As such, neo-liberalism is hostile to social justice. Given capitalism's rapacious and predatory nature and, in particular, given its advances made since the 1980s neo-liberal revolution, a revolution continued under Blair (Allen *et al.* 1999) and in some ways exacerbated by New Labour (Cole 1999). Capitalism will not retreat to its pre-1980s position.

My argument is not that capitalism cannot in theory be made more humane, nor that Blair's vision is insincere (this is neither here nor there). The point is that, in the words of Kevin Watkins of Oxfam, '[i]ndustrialised countries ... have collectively reneged on every commitment made' (*Guardian* 12 November 2001). In fact, organisations such as the World Trade Organization (WTO), the World Bank, and the International Monetary Fund (IMF) are constitutionally destined to fail in any attempt at addressing the marginalisation of 'the developing world'. The WTO can only set maximum standards for global trade, rather than the minimum standards that might restrain big corporations, while the World Bank and the IMF, entirely controlled by the creditor nations, exist to police the poor world's debt on their behalf. Rather than recognise these inherent defects, their backers blame the poor countries themselves. Peter Sutherland, former head of the WTO, has asserted that it is 'indisputable that the real problem with the economies that have failed [is] their own domestic governments', while Maria Cattui, who runs the

International Chamber of Commerce, insisted that the 'fault lies most of all at home with the countries concerned' (Monbiot 2001: 17).

In the context of global capitalism and the neo-liberal revolution, and, of course, the new imperialism (see, for example, Cole 2004a, for an analysis) any possible gain for poor and dispossessed workers in the developing countries and elsewhere as a result of increasing global political awareness after 9/11 is likely to be minimalist and short-lived.

Neo-liberalism and education in Britain

The tyranny of capitalism is masked by massive ideological apparatuses. Louis Althusser (1971) argued that in the current era, the educational ideological state apparatus is the most important apparatus of the state for transmitting capitalist ideology.

For it to function effectively and to protect its interests, capitalism needs to prevent the working class from becoming a 'class in itself'. This is a twofold process. First, a concept of the world is fostered in which capitalism is seen as natural and inevitable; second, false consciousness is nurtured, whereby consciousness is channelled into non-threatening avenues (for example, commercial ones; see Cole 2004b).

It is important for capitalism that the education system does not hinder this process. Indeed the current ideological requirements of capitalism are that the education system plays an active role both in facilitating the growth of consumerism (a material as well as an ideological benefit for capitalists) and in naturalising capitalism itself. This takes the form of bringing business into schools and in using schools to promote business values. This process has accelerated greatly under New Labour (Allen *et al.* 1999).

Hatcher (2001: 1) has identified three agendas for neo-liberal capital with respect to schooling in Britain. He describes them as the 'business agenda for *what* the school system should produce; an agenda for *how* it should do it; and an agenda for what business itself should do *within* the school system, that is make profit. Hill (2004) has renamed the first and third of Hatcher's agendas as Capital's Agenda *for* Education and Capital's Agenda *in* Education, and applied them globally. For the purposes of this chapter, I will deal with that which, I believe, applies particularly to Britain, namely, the capitalist agenda *for* education.

The capitalist agenda for education

This agenda relates to the role of education in producing the kind of workforce that is currently required by global capitalist enterprises. It is thus about making profits *indirectly*. In economic theory, this agenda is connected to *human capital theory*. In mainstream labour economics, human capital theory uses a restricted account based on skills and knowledge: creating workers who are flexible and meet the requirements of capitalist enterprises at any given time. Marxists have long argued that personality traits and attitudes should be added to skills and knowledge (Bowles and Gintis 1976). The capitalist agenda *for* education is thus about creating the kind of workers that will 'fit in' with capital's needs. In practical terms, the capitalist agenda *for* education means involving the private sector in the running of schools to ensure that government and institutional aims for education correspond to market needs. Not only governments regulate this process, but so also do (relatively) new State apparatuses. In the case of Britain, for example, there is the Office for Standards in Education (Ofsted), policing schools and teacher education, the Training and Development Agency for Schools (TDA) regulating teacher education and the Qualifications and Curriculum Authority (QCA) as a general overseer. As Hatcher (2005) puts it, control by teachers and local education authorities (LEA) has been displaced by two new categories of agents: Ofsted, the TDA and the QCA on the one hand, and private companies, on the other. Their role is 'to discipline and transform the old institutional sites of power' (Hatcher 2006).

As I have suggested, since the election of the New Labour Government in 1997, there has been a qualitative extension of the role of the private sector in the schools system in England. Indeed, in a 1998 background note on education services, the WTO and its Council for Trade in Services (CTS) expressed praise for the British Government for having promoted 'greater market responsiveness' and an 'increasing openness to alternative financing mechanisms' (cited in Rikowski 2001b: 28). As Hatcher (2005: 2) points out, 'almost every major government policy initiative has relied on private companies to translate it into practice'. Citing Smithers (2004) Hatcher gives the example of a five-year contract worth £177 million given by the Government to Capita to manage the delivery of the National Primary and Key Stage 3 strategies (Hatcher 2005: 2). Hatcher (2005: 3) also lists the chronological privatisation of LEA functions: the handing over of some functions, such as supply teachers and school inspections permanently to the private sector; the contracting out of entire LEA provision to private companies, which results when LEAs are designated as 'failing' by Ofsted; and the current dominant model of 'public-private partnership' between LEAs and private companies.

Resistance at the chalk face

In schools, colleges and universities throughout Britain, people are being miseducated. However the educational ideological state apparatus is neither total nor all-encompassing. While recognising the limitations to the power of educational institutions and teachers, I do consider that teachers have a valid role to play in challenging dominant inequalities and in raising consciousness in the quest for a more egalitarian economic, social and educational system. Socialist teachers in Britain have consistently and constantly challenged and continue to challenge the 'businessification' of education and education for compliance. This takes the form of organised resistance from activists within the teacher unions, campaigning groups such as the Socialist Teachers Alliance and the Promoting Comprehensive Education Network. In addition, teachers in groups and individually are creating and opening up space within the National Curriculum and the hidden curriculum to challenge education for compliance (Cole *et al.* 1997; Hill and Cole 1999; Cole *et al.* 2001).

Conclusion: an agenda for teacher education

Teacher education, of course, plays a pivotal role in schooling. Since the pockets of resistance outlined above remain marginal and relatively isolated, what follows is meant to provide suggestions of how socialist teachers in departments of education in universities might open further spaces of resistance in the current climate. What then should critical teacher educators, including Marxists, strive for in the future? How can we sustain resistance to neo-liberal capitalism and imperialism? Fischman and McLaren (2005: 351–353) have suggested four ways forward. First, student teachers need to engage in an analysis of the mechanics of capitalist production and exchange. Marxism would be an obvious starting point. In this context, they should be introduced to theories of power, and should be encouraged to investigate aspects of control, the process of commodification, the creation of violence in nation states, and destructive patterns in the earth's ecosystems. To this I would add, student teachers also need to be critically aware of systems of imperialism, past and present. Here also, Marxism would be a good starting point. For Lenin (1916), imperialism was the highest stage of capitalism and 'the eve of socialist revolution'. Before and since Lenin's major work, a number of other Marxists have analysed imperialism (for example Luxembourg (2003 [1913]).

Second, student teachers need to be able to relate shifting patterns of globalisation and their effect on local communities. Again, Marxism would be a logical starting point. Student teachers should not only be involved in struggles for a better education for *all* pupils, they should also connect their professional needs with local community struggles for better jobs, working conditions, health services, daycare facilities, housing and so on.

Third, there is a need to connect with local oppressed communities. What is required is reciprocal knowledge. This should involve moving beyond white, Anglo-Saxon, middle-class and heterosexist educational norms, and in Fischman and McLaren's (2005: 352) words, we should 'explore the subjugated knowledges of women [and] minority groups'. Identities other than class are now acknowledged in recent and current Marxist analysis and practice. In addition, the Marxist concept of racialisation is most pertinent in connecting with oppressed communities, since it helps understand how and why certain groups are oppressed (for an analysis, see, for example, Cole 2004a). A move beyond traditional educational norms would, by necessity, involve teachers and teacher educators in a number of struggles. Local struggles would, of course, relate to national and international struggles. It would be important to make interconnections between them.

Fourth, teacher education programmes need to emphasise a media literacy curriculum, in order to acquire the multiple skills required to engage critically with hegemonic discourses. Understanding such discourses can be facilitated by the transmodern concept of enfraudening (Smith 2003). As Smith explains (2003: 488–489), special circumstances require the coining of new language and new terminology. He has coined the phrase, 'enfraudening the public sphere' to describe 'not just simple or single acts of deception, cheating or misrepresentation' (which may be described as 'defrauding'), but rather 'a more generalised active conditioning of the public sphere through systemised lying, deception and misrepresentation'. Student teachers need to be able to find ways of breaking through these processes.

I would like to add a fifth suggestion for ways forward for teacher education programmes. I would like to suggest that, at the heart of teacher education, in order to counter global misinformation and false consciousness or weapons of mass distraction, space is created for a consideration, both historic and contemporaneous, of the varying theoretical understandings of society, provided by current theoretical approaches such as postmodernism, poststructuralism and transmodernism, as well as Marxism. This would not only stimulate debate about the nature of our world, it might encourage student teachers to transcend 'common sense' (Cole and Virdee 2006) and to move towards a critical understanding of all that envelops them. It might also engender a belief that a different world is possible, that 'history is always in the making' (Fischman and McLaren (2005: 356), in other words empowerment. As Darder has put it, with respect to school pupils/students, but equally prescient to student teachers:

empowerment ... entails participation in pedagogical relationships in which ... [student teachers] experience the freedom to break through the imposed myths and illusions that stifle (them) and the space to take individual and collective actions that can ... transform their lives.

(2002: 110)

And, of course, the lives of others.

References

Allen, M., Benn, C., Chitty, C., Cole, M., Hatcher, R., Hirtt, N. and Rikowski, G. (1999) *Business, Business, Business: New Labour's Education Policy*. London: Tufnell Press.

Althusser, L. (1971) *Lenin and Philosophy and Other Essays*. London: New Left Books.

Bowles, S. and Gintis, H. (1976) *Schooling in Capitalist America*. London: Routledge and Kegan Paul.

Carlin, B. and Hope, C. (2005) Modernise or die, Blair and Brown warn the unions. http://www.mobile.telegraph.co.uk/news/main.jhtml?xml=/news/2005/09/14/ntuc14 (accessed 22 Sept. 2005).

Cole, M. (1998) Globalisation, modernisation and competitiveness: a critique of the New Labour project in education. *International Studies in Sociology of Education* 8(3): 315–32.

Cole, M. (1999) Globalisation, modernisation and New Labour, in M. Allen, C. Benn, C. Chitty, M. Cole, D. Hill and J. Kelly (eds) *Business, Business, Business: New Labour's Education Policy*. London: Tufnell Press.

Cole, M. (2004a) 'Rule Britannia' and the new American Empire: a Marxist analysis if the teaching of imperialism, actual and potential, in the British school curriculum, *Policy Futures in Education* 2(3/4): 523–538.

Cole, M. (2004b) US imperialism, transmodernism and education: a Marxist critique, *Policy Futures in Education* 2(3/4): 633–643.

Cole, M. (2005) New Labour, globalisation, and social justice: the role of education, in G. Fischman, P. McLaren, H. Sunker and C. Lankshear (eds) *Critical Theories, Radical Pedagogies and Global Conflicts*. Lanham, MD: Rowman and Littlefield.

Cole, M. and Virdee, S. (2006) Racism and Resistance: from Empire to New Labour, in M. Cole (ed.) *Education, Equality and Human Rights: Issues of Gender, 'Race', Sexuality, Disability and Social Class*, 2nd edn. London: Routledge.

Cole, M., Hill, D. and Sharanjeet Shan, S. (eds) (1997) *Promoting Equality in Primary Schools*. London: Cassell.

Cole, M., Hill, D., McLaren, P. and Rikowski, G. (2001) *Red Chalk: On Schooling, Capitalism and Politics*. Brighton: Institute for Education Policy Studies.

Darder, A. (2002) *Reinventing Paulo Freire: A Pedagogy of Love*. Cambridge, MA: Westview Press.

Fischman, G. and McLaren, P. (2005) Is there any space for hope? Teacher education and social justice in the age of globalization and terror, in G. Fischman, P. McLaren, H. Sunker and C. Lankshear (eds) *Critical Theories, Radical Pedagogies, and Global Conflicts*. Oxford: Rowman and Littlefield.

Hatcher, R. (2001) *The Business of Education: How Business Agendas Drive Labour's Policies for Schools*. Stafford: Socialist Education Association.

Hatcher, R. (2005) *Business Sponsorship of Schools: For-Profit Takeover or Agents of Neoliberal Change? A Reply to Glenn Rikowski's 'Habituation of the Nation: School Sponsors as Precursors to the Big Bang?* http://journals.aol.co.uk/rikowskigr/Volumizer/entries/651 accessed on 21st May 2006.

Hatcher, R. (2006) Privatisation and sponsorship: the re-agenting of the school system in England, *Journal of Educational Policy*, in press.

Her Majesty's Government (2005) *Higher Standards, Better Schools For All – More Choice for Parents and Pupils*, White Paper, Cm 6677. Norwich: Stationery Office.

Hill, D. (2004) Books, banks and bullets: controlling our minds – the global project of imperialistic and militaristic neo-liberalism and its effect on education policy, *Policy Futures in Educaiton* 2(3–4): 504-522. http://www.wwwords.co.uk/pdf/viewpdf.asp?j=pfie&vol=2&issue=3&year=2004&article=6_Hill_PFIE_2_3-4_web&id=81.155.87.252 (accessed 4 April 2006).

Hill, D. and Cole, M. (eds) (1999) *Promoting Equality in Secondary Schools*. London: Cassell.

Lenin, V.I. (1916) *Imperialism: The Highest Stage of Capitalism* [Lenin Internet Archive, *Selected Works*, Vol. 1, pp. 667–766]. http://www.marxists.org/archive/lenin/ (accessed 4 April 2006).

Luxembourg, R. (2003) [1913] *The Accumulation of Capital*. London: Routledge Classics.

Martinez, E. and García, A. (2000) What is 'Neo-Liberalism' A Brief Definition, *Economy 101*. http://www.globalexchange.org/campaigns/econ101/neoliberal-Defined.html (accessed 29 March 2005).

Marx, K. (1965) [1886] *Capital*. Moscow: Progress Publishers.

Marx, K. and Engels, F. (1977) [1888] Manifesto of the Communist Party, in *Karl Marx and Frederick Engels Selected Works*. London: Lawrence and Wishart.

Monbiot, G. (2001) Tinkering with poverty, *Guardian* November 20.

Rawnsley, A. (2001) Missionary Tony and his Holy British empire, *Observer* October 7.

Rikowski, G. (2001a) After the manuscript broke off: thoughts on Marx, social class and education. Paper presented to the British Sociological Association Education Study Group Meeting, June 23.

Rikowski, G. (2001b) *The Battle in Seattle: Its Significance for Education*. London: Tufnell Press.

Smith, D.G. (2003) On enfraudening the public sphere, the futility of empire and the future of knowledge after 'America', *Policy Futures in Education* 1(3): 488–503.

Sweezy, P. (1997) More (or less) on globalisation, *Monthly Review* 49(4): 1–4.

17

ANIL KHAMIS

Pakistan: whither educational reforms?

Introduction

This chapter critically reviews the history, profile, state and proposed reforms of education in Pakistan, in the context of a developing Muslim country. It draws upon lessons from innovations as well as current challenges facing Pakistan as an illustrative case to improve educational provision, particularly teacher education, as the principal means to improve the state of education and encourage reform. The chapter concludes by a critical analysis of the role of international agencies, including bilateral donors, to determine their influence on current directions in education reform and their implications.

Planning in Pakistan is often considered to meet the learning needs of children and teachers only in extraordinary situations. These are situations where a region or locality, for example, is in a post-conflict situation or recovering from a natural disaster. This chapter brings to light another consideration in the context of South Asia that has been missed by development planners and educators. In this region, prolonged low-intensity trauma with the occasional conflagration of violent hostilities has been the experience. South Asia, along with other developing countries, has witnessed a host of disasters as well as chronic conditions which have not only been debilitating but have had a deleterious effect on educational provision without its having been factored into planning regimes. Many of these factors are related to social and economic conditions facing these regions and have a critical impact on their populations' welfare. Contributing factors to this chronic and at times debilitating state include:

- the foreign debt burden and growing rates of poverty
- the depletion of resources: human (brain drain); land (pollution, desertification, limited renewable fresh water); and capital (net flow of capital outside of these regions)
- the rise in insecurity and instability arising from increased armed conflict and crime; lack of disease control which results in rising mortality rates and a reduction of life expectancy; unpredictability in growth rates particularly due to

HIV-AIDS as well as rises in the number of internally displaced people, movement of refugees, and migration.

These factors affect directly the supply and demand of teachers and it has been estimated that the numbers of teachers relative to the growing numbers of children in school has consistently reduced in the most vulnerable countries. Significantly however, and more indirectly, they affect teacher morale, motivation and professionalism. Teachers are reported to be despondent, disempowered and unfulfilled in their work (Retallick and Datoo 2005).

No teacher education or certification programme prepares teachers to confront this array of concerns that they face on a daily basis. Teachers are thus unable to respond to their own or to their pupils' learning needs and this lack of competence results in untold and unaccounted abuses, physical and verbal, perpetrated by teachers on the very people they are serving – the children.

Acknowledging that these are the situations confronting us, teacher education is required to respond appropriately and with urgency. This paper considers and analyses the state of education, including teacher preparation, in Pakistan and the lessons that remain to be learned as security concerns once again take on greater global prominence.

Education in Pakistan: a brief profile and history

Pakistan has been a sovereign state since its independence from Britain in 1947. With considerable evidence of the severe poverty of its education system, Pakistan affords us an opportunity to study a context that is important in terms of educational development that is arguably representative of a much larger constituency and region. In the context of Pakistan – a developing Muslim country which inherited an infrastructure upon its independence and has had no comprehensive reforms to its education sector to date – many questions arise. Such questions include: what improvements and developments in educational provision are required; how can this be done and with what envisaged outcomes; and whether such thinking and subsequent investment would be effective. A review profile and history of education in Pakistan will reveal concerns that have been expressed and approaches or innovations that have been attempted earlier and which have yielded variable results. Such a review also helps to establish parameters to discuss reform and assists in analysing the current reform strategies that are being pursued.

To answer the question why Pakistan has failed to reach its stated aims for education, one has to step back a little in history. The precise events that led to the development of a separate nation state have been much debated; however, Pakistan had its genesis, in part, in the recognition of the specific needs of the minority community of Muslims of the subcontinent. Today, the nature and character of this eventuality, a separate nation state built explicitly on a Muslim ideological orientation, has important ramifications for the educational provision to be offered to its citizens.

Prominent Muslim intellectuals such as Sir Sayyid Ahmad Khan and Fazlur Rahman, as well as non-Muslim scholars, have argued that upon the decline of

Muslim rule and civilisations, particularly the Mughals of India, the Qajars of Iran, and the Ottomans of the Middle East, at the onset of the Imperial Age, Muslims resisted the new political order and their communities resisted formal modern education as it was seen as a threat to their identity and their faith. Regardless of the veracity of this claim, it is evident that all Muslim countries did engage in modernising their polity, social institutions and infrastructure and therefore their educational systems upon independence (OIC 2005). What has resulted in South Asia – Pakistan, Bangladesh and India – however, is the existence of separate and parallel education systems: traditional Muslim education known as *madrassah* that predates colonisation, and the continuation and expansion of the formal education system established by British rule.

At independence Pakistan was a very poor country with an ill-educated population. The founding father of the nation and its first president, Muhammad Ali Jinnah, at the first Educational Conference in November 1947, urged the State to take a critical look at the aims of education:

> If we are to make a real, speedy and substantial progress we must earnestly tackle this question and bring our educational policy and programme on the lines suited to the genius of our people, consonant with our history and culture and having regards to the modern conditions and extensive developments that have taken place all over the world South Asia ... There is immediate and urgent need for giving scientific and technical education to our people in order to build up our future economic life and to see that our people take to science, commerce, trade and particularly, well-planned industries. We should not forget that we have to compete with the world which is moving very fast in this direction. At the same time we have to build up the character of our future generation. We should try, by sound education, to instil into them the highest sense of honour, integrity, responsibility and selfless service to the nation. We have to see that they are fully qualified and equipped to play their part in the various branches of national life in a manner which will do honour to Pakistan.
>
> (quoted in Curle 2001)

The course of development proposed was to expand, in essence, the colonial provision that had been earlier resisted or which was not accessible to many Muslim communities. Thereby, schools were divided into state-sponsored formal modern schools and alternative or traditional and disenfranchised *madrassah* schools. In 1947 the country did not have the institutional infrastructure or the resources to serve the rhetoric of the leadership nor does it have that capacity today after more than five decades (Government of Pakistan 1998; UNESCO 2000; 2005). The majority of the population in 1947 (80%) did not have access to modern sector schools and today there is a great unmet demand for education.

The present system of education

To cope with the growing needs and aspirations of its citizens, Pakistan developed its education system along the models of more industrialised Western countries.

That is, a system of mono-grade progression from primary education through to secondary and tertiary education including specialised streams for professionals such as teachers and engineers and the like. The main distinguishing characteristic of this formal education system today is the high dropout rate. It is estimated by the local media, in the light of unreliable and incomplete Government databases, that less than half of children enrolled in primary school progress to the secondary stage of their education and that a virtually equivalent number do not have any access to formal schools.

The predicaments for teacher education is that prospective teachers in formal public schools receive low salaries, have limited prospects for promotion, and occupy a low status within society. Consequently, teachers are ill-trained or untrained, unavailable in the most disadvantaged and rural areas, and younger talented student cohorts are not attracted to teaching. Given these conditions, it is not surprising that the quality of available teachers is suspect as is the training offered to prospective and in-service teachers and indeed there are no observable differences between trained and untrained primary teachers; the years of formal schooling that a teacher possesses is a more significant variable of good teaching (Qaisarani 1990).

From an international perspective, Pakistan faces issues similar to most low- and middle-income countries across the world: inequity between urban and rural provision; excessive dropout rates and low adult literacy; inequity between private and state provision; poor-quality curriculum and textbooks; overcrowded class-rooms; and poor school facilities and materials. To compound this situation, primary schools in Pakistan are chronically understaffed and there is additionally a dearth of trained female teachers due to the initial low enrolment rates for girls, within a gender stratified society, thereby exacerbating the problem of attaining quality schooling for all children. This renders educational change approaches that expect more from teachers than they are in a position to offer, not only bound to failure but probably to be met by actual or covert resistance.

Successful innovations and field conditions

In the 1980s and 1990s, Pakistan, in an attempt to increase access to education, initiated a number of innovative projects that resulted in varying degrees of success. Although numbers vary and are contested, it is estimated that formal primary schools cater for only 50% of school-age children and that the net enrolment has remained at approximately 40% over the last decade; that is, less than 50% of school-age children have access to formal schools. Government sources place this figure slightly higher; however, its own reports conclude that at least 6 million children either do not have access to or drop out before completing primary school (UNESCO 2005). Whilst Pakistan, as well as other developing countries, has reported increases in access to education by way of newly constructed schools, increasing training facilities, and proposing alternative routes to formal education, the available figures identify factors beyond the sector that influence provision, for example, the burgeoning population growth. This then also highlights that social sector endeavours interface with each other in complex and non-stochastic ways that affect society as a whole.

Net spending on education over the last decades has witnessed a drop in the annual budget, which is itself under-spent because of the lack of capacity in the educational system to utilise more resources. One argument for this is that the education sector as an integral part of Pakistan's national development strategy has received low priority for decades. Another argument forwarded is poverty and thus the limited funds available for development expenditure. The resource base is further strained by increased security costs given Pakistan's longstanding clash and three wars with India as well as its porous borders with Afghanistan and the former Soviet Central Asian states. However, one clear indicator is that in the public sector there is a virtually total absence of expenditure on development of new textbooks and teaching aids with some 90% of the budget devoted to teachers' salaries; consequently the education system has been subject to chronic neglect. Given the weaknesses of the public sector as well as international agreements to engender greater competition, the last decade has witnessed a proliferation of private schools that target all income levels from the very poor in rural areas to those wishing and willing to pay for an education that provides international standards of excellence. Providers include market-orientated businesses, religious organisations, community groups and secular philanthropists (Khamis 2003).

Towards reform

Pakistan has invested in education in the past. The reasons for this were either international pressure such as the 1990 Jomtien Declaration to meet Education for All targets by the year 2000 or because it was seen to be an investment for the rapid industrialisation of the country, which was thought to be possible with increased managerial efficiency. That is, it was thought possible to increase access to greater numbers of children with the same level of expenditure and thereby also meet Pakistan's international commitments. However, until now, nothing pragmatically was done to reform the education system as a whole.

In 2003, the Government of Pakistan, in liaison with USAID, launched the ESRA programme. Initial funding to the amount of US $60 million has been agreed by the US Senate for what is deemed to be a Pakistan Government initiative. The ESRA programme itself, not surprisingly, is lauded as a comprehensive initiative and targets all the areas of weakness identified above. Given the history and context of the country, it is pertinent and crucial for us to ask whether this initiative will encourage greater access to quality education that is relevant to its supposed beneficiaries, the children who attend school.

To come to such an understanding, it is important to note that whilst this is a bilateral aid reform programme the oversight for ESRA's programme delivery and financial management is contracted to a private firm in North Carolina, USA. In the current international security climate, and with regard to Pakistan's geo-political position and its stated fiscal and budgetary weaknesses, the question immediately arises as to whether this is a Pakistan Government reform initiative or one that Pakistan is willing to support for other, as yet unknown, purposes. The answer to this question will then determine whether the reform has any chance of succeeding where other similarly designed initiatives have failed and, secondly, what can be the anticipated consequences of this strategy. A lesson from history is that the legacy Pakistan inherited from its colonial past was adopted for national development; the innovations and reforms being attempted in Pakistan presently will necessarily need to be aware of these experiences and the outcomes of this line of thinking.

In the recent past, however, genuine and significant improvement in education provision has come from identifying the intended and ultimate beneficiaries of programme innovations. To meet the increasing demands being placed on education both national and international agencies have attempted novel and innovative approaches to enhance educational provision. Warwick (1995) discusses five major innovations attempted in Pakistan:

- the teaching kit – a box with about 100 instructional aids
- mosque schools – a policy designed to increase primary school enrolment at low cost
- building residences to solve the shortage of housing for women teachers in rural areas
- the Nai Roshni (New Light) programme of drop-in schools for students who had never attended or had left school
- learning coordinators – a cadre of people to make a management link between the Department of Education and schoolteachers to provide professional support.

Warwick (1995) considered the lessons for implementation and relevance of educational innovations and reform strategies in the context of Pakistan. He concluded that the concepts of the innovations/reform must be clear. Firstly, all involved in the education programme, the organisations and individuals that will be responsible for implementation must have the same idea of what the project means. Secondly, the innovation/reform must be integrated into the larger organisation of which it is a part. If the programme calls for additional organisational and management tiers, alternative authority structures, curriculum enhancement, sharing of facilities and the like, it cannot supplant or compete with an established organisational frame unless that organisation is completely revamped. Thirdly, innovations/reforms must be compatible with the region's culture. Programmes must be seen to be harmonious with the prevailing culture in order to be credible, and must not be seen as hostile

Another lesson that emanates from the work done over the last two decades suggests that an innovation/reform must build user understanding and motivation. Those who are to be responsible for accomplishing success must understand the purpose and the content of the programme, and its methods of operation. Politics has a mixed effect on innovations/reform; when the political will favours an innovation, its chances of success rise. However, if the political intervention is perceived to be for dubious motives then the innovation/reform is sensed as a corrupt practice.

More practical lessons are that effective implementation requires sensitivity to pivotal field conditions. Innovations/reforms need certain facilities to be carried out or require sensitivity to local circumstances and culture and an awareness of the dynamics of the relations that will unfold.

Finally, there are no teacher-proof innovations. For example, the teaching kits purportedly provided teachers with resources but were actually developed to entice teachers towards activity-based learning. This innovation failed because the purposes of the kits was known or understood by teachers and strategies cannot be used to subversively or covertly entice, spur or press teachers to change their practice through technical devices.

From the analysis of the innovations attempted in Pakistan, which were encouraged and supported by the international community, mosque schools were evaluated to be the most successful in increasing access to education. This presents an important overarching lesson from the past; to critically appraise from where the drive for reform is emanating and for what particular purposes. Warwick (1995) suggests that despite certain setbacks, mosque schools were considered to be a successful innovation because they reflected and respected cultural and contextual sensitivities whereby both boys and girls equally, for example, can go to the mosque together. This innovation was conceived around the idea that it would increase enrolment rates without the need to build separate schools for each sex (managerial efficiency). The Government also further planned to save substantial sums by eliminating the need to acquire land and build new school buildings by using the existing mosques as schools. The implementation of this and all the other innovations differed markedly from the official strategy. Religious leaders disturbed that the sacredness of the mosque would be defiled by the poor hygiene of the children had separate premises built at some distance from the mosque; some close to existing schools. Mosque schools were successful in increasing enrolment and facilitating access for girls; however, the problem noted was that the quality of education delivered in these schools was of a lower standard primarily because of the educational attainment of the religious leaders and other teachers who taught in these schools.

Clearly a more fundamental concern is what is taught in these schools. Rashid (2003) contends that many new *madrassahs* were established during the military regime of General Zia ul Haq. Indeed, Rashid, amongst others, contends that it was the explicit intent of Pakistan, supported and encouraged materially by its Cold War ally the United States principally but also other Western powers, to use the graduates of these new *madrassahs* as the breeding ground of the *mujahadin* to force the Soviet Union's withdrawal from Afghanistan. The Taliban regime in Afghanistan, then, can be seen to be a direct outcome of the educational aid and development agenda pursued primarily by the United States and which has since created a new nomenclature, *madrassah*, which is poorly understood and confused in terms of the legitimate search for knowledge in traditional educational systems and those devised for ulterior purposes.

Whither reform?

The learning, education and development needs of the nation and its people seem to have been perversely manipulated and subverted and yet we are once again at a similar nexus. The current reform plans seem neither to have been informed by Pakistan's immediate past experiences or its history of development of education nor to have paid heed to emerging lessons. When one investigates the current reform proposal in Pakistan, the basic question of its aim and who owns it is mired in confusion. If one consults Government of Pakistan sources, the reform is deemed to operate through its agency. The international community cites a number of bilateral aid agencies involved in the initiative and seems to give it their blessing. The main sponsor, USAID, has little available information for the public. If such conditions are present at the outset of the introduction of the reform – reminiscent of Warwick's (1995) first lesson – then it is very probable that this confusion will deepen, if not precipitate subversion as the strategy is pursued.

As the other lessons noted above inform us: politics is a mixed blessing for government-sponsored development programmes. Without the involvement of government and its explicit role, innovations and reforms will not develop the necessary momentum towards implementation. Properly applied, politics can give educational development programmes public legitimacy, help raise the funds for implementation, and support and encourage teachers and teacher educators to become active and responsible promoters of the available provision. The foregoing analysis reveals that in the post-colonial era and as we contend with the increasing globalisation and interconnectedness of the world's communities, ideas of reform in less developed countries still mirror or mimic Western models. The applicability and efficacy of these models, if they fail to consider (unique) contextual conditions, cultural and social aspirations and fail to learn from the past, will be severely undermined.

Ultimately it is teachers and teacher educators who have to confront the 'chalk face' or the arena of teaching-learning that is the subject of these intended reforms. As Kanu (2005) notes of her experience in Pakistan as an expatriate educator who unwittingly found herself promoting hegemonic transnational knowledge transfer, this was variously resisted by the candidates and the expatriate educators' own intent was consistently subverted. The conclusion, having reviewed educational development in Pakistan, must be that 'education in current global and postcolonial contexts involves the abandonment of hegemonisng forms of knowledge that are rooted in Eurocentricism, in favour of dialogue with knowledges and identities which have been submerged or marginalised in the global power/knowledge relations' (Kanu 2005: 20).

In developing country contexts, as highlighted by the case of Pakistan, teachers must be supported to work with their communities and it is these teachers who will still be there to teach children long after the reform programmes, the funding agencies, and indeed the government of the day are long gone.

Conclusion and recommendations

If it is aimed to help teachers cope better with the task of teaching and educating their pupils then it is essential to urgently support them with at least the following measures:

- Teachers themselves must be supported to deliberate and take action against the chronic state of instability in their environments (psycho-social support). This can be effected by establishing peer groups, discussion forums, school clusters and the like that help teachers focus and direct their energies to self-learning and empowerment – this is a necessary first step if we are to expect teachers to support their pupils' learning and development needs.
- Teachers must be enabled to acquire greater professionalism and control of their vocation. This has to be supported by tertiary institutions that have to be ready to learn from teachers' working conditions and to shift the school–university power relations. The encouragement of teachers as research collaborators in action research projects is an example. Accreditation and certification agencies can then recognise their involvement materially and thereby incentivise and facilitate the uptake of such novel opportunities. There needs also to be regular system of follow-up and sharing good practices across schools and districts.
- Teacher education programmes must
  - maintain links and engage sympathetically but critically with local knowledge, skills, traditions, cultures and customs to build bridges between the school and community
  - share and link school knowledge with community knowledge
  - build on the collective resources of the community to assist teachers in their task of meeting educational and psycho-social needs of the community as a whole.

The current international discourse places too great a burden on the teacher to meet all the needs of learners which are to be conveniently facilitated at 'school'. Such expectations are neither supported with further training opportunity nor are the necessary resources effectively deployed, which is the irony of rational reform plans! Teachers' burdens need to be reduced and they need to be supported and encouraged to focus on the principal task of engaging in teaching and learning including their own learning. Such an approach in developing countries can lead to the promotion of learning for the whole community that allows them to build on their collective experiences. The dichotomisation of reforms that posit individual versus collective natures; national versus global needs; rational planning regimes versus the value of local traditions that seek to control the community's actions and behaviours are not supportive of any meaningful and lasting improvement in the system of education to which people aspire and which ultimately they own.

References

Curle, A. (2001) [1966] *Planning for Education in Pakistan*. London: Replica Books.
Government of Pakistan (1998) *National Education Policy 1998–2010*. Islamabad: Ministry of Education.
Kanu, Y. (2005) Tensions and dilemmas of cross-cultural transfer of knowledge:

post-structualist/postcolonial reflections on innovative teacher education in Pakistan, *International Journal of Education Development* 25: 1–21. http:// www.sciencedirect.com/science (accessed 14 July 2005).

Khamis, A. (2003) Final evaluation of Project 200 Community Education Programme of the National Rural Support Programme funded by the Department for International Development and Learning for Life, London.

OIC (2005) Final and approved recommendations of the OIC Commission of Eminent Persons, adopted in Islamabad May 29 2005. http://www.oic-oci.org/ (accessed 22 July 2005).

Qaisarani, M.N. (1990) *Effect of Teacher Level and Quality of Formal Schooling and Professional Training on Students' Achievement in Primary Schools in Pakistan*. Harvard: Bridges.

Rashid, A. (2003) *Jihad: The Rise of Militant Islam in Central Asia*. Harmondsworth: Penguin.

Retallick, J. and Datoo, A. (2005) Transforming schools into learning communities: focus on Pakistan, in J. Retallick and I. Farah (eds) *Transforming Schools in Pakistan – Towards the Learning Community*. Karachi: Oxford University Press.

UNESCO (2000) *The Dakar Framework for Action: Education for All*. Paris: WCEFA, UNESCO.

UNESCO (2005) *Global Monitoring Report 2005: Education for All – The Quality Imperative*. Paris: UNESCO.

Warwick. D.P. (1995) *Hope or Despair? Learning in Pakistan's Primary Schools*. New York: Praeger Publishers.

18

SUSAN ROBERTSON
AND ROGER DALE

Changing geographies of
power in education: the
politics of rescaling and its
contradictions

Introduction

Our concern in this chapter is with the implications for education of the expansion
of 'globalisation' as a particular kind of political project, process and product.
Specifically, we will be addressing the way in which globalisation is affecting what
gets done at what scale in the education sector, arguing that these shifts represent a
changing geography of power in education. We will be arguing that in the post-
Second World War period, the scale and governance of education was primarily
national (though federal systems, such as in Australia, the United States, Canada
and Germany, where compulsory education and in some cases higher education
was a regional or local responsibility are exceptions): they were tied to nation
states, national economies, national territory and nation-building (see also Brenner
2003). The governance of education, particularly in developed economies, was also
informed by a Keynesian model of economic and social development. However, in
the current, 'globalisation', phase of capitalism, a series of linked and overlapping
dynamics associated with the rescaling globalisation (Cerny 1997), from the local
to the global, are tied together by the 'constitutionalisation of neo-liberalism' (Gill
2003).

While considerable attention has been paid to the way in which national
education systems and citizens have been subject to the discipline of the market as
a result of displacements of power downward (see Jessop 2000) in what Gough
(2004: 197) has called 'neo-liberal localism', in this chapter we are interested in
understanding the changing social relations arising as education is mobilised
upward to different scalar locations to play a more direct and functional role in
capital accumulation. In particular we will be arguing that processes of *upscaling*

and the governance of education to supra-regional (in this case the EU) and global scales (for instance through the World Trade Organization (WTO) can be understood as a new *functional, institutional and scalar division of the labour of education systems* (Dale 2002)). We will also be suggesting that this emerging geography of power generates new contradictions that will become increasingly difficult to absorb at these new scales of activity, generating important challenges at the door of the new global world 'order'.

In order to make our case, the chapter will proceed in the following manner. We will begin with some brief opening remarks on the changing nature of the world order; from an international political economy (1975–90) to a global political economy (1990 onward) powered by neo-liberalism as an ascendant ideology (see Gill 2003). We will then focus on the emergence of new forms of governance and processes of rescaling, in particular the embedding of neo-liberalism in these new governance mechanisms. Then we develop a case study on 'configuring' and 'constructing' the 'European education space'. We conclude by examining the contradictions of these new scalar and governance shifts for states and their education systems.

Scale and governance in the new geography of power in education

There is a considerable amount of writing now on globalisation and agreement that globalisation is the latest phase in a long process of capital accumulation (e.g. Held *et al.* 1999). As some writers have also pointed out (e.g. Harvey 1982) in order for capital to continue to expand, it must be mobile while at the same time requiring points of fixity in order to reproduce itself and the necessary social relations of production and reproduction. This generates a dynamic of perpetual motion and points of fixity that, over the long term, can be viewed as sets of temporary settlements punctuated by periods of restructuring and transformation.

In Jessop's (2000) terms, and in reference to the developed economies, the 1970s signalled a collapse in the existing state–economy–civil society relation, or what he terms the Keynesian Welfare National State settlement. Over the period from 1975 to 1990, a period of significant 'rolling back' occurred (Peck and Tickell 2005). Markets and institutions were transformed as the remit of state intervention was withdrawn, while financial markets assumed a new role disciplining states. However, Peck and Tickell (2005: 174) note, for all this the political reproducibility of neo-liberalism in countries such as the UK and the US looked rather fragile.

The 1990s signalled a sea change in events. This was shaped by on the one hand, the 'Fall of the Wall' and with it the end of the Cold War and the removal of any alternative, and on the other, the new technologies that made possible not only the rapid flow of finance around the globe, but the creation of new industries and patterns of consumption. This was also a period characterised as much by an expansionary as a defensive 'West'. With the abandonment of the various 'client states' in the least developed countries, the 'West' – in particular the US and Europe – worked to protect existing markets while expanding into hitherto untrodden, or at least previously 'off-limits', territory advanced through a vigorous round of negotiations and treaty-making activities such as the North America Free Trade Agreement (NAFTA) in 1991, the World Trade Organization (WTO) in 1995 and the expansion of the EU through Maastricht 1993, and the Stability Pact 1999.

Over this period it might be argued that economies moved from being part of an 'international' world order to being part of a new 'global' order, a shift that writers like Held *et al.* (1999) sought to capture in the book *Global Transformations*. While there is considerable contestation, still, about the nature and extent of the transformations taking place and its underlying logics, there can be little doubt that the globalisation is not a myth (Weiss 1998) or indeed that its opposite is the case (Omhae 1990); that there are few borders and barriers and that states, by implication, have simply ceded power to the 'global'.

What has emerged over this period has been a set of tools that we feel contribute to a better understanding of the nature of the transformations taking place. One is the idea of *scale* (see Lefebvre 1991; Brenner 1998) to talk about the changing spatial arrangements that the notion of 'global' invokes. Most importantly, the idea of scale enables us to see that social activity is organised spatially, and that this spatial organisation is produced. It is thus highly political – despite our tending to see the organisation of particular activities at certain scales as natural. A case in point is the idea of the national as the firmly fixed 'centre' of all political activity.

So, too, with the idea of governance: as once fixed to government at the national scale. If the changes over the past decade have shifted anything, it is that ideas like *where things happen* (space/scale) and *who does them* and *how those things are regulated* (governance) are themselves shown to be socio-political constructions. In the following section we show that space, scale and governance are also subject to particular ideas, in this case neo-liberalism, about the preferred nature of these arrangements and their social relations.

Disciplinary and constitutional neo-liberalism

While globalisation and neo-liberalism are often elided (Scholte 2002; Peck and Tickell 2005), largely as the advance of neo-liberalism for the developing and least developed economies has been the most discernible face of globalisation, we want to prise these two ideas apart in order to better understand neo-liberalism as a more complex set of processes that has been deeply implicated in developing globalisation but is not reducible to it.

A basic definition of neoliberalism is given by Unger:

[i]n its most abstract and universal form, neoliberalism is a program (and it is crucial to recognize that neoliberalism constitutes a new programme rather than merely a new set of policies) committed to orthodox macroeconomic stabilization, especially through fiscal balance, achieved more by containment of public spending than by increases in the tax take; to liberalization in the form of increasing integration into the world trading system and its established rules; to privatization, understood both more narrowly as the withdrawal of government from production and more generally as the adoption of standard

Western private law; and to the deployment of compensatory social policies ('social safety nets') designed to counteract the unequalizing effects of the other planks in the program.

(1998: 53)

The key idea here is that neo-liberalism has been mobilised as an ideology and practice so that patterns of privilege on a multiplicity of scales can be extended and defended from encroachment and possible expropriation (Gill 2003: 129). We also find it helpful, for the purposes of thinking about the shifting pluri-scalar governance of education, to use Gill's distinction between two forms that neo-liberalism takes in regard to governance – *disciplinary neo-liberalism* and *neo-liberal constitutionalism*.

Disciplinary neo-liberalism refers to the way in which neo-liberal forms of order and ordering are institutionalised and operate across both public and private spheres in various state and civil society complexes. Drawing on the work of Foucault, Gill uses the idea of disciplinary neo-liberalism to refer to 'a terrain of knowledge and a system of social and individual control' (2003: 130); in other words, a type of governmentality (see, for example, Rose 1999).

The new constitutionalism, on the other hand, refers to the way in which 'neoliberalism is institutionalized in the quasi-legal structure of state and international political forms' (Gill 2003: 131). While Gill's examples are largely drawn from the wider global political economy, for example the (International Monetary Fund (IMF) and the World Bank (WB) and quasi-constitutional regional arrangements such as the NAFTA, Maastricht and the WTO, we argue in the following section that processes of constitutionalising neo-liberalism have been prominent in the changes in governance at the national scale.

In essence what Gill means by constitutionalising neo-liberalism is that the requirements of neo-liberalism have been increasingly made legal instruments rather than contested/contestable policy preferences. It is 'the move towards the construction of legal or constitutional devices to remove or insulate substantially the new economic institutions from popular scrutiny or democratic accountability' (Gill 2003: 132). The effect, Gill argues, is to confer privileged rights of citizenship and representation to corporate capital while constraining the democratisation process that has involved struggles for representation (Gill 2003). As we will see when we look at the processes of negotiation in the WTO, key players in the services industry in the US have had unprecedented influence on shaping the negotiation rounds within the WTO through the 'consensus'-building rounds in Geneva and at the negotiation meetings. Gill goes on to argue that 'the new constitutionalism can be defined as the political project of attempting to make transnational neo-liberalism, and if possible liberal democratic capitalism, the sole model for future development' (2003: 131–132). Our tracing through of these processes across scales suggests there is evidence for this view, though clearly the ongoing internal political struggles, as well as those across nations and regions, also shape both the political project itself, as well as its outcome.

Gills argument's around the constitutionalism of neo-liberalism sit well with those of Jayasuriya who suggests that it is necessary to differentiate between two notions of constitutionalism:

a political notion of constitutionalism (that) emphasizes issues of participation and accountability (and) an economic notion of constitutionalism which places emphasis on issues of market transparency and the juridical limitations on the influence of rent-seeking coalitions or discretionary political intervention in the functioning of the economy.

(1999: 109)

As we will show in the case study, both of these forms of neo-liberalism act in a pincer-like way on national states as well as in constructing education at these new scales in that the rules of the game as well as the possibilities for action work in the interests of the powerful developed economies.

The implications of neo-liberal constitutionalism for education governance

The first and basic element of neo-liberal governance that had important consequences for education was that, in common with all other sectors of the state, it became mainstreamed. That is, the whole public sector was to be administered and managed according to the same principles with no exceptions or concessions to be made in respect of sectoral special pleading. This was a means of reducing state intervention and, especially in education, of undermining provider, or portfolio, capture.

Mainstreaming then meant that all sectors were subject to the same administrative disciplines, and typically to enhanced surveillance from the treasury or finance ministry (which became dominant under New Public Management [see Hood 1991], the form taken by neo-liberal governance in most Anglo-Saxon countries). The pressure was in the direction of introducing markets or market-aping competitive structures, maximising competition and choice, and minimising state influence – even on state-funded, provided, regulated and owned education systems. This can be regarded as a classic case of one form of constitutionalising the neo-liberal; that market-making, state-inhibiting rules are put into place through legislation and largely administered by the state.

However, this is still not the ideal situation for neo-liberals; there is still 'too much state'. Regulated and quasi-markets are a great advance on 'state control', but they are not the same as open markets and 'pure' competition involving the private sector. This can be illustrated most relevantly through the impact of the Maastricht Treaty and the Growth and Stability Pact in the EU, which are further examples of the constitutionalisation of the neo-liberal. In essence, they limit the level of public expenditure as a proportion of overall spending, which has the effect of 'forcing' governments to obtain finance from the private sector. The clearest example of this is the Private Finance Initiative (PFI) and Public-Private-Partnership (PPP) in the UK.

In a sense, PPPs in education represent the acme of what we refer to as the functional/institutional/scalar division of labour of education. They are a very clear example of one form of *division of the responsibilities* for the *activities* of running education – funding, provision, ownership and regulation – which traditionally were all assumed to be carried out by the national state, *between the state and a range of different institutions* – for-profit, not-for-profit, community, household and so on. Further than this, there is increased division of responsibility within each of the activities, and much of this may be shaped by the substantive as well as formal elements of neo-liberalism. In this case, the subjugation of social to economic policy is a crucial feature. Funding is an obvious case, but provision and regulation may be more significant. In terms of provision, for instance, we are witnessing various forms of division of responsibilities between public and private providers, for instance in the running of local education authorities. We shall argue more formally below that these divisions will continue to grow within the activities of governance, and one significant implication of this institutional/functional division of labour in education is a fragmentation of the sector and the constitution of education as a service. We might say that it moves from operating on the principles of an integrated code to those of a collection code (Bernstein 1996).

The emergence of PPP is also a very good example in terms of what it indicates about the rescaling of educational governance. It is brought about as a direct consequence of decisions made at the European rather than the national level which, again, is where it has traditionally been assumed that education is governed. And it thus illustrates a further outcome of neo-liberalism; the separation of sovereignty and territory. The EU is the most fully developed example of this, with European law overruling UK law in some areas. And a further example of this priority of supranational rule is found in the WTO, where countries are subject to binding rules (albeit rules that they have 'voluntarily' accepted (just as EU member states all agreed to cede elements of their sovereignty) that continue to bind irrespective of changes of government (and indeed this is precisely the point for putting such rules into place to begin with).

Finally, we should note that while the EU and the WTO have formal sovereignty over national states, the neo-liberal agenda as implemented by the WB/IMF in the form of the Washington and post- (or augmented) Washington Consensus, has had effective sovereignty over many of the developing countries. Furthermore, it is the dominant ideology of such organisations as the Organization for Economic Co-operation and Development (OECD) which, while they have no formal control over countries' policies, nevertheless exert considerable pressure in a number of ways, for instance through techniques of soft governance such as comparisons between countries in terms of student achievement (Schafer 2006). And of course, as we shall elaborate later, the EU has no formal control or right of intervention in national education systems, which are formally strictly subject to subsidiarity. All of which is to make the point that the rescaling of the governance of education is not dependent on a single mechanism, such as regulation, but may be associated with a range of different mechanisms.

Configuring the European education space

A central argument of this chapter is that just as control over the rules of trade and currency have been 'rescaled' to the supranational level, so the means of addressing the extra-economic conditions that they depend upon have to be rescaled too. And while education remains emphatically a national matter within the EU, and especially subject to the principle of 'subsidiarity', we will be suggesting that recent shifts in both the European social model as a goal of EU policy and in the means of bringing about greater policy effectiveness – particularly soft governance tools such as the Open Method of Coordination – will have the effect of bringing about a re-division and rescaling of responsibility for the existing functions of national education systems around an agenda that seeks to maximise the likelihood of their facilitation of, and minimises the likelihood of their acting as significant obstacles to the development of the overall agenda of making Europe the most competitive economy in the world (see Dale 2003).

In particular, we will suggest that as key aspects of the mandate, capacity and governance of education (particularly around the idea of a competitive European knowledge-based economy) move to a European level, the education sector settlement – the arena on which the agenda for education comes into contact with the means of achieving the agenda – *selectively* shifts from the national to the European level. Very broadly, we suggest that those elements linked directly to the reproduction of national social formations appear to remain largely at the nation state level, while those more directly associated with the extended reproduction of the mode of production are moving to the European level. At the same time, those elements particularly associated with constructing/embedding the social integument/extra-economic conditions of the mode of production (such as the ideal citizen), will remain national responsibilities, pending the (highly unlikely) development of a 'European State'. However, it will be a central argument of this chapter that the European Commission is creating, in the form of the Open Method of Coordination (OMC), a mechanism that will not only allow for but even encourage a gradual convergence of the various national education systems' contributions to building the social integument.

Specifically in the area of the European Education Space (EES) (this will involve new and possibly converging institutional configurations, with both the individual bases of, and the relationships between, the three fundamental elements of the EES (the education system's *mandate*, what it is desirable for it to achieve; its *capacity*, what it is feasible for it to achieve; and its *governance*, how it is organised to achieve its mandate and capacity) recalibrated and redistributed both internally and across geographic scales. In terms of the education sector settlement, we will suggest that as well as a scalar shift of responsibility of the accumulation problem, there is considerable evidence that the focus of European activity in the educational sphere at both the supranational and the national levels will be on the *capacity* of education systems rather than their *mandate* or their *governance,* and on their *effectiveness* rather than their efficiency (see Robertson 2002). The shifts in focus, methods and consequences of rescaling educational policies and practices in Europe are shown in Figure 18.1.

At the supranational level, these major changes might be seen as bringing about the creation of a 'European education space' that has as its main responsibilities a more direct link between education and the regional economy within the wider context of global economic competition. This will in turn entail a massive

FROM	TO
FOCUS	
ESM (DELORS) As social redistribution	ESM (NICE) As economic policy
Mandate/governance	Capacity
Nation state	State and other actors
Common indicators of national system Efficiency Effectiveness	Common targets for a supranational space of output
International coordination	Supranational cooperation
METHOD	
Harmonisation Convergence	
Regulation Governance	Soft
System-wide Selective	
CONSEQUENCE	
EU-level 'collection'* of cohesive national systems	(EU) level 'integration' of elements of fragmented national systems

* The terms 'collection' and 'integration' are from Basil Bernstein's celebrated essay on the classification and framing of educational knowledge, where a 'collection' code is characterised by strong classification (insulation

Figure 18.1   Rescaling of education

reconstruction of different national education systems as we have known them for the past 150 years.

In terms of the implications for national education systems we shall suggest that what we are witnessing is neither a Europeanisation of national systems nor a unified European system (Streeck 1999; Pochet 2000) as much as an EU division of labour that sees: positive supranational coordination of the development of a knowledge economy (Kne) energised through lifelong learning (LL) or KNeLL (that is accumulation and capacity); a negative/exclusive/proscriptive convergence at international level (agreed 'quality' benchmarks); and within this responsibility for social and societal cohesion variously (following national traditions) divided between national and subnational levels.

This is also to suggest that the effects on national education systems will not be confined to the 'spillover' (see Leibfried 2000) from action at other levels, but will be fundamentally shaped by the 'new' structure of the governance of education (Robertson 2002). In other words, we should approach what is happening at the level of national education systems as neither incidental 'effects on' them, nor as some form of 'collateral damage', but as distinct emergent properties of the new functional, institutional and scalar divisions of labour. This also suggests that *the key area of contestation is likely to be legitimation*, the contingent consent given to the form and outcome of (re)distributive policies, and through that the stability of the (national and supranational) political economy as a whole.

New contradictions for education systems of different 'politics of scale'/ geographies of power

In this final and concluding section we will point briefly to four sets of contradictions generated by the changing geographies of power in education. On the face of it, rescaling appears to offer a means of 'escaping' the existing contradictions between the 'solutions' to the three core problems of national education systems, assisting accumulation, ensuring order and legitimation. This promise might be perceived in the possibility of rescaling one of the core problems, say accumulation, to the supranational scale. This would then enable the national State to tackle the problems of order and legitimation in new ways and possibly to come up with new 'solutions' that were not mutually contradictory. However, it seems more likely that such moves will intensify rather than mitigate the contradictions between the solutions to the three core problems.

First, it seems extremely unlikely that any set of problems could be so comprehensively 'exported' that they left no trace behind at the national level. Given this, the contradictions between the solutions are likely to be exacerbated by the introduction of a further, complicating dimension – the global. More than this, it seems likely that if such an export were to take place successfully that would have the effect of highlighting the contradictions rather than concealing them – and a major element in the national State's ability to maintain a coherent and cohesive system in the face of the contradictions is that they are not readily apparent. If they were to become so as a result of the export of at least part of one set of problems, the contradictions might thereby be intensified.

Second, it seems likely, too, that the existing contradictions between education as a public service and as a private commodity will be qualitatively altered. The notion of education as a public service might be seen to have at least four central components that, separately and collectively, are difficult to combine with an emphasis on education as a private commodity. One component is that a public service essentially depends on its supplying *public goods*; that is, goods that are non-rivalrous and non-excludable, and that would not therefore be supplied by the market. A second component of a public service is that it has an instrumental role, in that it *serves and enables* a range of other services and activities, personal, organisational, communitarian, recreational and so on.

Third, the idea of education as a public service implies that education systems are *publicly and democratically accountable*.

The fourth component, one that draws on the French sense of public service, is that it is provided *disinterestedly* in terms of both planning and delivery. While clearly such a system can co-exist with the provision of education as a private commodity, it is not so clear that this co-existence would be so peaceful if the public service and private commodity emphases were located at different scales and subject to different forms of governance. It is not inconceivable, for instance (indeed it may already be happening), that the suppliers of particular forms of education, in specialist institutions with no responsibility to any other stakeholders other than their students and their shareholders, might cream-skim the lucrative areas of provision. This would place enormous pressure on the economies of scale and scope of nationally regulated systems, whose informing ideology of public service denies them the right to cream-skim and requires them to provide a broad curriculum.

The third contradiction is between education as a force for the equalisation of opportunities, and education as the means for allowing differences in initial endowments to flourish. The first is, of course, the traditional legitimating function of education. However, we should not forget that it is the legitimation of *national* education systems. Private and for-profit education has no legitimating responsibilities beyond those it owes its own patrons and shareholders, and indeed its success is, to a considerable degree, dependent on the degree to which it is able to exaggerate the socially polarising possibilities of education for the benefit of its clients. However, the conditions under and the degree to which it is able to do this is limited in every national system by the very legitimating responsibility the State owes the population in respect of educational provision. This restraint would not, though, apply with respect to systems governed by different institutions at different scales.

The tension between education as a contributor to 'economy-building' and to 'nation-building' is already quite acute at a national level, but it seems likely to become more so in the developing circumstances of a supranational economy. In this case, the contradictions would be across as well as within scales. The contradiction would be clear in the formation of human capital, for instance, where the pressure from neo-liberalism is very much in the direction of the flexibility and free movement of labour. However, it would also be a matter of considerable strain in the area of the 'extra-economic' embedding that education extends to the economy. This has traditionally been related to a national economy, but given the increasing but partial and concentrated 'denationalisation' of the economy we are experiencing, it seems likely to be a matter of considerable tension in much the same way as the first contradiction we outlined.

A final set of contradictions concerns the way in which the different governance regimes which operate at different scales map on to each other and the extent to which they are themselves contradictory in their intentions and their effects. While it might be argued that constitutionalising neo-liberalism will, probably, produce a greater articulation between scales, from the local to the global, there is some evidence to suggest that the different politics of scale are precisely that, the outcome of different political struggles over the precise nature and form of neo-liberalism in these different arenas. An example here are the different, though no less neo-liberal, political projects at the heart of the construction of Europe and the European education space, compared with the global.

Furthermore, which rules, regional or global or local, take precedence? At present there are a multiplicity of regional and bilateral treaties being negotiated to secure the conditions for trade. For example while Singapore is part of APEC, it is also part of ASEAN and a recent Singapore–US trade treaty. It is also a member of the WTO. These potential 'legal' complications are likely to keep trade lawyers busy for years! The fundamental point to make here, particularly in relation to the WTO, is that these are legal and binding rules into the future. Renegotiating one's position is not possible. What will possibly emerge is that the WTO will become an orientating point on the compass from which all other rules and policies begin. In education this will really change the geography of power – upward.

Conclusion

In this chapter we have sought to examine the implications for nationally located education systems of an emerging functional and scalar division of the labour of education through a project of rescaling. More particularly, we have argued that this new and emerging geography of power in education is both shaped by and reflects neo-liberalism ideology (see Gill 2003) – in the forms of soft governance at the European scale and the constitutionalisation of neo-liberalism in the rules of global governance that extend to the education sectors of national states. We have also argued, however, that these movements are likely to generate new contradictions, particularly as in the case of the WTO, there is limited policy space in which to absorb contradictions and tensions that inevitably shape the education sector.

References

Bernstein, B. (1996) *Pedagogy, Symbolic Control and Identity: Theory, Research, Critique*. London: Taylor and Francis.

Brenner, N. (1998) Between fixity and motion: accumulation, territorial organisation and the historical geography of spatial scale, *Environment and Planning D: Society and Space* 16(1): 459–81.

Brenner, N. (2003) *New State Spaces*. Oxford: Oxford University Press.

Cerny, P. (1997) Paradoxes of the competition state: the dynamics of political globalisation, *Government and Opposition* 32(2): 251–74.

Dale, R. (2002) The construction of a European education space and education policy. Paper presented to the European Science Foundation – Exploratory Workshop, Globalisation, Education Restructuring and Social Cohesion in Europe, Barcelona, Spain, 3–5 October.

Dale, R. (2003) The Lisbon Declaration, the reconceptualisation of governance and the reconfiguration of European educational space. Paper presented to the RAPPE seminar, Governance, Regulation and Equity in European Education Systems. Institute of Education, London University 20 March 2003. http://www.genie–tn.net (accessed 4 April 2006).

Gill, S. (2003) *Power and Resistance in the New World Order*. New York: Palgrave Macmillan.

Gough, J. (2004) Changing scale as changing class relations: variety and contradiction in the politics of scale. *Political Geography* 23(1): 185–211.

Harvey, D. (1982) *The Limits to Capital*, 2nd edn. London: Verso.

Held, D., Mcgrew, A., Goldblatt, D. and Perraton, J. (1999) *Global Transformations*. Cambridge: Polity Press.

Hood, C. (1991) A public management for all seasons, *Public Administration* 69: 3–19.

Jayasuriya, K. (1999) The rule of law and governance in the east Asian State, *Australian Journal of Asian Law* 1(2): 107–123.

Jessop, B (2000) The changing governance of welfare: recent trends in its primary functions, scale and modes of coordination, *Social Policy and Administration* 33(4): 346–59.

Lefebvre, H. (1991) [1974] *The Production of Space*, translated by D. Nicholson Smith. Oxford: Blackwell.

Leibfried, S. (2000) National welfare states, European integration and globalization: a perspective for the new century, *Social Policy and Administration* 34(1): 44–63.

Omhae, K. (1990) *The Borderless World*. New York: Harper.

Peck, J. and Tickell, A. (2005) Making global rules: globalisation or neo-liberalism, in J. Peck and H. Yeung (eds) *Global Connections*. London: Sage.

Pochet, P. (2000) Three portraits of the future of Europe, *Infos 5, May: 1–2*.

Robertson, S. (2002) Changing governance/changing equality? Understanding the politics of public-private-partnerships in education in Europe. Paper presented to the European Science Foundation – Exploratory Workshop, Globalisation, Education Restructuring and Social Cohesion in Europe, Barcelona, Spain, 3–5 October. http://www.genie–tn.net (accessed 4 April 2006).

Rose, N. (1999) *Powers of Freedom: Reframing Political Thought*. Cambridge: Cambridge University Press.

Schafer, A. (2006) A new form of governance? Comparing the open method of coordination to multi-lateral survelliance by the IMF and the OECD, *Journal of European Public Policy* 13(1): 70–88.

Scholte, J.-A. (2002) *What is Globalisation? That Definitional Issue Again*. Working Paper. Warwick: Centre for Globalsation and Regionalism.

Streeck, W. (1999) *Competitive Solidarity:* Rethinking the 'European Social Model'. Presidential Address to the Society for the Advancement of Socio-economics (SASE), Madison, Wisconsin, June 8–11. http://www.scase.org/conf1999/streeck.html.

Unger, R.M. (1998) *Democracy Realized: The Progressive Alternative*. London: Verso.

Weiss, L. (1998) *The Myth of the Powerless State*. Cambridge: Polity Press.

19

JOHN ROBINSON AND
TONY SHALLCROSS
Education for sustainable development

Introduction: clarifying some terms

2004 saw the launch of what has become referred to as Third Generation Environmentalism (3GE). This move posits a first generation environmentalism located in the conservationist movement which began in the US in the nineteenth century, with Henry David Thoreau and Ralph Waldo Emerson, and spawned a series of wilderness approaches to environmentalism. The second generation of environmentalism is seen as developing in the 1970s with the rise of Green politics and a focus on individual responsibility to refuse, reduce, reuse, recycle or repair. 3GE argues for an alliance of government, business and individuals to achieve the goals that have become almost taken for granteds as a consequence of the awareness raising undertaken by second generation pressure groups.

This chapter takes up the challenge of 3GE thinking to ask what sort of sustainability education would both support the goals of 3GE and challenge the thinking at the same time. In doing so we argue for a whole educational institution approach to these issues, as an exemplar for bringing together the different dimensions of 3GE thinking. The chapter will explain that whole institution approaches mean 'practising what we teach' by trying to minimise the gaps between espoused values and values in action through the integration of formal and non-formal curricula. Whole institution approaches shape our interaction with the environment in an intellectual, material, spatial, social and emotional sense to achieve a lasting/sustainable quality of life for all by integrating pedagogy with the social/organisational and technical/economic aspects of institutional practice, within a context of communities of action.

Arguments about terminology abound in the environmental education/education for sustainable development (EE/ESD) literature. We do not intend to indulge in definition dementia or debate about which of the many terms used to describe approaches to education that address the environment and/or sustainability are correct. Some understanding of terms such as EE (UNESCO 1978), earth education (van Matre 1990), education for sustainability (EfS) (Huckle and Sterling 1996), sustainable education (Sterling 2001), sustainability education (SE) (Shallcross 2004), education as sustainability (EaS) (Foster 2001), education for a sustainable future (ESF) (UNESCO 1997), ESD (UNESCO 2004) and learning for sustainability (LfS) (WWF 2005) and others is needed, however.

Why do we need ESD?

It has been widely recognised since Rachel Carson's classic book *Silent Spring* (1991) was published in the 1960s that the Earth is facing an environmental crisis. Although *Silent Spring* described how insecticide and pesticide use were causing the decline in songbird populations in the US, it increased concern about other environmental problems such as deforestation, loss of biodiversity and global warming. Educational movements such as EE and conservation education (CE) emerged in response to the environmental crisis leading to the first UNESCO conference on EE in Tbilisi in 1978.

However, during the 1980s although some approaches to EE emphasised the need to look at environment in its widest sense; social, economic and built as well as natural, there was a feeling that EE was too preoccupied with the natural world. Some argued that EE overlooked social and economic problems such as poverty, gender and racial discrimination, high infant mortality and HIV-AIDS and the ways in which these problems were linked with each other and with environmental problems. Others criticised EE because it failed to practise what it taught, was more concerned with knowledge than feelings and actions and counter-productive because it created helplessness by focusing on the global and structural nature of problems such as deforestation and global warming. Whatever the accuracy of these criticisms, they triggered an interest in education and development which addressed not only the natural, but the social and economic environments. Sustainability and ESD were seen as answers to these criticisms.

Before we consider a whole institution approach to ESD we need to consider what the difference is between sustainability and sustainable development. Sustainability means a state of affairs that can continue indefinitely into the long-term future. Sustainable development (SD) is the process that societies must go through to achieve sustainability (Porritt 2006). SD became much more important politically in the UK after the First UN Earth Summit in Rio de Janeiro in 1992. This conference focused on the critical issues of sustainability and natural resources and established a plan of action to try to achieve SD, called Agenda 21. Although Agenda 21 acknowledges that individual nations cannot achieve SD on their own, the UN stated that the successful implementation of Agenda 21 was 'first and foremost the responsibility of Governments' (Quarrie 1992: 46). Population growth, consumption and technology were identified as the primary driving forces behind environmental change. Agenda 21 proposed what needs to be done to reduce wasteful and inefficient consumption patterns in some parts of the world whilst carefully managing natural resources. Education was addressed in Section Four of Chapter 36 of Agenda 21 which states:

Both formal and non-formal education are indispensable in changing peoples' attitudes so that they have the capacity to assess and address their sustainable development concerns. It is critical for achieving environmental and ethical awareness, values and attitudes, skills and behaviours consistent with sustainable development and for effective public participation in decision-making.

(Quarrie 1992: 221)

Whilst Chapter 36 makes no specific reference to whole institution development it recognises education as a process that will improve the 'capacity of the people to address environment and development issues' (1992: 221). The recognition that 'both formal and non-formal education are indispensable to changing peoples' attitudes' (1992: 221) could be taken as implicit support for approaches to ESD with strong community links and effective participation in decision-making. The 2002 Earth Summit in Johannesburg reinforced ESD by emphasising the need to integrate SD perspectives at all levels in societies to promote education as a decisive factor for change.

Kofi Annan, the UN Secretary General, has stated that SD is the single most important challenge facing humanity. The UK Sustainable Development Strategy (DETR 1998) demonstrates the attempt to address SD through natural, social and economic goals:

- social progress that recognises the needs of everyone
- effective protection of the environment
- prudent use of natural resources
- maintenance of high and stable levels of economic growth and employment.

UK schools are expected to try to address the Government's goals for SD especially the DfES *Sustainable Development Action Plan for Education and Skills* (2003); this action plan commits the DfES to exploring whole school approaches as a way of promoting SD in schools. The action plan aims to address four objectives:

- ESD
- the environmental impact of DfES and its partner bodies
- the environmental impact of the education estate
- local and global partnership activity.

There is a strong commitment to participation in the action plan:

It is also clear that schools should enhance pupil/student participation in both policy development and its implementation and that staff should: actively involve children and young people in developing and delivering the sustainable development agenda . . .

(DfES 2003: 17)

Another powerful reason for addressing ESD in the UK is because 2005–2014 is the UN Decade of ESD (UNDESD). The UNDESD which was launched in the UK in December 2005 has five objectives, to:

- give an enhanced profile to the central role of education and learning in the common pursuit of SD
- facilitate links and networking, exchange and interaction among stakeholders in ESD
- provide a space and opportunity for refining and promoting the vision of, and transition to SD through all forms of learning and public awareness
- foster increased quality of teaching and learning in ESD
- develop strategies at every level to strengthen capacity in ESD. (UNESCO 2004).

The UNDESD identifies society, environment and economy as the three key areas of SD 'with culture as an underlying dimension' (UNESCO 2004: 5) and argues that the processes of 'learning/teaching in ESD must model the values of SD' (2004: 21) and that ESD should be reflected in daily decisions and actions. It also states that ESD should be interdisciplinary, holistic, values-driven, critical, multi-method, participatory and locally relevant. This vision of ESD gives clear support for whole institution approaches.

What is unusual in educational terms about this vision of ESD is that it allots education the lead role in implementing SD when traditionally education has been seen as a following discipline led by politics, economics and technology (Sterling 2001). This vision raises the question of whether UK education, with its current emphasis on economic growth and increased standard of living, is partly a contributor to the environmental crisis. Table 19.1 shows that the higher a country's level of educational achievements, the greater its environmental impact. ESD will need not only to change knowledge but to transform societal values and actions; the entire way in which we perceive relationships between human driven social and economic systems and the natural environment.

While the level of CO_2 emissions shown in Table 19.1 contribute to the global warming that causes climate change we are all responsible to a greater or lesser degree for these emissions. All who live in the UK use energy and so are responsible to a greater or lesser extent for global warming. Something can be done to reduce energy use and hence CO_2 emissions by switching off lights and electrical appliances when these are not being used. Schools can not only teach their pupils about the causes of climate change and promote energy saving, they can also purchase their electricity from environmentally friendly electricity suppliers that invest exclusively in renewable sources of electricity generation such as wind and solar power. Making such links between the formal curriculum and institutional practice in schools is not only a way of modelling SD but it is also an example of an aspect of a whole school approach that we will examine late in this chapter.

Analyses, however, should go beyond definitions and examine the concepts and practices that inform such definitions as we have illustrated here with EE/ESD. If the 1997 UNESCO description of ESD is compared to the 1978 UNESCO description of EE some strong similarities emerge:

Table 19.1 Relationships between education, income and CO_2 emissions in 2000

Country	School enrolment secondary (%)	Rank	Gross National Income per capita (US$)	Rank	CO_2 emissions (metric tons per capita)	Rank
Argentina	79.06	7	7,490	7	3.76	9
Bangladesh	43.07	12	390	11	0.22	13
Brazil	69.23	8	3,650	9	1.81	10
Burkina Faso	7.99	15	250	14	0.09	14.5
Ethiopia	13.32	14	110	15	0.09	14.5
Finland	94.61	1	24,940	4	10.33	2
Germany	88.32	5	25,140	3	9.55	4
Kenya	23.09	13	360	13	0.31	12
Republic of Korea	90.90	4	9,790	6	9.08	5
Malaysia	69.11	9	3,390	10	6.21	7
Mexico	58.22	11	5,110	8	4.33	8
New Zealand	91.58	3	13,700	5	8.31	6
United Kingdom	94.58	2	25,410	2	9.64	3
United States	87.13	6	34,400	1	19.85	1
Vietnam	62.46	10	380	12	0.73	11

Source: World Bank

The effectiveness of awareness raising and education for sustainable development must ultimately be measured by the extent to which they change the attitudes and behaviours of people as both consumers and citizens. Changes in lifestyles as reflected in individual behaviour, households and at a community level must take place (UNESCO 1997: 4).

Although the description had changed by 1997, the commitment to changing knowledge, attitudes and actions so that these support sustainable lifestyles can be traced from the discussions of EE in 1978 to deliberations over ESD in 1997 and in the UNESCO Draft Strategy on the DESD (2004). If learning institutions are to become places that debate, promote and enact sustainable actions there has to be a stronger focus on whole institution development to model sustainable living in EE/ESD with self-evaluation as a key process. Whole institution approaches emphasise processes rather than the outcomes of learning. It is crucial that values, attitudes and actions change in ways that equip learners with the personal, social and environmental competences to live in harmony with the world around them. Change of this magnitude in education entails the professional development of learning institutions' staff. However the focus on process in EE/ESD is not a panacea, because processes can be hierarchical or participatory and linked to a passive or empowered citizenry as shown in Figure 19.1.

The conceptions of sustainability and ESD in the top left quadrant of Figure 19.1 are those in which experts would determine outcomes, which would then be prescribed to passive institutions and their staff. The dominance of this

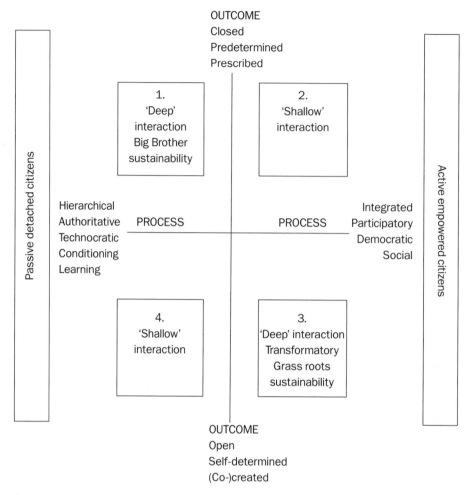

Figure 19.1   A process-based typology of sustainability
Source: Adapted from Walls and Jickling (2002)

authoritative and universal approach to ESD, in which educational authorities use their power over learning institutions, like schools, to expect all to do much the same thing, can result in Big Brother sustainability.

The bottom right quadrant is associated with bottom-up, grass roots approaches to sustainability and ESD in which active citizens decide on local, more open outcomes. With such a participatory approach in which each school decides what its most appropriate outcomes are, grass roots sustainability results that requires educational authorities to devolve power to learning institutions. Then institutions devolve power to learners.

The other two quadrants represent forms of ESD or sustainability characterised by limited openness and/or involvement. This can occur when learners are encouraged to participate in activities that have been determined by others without the involvement of the learners themselves. In these circumstances limited, token participation or even non-participation might result. An example of this shallow interaction can occur when learners become involved in a corporate-sponsored recycling programme. While their involvement might provide them with opportunities to consider recycling and develop a recycling action plan, they may not critically examine reducing consumption as part of this programme. An emphasis on the critical consideration of one or more of the four Rs: refuse, reduce, reuse, or repair might be a far more effective strategy for learning institutions concerned with promoting sustainable lifestyles than a strategy that concentrates only on the fifth R: recycling.

An imposed environmental awareness approach may not engage critically in this discussion, let alone examine these other four forms of action. The environmental awareness approach to recycling may avoid critical, deeper engagement with the recycling issue. What results is 'feel good' sustainability, because the corporate sponsor is proud of its support of community recycling as this improves the company's image without it having to worry about challenges to the pursuit of economic growth. The learners and their institutions feel good because they have done something positive for the environment and perhaps raised some money for their school. The irony is that an approach that only encourages recycling may actually increase consumption: the more soft drinks you consume the more cans you can recycle. A more critical approach might be to consider reducing school consumption in addition to recycling, perhaps by reducing or refusing highly carbonated sugar-rich drinks because of their possible detrimental effect on teeth. The consequence ironically, might be to reduce the number of drink cans that the institution recycles.

Such initiatives may originate externally to the learning institution. Drink vending machines in Scottish schools only retail water and fruit juices as a result of changes in policy to promote healthy food consumption in schools. In England, from 2006, in maintained schools, food that is high in fat, salt and sugar will be banned from school canteens and vending machines following a recommendation from the School Meals Review Panel (www.teachernet.gov.uk/healthyliving). In Italy school kitchens are banned from serving fried food and all pasta and olive oil used must be organic.

How can whole institution approaches provide an answer?

In order to promote sustainable actions learning institutions need to become active agents of change rather than passive transmitters of information and/or values (Uzzell et al. 1994). Whole institution approaches are one way in which learning institutions can become such agents of social and environmental change. A key feature of institutional agency is democracy (Aspin 1995; Beane and Apple 1999) that grants power to learners and leaders of learning, not only to make decisions, but also to act on these decisions. This is democracy in the participative sense that can be implemented in institutions through participation and active citizenship (DfEE and QCA 1999), not democracy confined to voting and representation.

Learning institutions have a crucial role to play if children are to play their part in democracy (Council of Europe 1999). Active citizenship needs to be founded on notions of both learners' rights and responsibilities and rooted in actions that are authentic because these actions relate to real issues arising in learning institutions and their local communities (Uzzell *et al*. 1994). What this section of this chapter will seek to do is to outline a vision of what whole institution approaches should entail, to present a rationale that explains why these approaches can make an important contribution to environmental education (EE) or education for sustainable development (ESD) and to outline a design for whole institution approaches.

The rediscovery and extension of community to include the natural world combined with greater attention to active citizenship in education may redress the educational problems that may arise through some forms of EE/ESD. We need to explain what we mean by this. Although most descriptions of EE/ESD, from the first UNESCO conference on EE in Tbilisi in 1978 to the UNDESD, seek to promote the change to more environmentally friendly lifestyles, the mistaken assumption still exists that if people learn about environmental problems they will act for their resolution (Sterling 2001). Yet even when people support environmental changes they frequently lack the range of skills necessary to make these changes (Uzzell *et al*. 1994). So while knowledge and positive attitudes to environmental issues are necessary these have not been sufficient to promote the change to more sustainable actions on a societal scale. Until relatively recently education has been driven by an ideology of childhood that considers pupils to be citizens in waiting rather than present citizens (Alderson 2000); it has not treated children as equal and responsible partners in the process of change. Modern education generally subscribes to this conventional ideology of childhood that assumes that children are minors, passive receivers of knowledge who are under the hierarchical influence of adults. Consequently although environmental concerns have high priority for young people, many feel powerless to act on these concerns as no one will listen to their ideas about environmental change (Freeman 1999).

Another difficulty in EE/ESD can be the focus on environmental problems. While on one hand education should not seek to make learners feel personally responsible for the environmental crisis, apathy can result if education focuses on apparently intractable environmental problems, because these problems appear to be caused by governments and/or large corporations. Children, like other people, become depressed if they cannot change what happens to them, which can lead them to give up even in situations where they can make a difference. So not only do learning institutions fail to prepare learners for the future, they often undermine the personal worth that learners, particularly younger, school-aged learners, need for the continued self-development (Bandura 1986) that leads to sustainable actions. A further problem for EE/ESD is that modern education is associated with personal advancement and the promotion of economic growth. Is it a coincidence that many European nations, with some of the world's highest levels of education are responsible for much of the planet's environmental degradation? In short is education part of the cause of the environmental crisis?

By contrast, debates about community-focused citizenship, education-orientated EE or ESD often distinguish between process and outcomes. The danger with focusing on outcomes alone is that this approach splits theory from practice 'seeing citizenship as a set of ideas which adults instruct pupils about, not as relationships which pupils already experience in schools' (Alderson 2000: 114). A focus on process in EE/ESD is crucial because, as yet, we do not fully understand what sustainable development looks like and even when we think we understand sustainable development, sustainable solutions will differ from one community and context to another. By focusing on processes, on how societies educate their young generation, education can empower learners by equipping them with the skills they need to assist learning institutions, themselves and their local communities to become more sustainable. Whole institution approaches that focus on educational processes such as participation and collaboration offer one very attractive way of closing the gaps between knowledge, attitudes and actions in EE/ESD.

Whole institution approaches

In simple terms whole institution approaches mean that learning institutions practise what they teach by trying to minimise the gaps between the values they profess and those values implicit in their actions (Posch 1993). Whole institution approaches seek to integrate all aspects of school life by making links between the formal curriculum (what happens in classrooms) and the non-formal curriculum (what happens in other aspects of school and community life that have an influence on learning) (see Figure 19.2). Such approaches integrate teaching and learning with the social/organisational and technical/economic aspects of institutional practice (Posch 1999). If the formal curriculum addresses climate change how is this concern reflected in the way in which energy is used in learning institutions? If curriculum guidelines include active citizenship how are learners encouraged to participate in deciding and implementing sustainable actions in their places of learning? Whole institution approaches are education as a way of life; they are approaches in which such places become a microcosm of a sustainable rather than an unsustainable society (Sterling 2001). These approaches involve processes of development that shape 'our interaction with the environment in an intellectual, material, spatial, social and emotional sense to achieve a lasting/sustainable quality of life for all' (Posch 1999: 341–342). The socio-organisational strand in Figure 19.2 is arguably the key to whole institution approaches because it promotes the participation and collaboration that lead to the other strands not only being addressed but also integrated with each other.

Whole institution approaches are not just the preserve of teachers/educators, they involve learners, parents, carers and all those who manage the infrastructure of the institutions and the services that they offer to support education, such as catering, energy and estate management. Thus EE/ESD has to transform not only the content and processes of the formal curriculum and the purposes of learning but also the ways in which educational institutions and educational buildings work (Orr 1994). But these changes will only come about if people think critically about values, participate in decisions and understand their consequences. Evaluation is also included in any model of whole institution approaches as it is integral to a plan-do-review cycle in educational places (see Figure 19.2). After all most

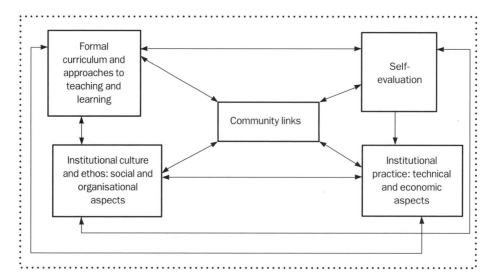

Figure 19.2 The five strands of a whole institution approach to EE/ESD
Source: Shallcross (2003)

proposals for educational change are responses to someone's evaluative critique of current provision.

EE/ESD is committed to sustainable actions but what does the word action mean? Action is the continuous flow of conduct (Argyris and Schon 1996), of actual interventions that should not be confused with behavioural change that occurs in a direction determined by somebody else (Uzzell *et al*. 1994). Some describe action as intentional and behaviours, such as coughing, as instinctive (Schnack 1998). However, this distinction between the instinctive and the intentional misses the crucial notion of culturally intuitive actions, for example, covering one's face after sneezing. This is not an example of an instinctive response to a stimulus, but a culturally and contextually shaped action that we do not consciously consider before performing. Through learning that is contextually situated, many socially and environmentally sustainable acts can become culturally intuitive, second nature actions. These acts will only become widespread and second nature if they are reinforced by seeing what is learned in the classroom being applied in the non-formal curriculum, in the routine, daily life of the place of learning. Such integration is often apparent in the mutual care that is apparent in the actions of young learners, such as pupils and adults in many schools. Such caring does not just result from considered rational actions, many of these acts of caring are second natured actions. The crucial thing is that these many of these actions have been learned in educational institutions, often through the non-formal curriculum.

Action perspectives

Actions can be individual or collective, direct (the actions of people on the environment such as the planting of trees) or indirect (when people seek to influence others), for example, writing that advocates alternative, sustainable lifestyles. Actions can also be divided into political (those which are intended to influence others) and personal (those which we do for ourselves). While knowledge that leads to direct action is critical in the promotion of sustainable lifestyles it is not necessarily superior to knowledge that only promotes reflection (Clover 2002). Sustainable lifestyles are not just about recycling, especially if such recycling results from authoritative interventions from outside or within schools that limit the participation of children. Reflective knowledge may sow seeds in childhood that blossom direct into sustainable actions in the future.

Although all sustainable actions need not be direct, sustainable lifestyles will only happen when there are substantial, societal changes in direct sustainable actions. But privileging direct over indirect action may also have a social bias, for example, most people on limited incomes may not be able to buy organic food. It is inappropriate for schools, for example, to advocate actions, such as recycling, unless pupils and staff have the capacity and capability to perform these actions. In short, saying that people ought to do something implies that they can (Des Jardins 1993). It is those societies, individuals and learning institutions whose actions contribute most to the environmental crisis that need to make the biggest shifts in developing personal, organisational and societal capacity and capability for direct sustainable actions.

Local actions have authenticity because they are usually directed at real issues and decided by those who intend to implement them (Jensen 2002). Conserving energy, developing school grounds or supporting local old people is more tangible and immediate than learning about the deforestation of the Amazon Basin for pupils in European schools. This is not to suggest that the problems of planetary deforestation should be ignored but simply to acknowledge that for most people their immediate locality is their most significant action field (Vognsen 1995). Humans may also be genetically hot wired for local action because of their powerful emotional commitment to that which is socially, spatially and temporally immediate (Wilson 2002). It is interesting to note how often a local crisis such as environmental vandalism or the death of a pupil has become a driver for whole institution development (Shallcross 2004).

Authentic community links involve interpersonal, interagency and inter-institutional networks (Uzzell *et al.* 1994). However, local community-based actions may be most effective when they are linked with knowledge about wider, regional and planetary socio-economic and environmental issues. Thinking globally must be related to practice, this is why EE and ESD have made working through the near environment a virtue. Some argue that EE/ESD that is not applied beyond the educational institution's gates is not authentic (Elliot 1999; Posch 1999).

However, emphasising local action can sometimes raise problems for educational institutions. It can be difficult to see what is near, precisely because it is so well known and ordinary. Under these circumstances the art of teaching in schools, for example, is to help pupils to see the ordinary as extraordinary. But working with highly controversial local issues, such as discussing over-fishing in a school in a fishing community (Schnack 1998), can be difficult for schools if these issues create friction and conflict with parents, local citizens and/or politicians because the emotional immediacy of the issue disrupts considered judgment.

Conversely, the separation of environmental knowledge in formal curricula from sustainable actions in non-formal curricula and local communities socialises hypocrisy (Shallcross 2003). Pupils in schools can come to accept that expressing concern about the environment while defecting from sustainable practices is normal adult action. Whole institution approaches, by modelling sustainable lifestyles (UNESCO 2004), become a socialising process that can break this cycle of defection. The continuity of social relationships in whole institution approaches not only reduces defection, it increases mutual trust and leads to cooperation (Ridley 1996). By belonging to a functioning social community pupils become agents of change (Uzzell et al. 1994). For example, if the pupils in a school decide to make their school litter free it becomes easier to persuade those who might litter not to do so because their defection would be socially unacceptable. But if defection occurs and is not addressed, social pressure diminishes and an increase in littering may follow (Clayton and Radcliffe 1996).

An action perspective is also important in EE/ESD because it reduces the sense of powerlessness as learning and action proceed hand in hand, strengthening the attachment to sustainable practices. This is a bottom-up approach that respects democratic values more than a top-down prescriptive approach. Values education in whole institution approaches is not a passive process concerned with imposing predetermined attitudes, but a dynamic process in which values are caught rather than taught through engagement with decision-making and action. Through whole institution approaches, for example in primary schools, ethical education rooted in democracy and cooperative relationships between communities, teachers, parents and pupils can begin at an early age (Farrer with Hawkes 2000). Here pupils learn to respect each other, to cooperate, to listen and discuss; attributes that are essential to a true working democracy (Brain 2001). The personal commitment to sustainable actions is promoted because habits are established early in life when the routine practices that are often most effective appear least obtrusive to young children (Giddens 1979). In whole institution approaches most pupils accept these practices as second nature because they are integral to the school's culture.

However, it is crucial that such practices are not thwarted by the non-formal curriculum. The social, economic and environmental strands of sustainable development need to be integrated not only with formal learning and teaching but also with other institutional practices (see Figure 19.2). This integration does not just involve changing from a fragmented to an integrated view of knowledge; it has to connect learners' experiences of school and community so that these form a web of coherent experiences. In this way learning institutions can become communities of practice (Wenger 1999) in which people learn how to act by participating in learning rather than experiencing teaching. In such communities of practice, learning takes place through many modes including observation, demonstration and application rather than through the passive transmission of knowledge. Most modern schools, for example, are not communities of practice because their hierarchical, often passive relationships between teachers and learners place schools and teachers in a uni-directional position of authority and power over pupils.

However, through whole institutional development learning institutions can become communities of practice in which pupils are legitimate participants (Lave and Wenger 1991), active citizens in a process of learning by doing (John 1996). In communities of practice learning is contextually situated as knowledge is socially constructed through learners' active participation in actions that are considered in and applied to local contexts. The consequence is that the outcomes of whole institution approaches to EE/ESD will differ from one socio-environmental context to another. Learning is neither socially constructed nor simply a response to stimuli from the social or natural environment. Learning is situated because it is both socio-culturally constructed and located in a community of practice that derives its legitimacy from its integration of local socio-cultural and environmental issues.

Conclusion: third generation environmentalism – a critique

In the introduction to this chapter we argued that whole institution approaches to ESD might be one way of achieving the integrative goals of 3GE. This is because learning institutions can provide that integration between the State (Government), business and the individual or individuals. However, what we have hoped to show here is that individuals' actions are part of a larger collectivity. So how possible might it be for learning institutions to act as the focus for the integration of the state, business and individual action (in communities of action) to achieve the goals of 3GE? In order to begin to answer this question, we need to see ESD within a set of spheres of influence which include the socio-political, the economic and the technical-scientific spheres of society. Seeing ESD this way enables us to recognise that learning institutions, through the whole institution approach explained above (Figure 19.2), can and do act as the places where the three spheres of influence come together. The socio-political dimension is clearly present through the formal curriculum and approaches to teaching and learning and the institutional culture and ethos, the economic dimension is present through community links and institutional practices and the technical-scientific dimension is present through institutional practices.

It would appear that whilst some elements of the technical-scientific and the economic spheres of influence are positive about changes which would help to slow down the changes which humans have initiated that are bringing about climate change and global warming by trying to achieve stringent targets on reducing greenhouse gas emissions (Monbiot 2005; WWF 2005), the British Government has reverted to seeing sustainability as related to economics not ecology (see above). Recently the Stop Climate Chaos Group (a coalition of twenty organisations including the World Wide Fund for Nature (WWF), The Women's Institute, The Royal Society for the Protection of Birds (RSPB), Oxfam, Friends of the Earth, Tearfund, Planet and People, Christian Aid, Greenpeace and CAFOD) have argued the UK Government, during its Presidency of the European Union and leadership of the G8 Group of Countries (June–December 2006), has done little to promote sustainability. Tony Blair has suggested that legally binding targets would make people 'very nervous and very worried' (WWF

2005). This is in comparison to a statement made by Tony Blair in 2004 that world climate change is one of the most significant issues facing human beings that will change the lives of many of the world's population irrevocably. Monbiot (2005) argues that rather than the business sector, especially large transnational and transglobal corporations, dragging its heels about stringent climate change targets, they would prefer to operate to exacting targets that apply to all businesses, rather than just those that are trying to be more environmentally sustainable. Furthermore, Monbiot argues that it is the UK Government that is going soft on its international climate change commitments. So where does this leave a 3GE approach to sustainable development and learning institutions as pivotal in the educational processes for sustainable development?

It is clear from strategies like Every Child Matters in England (www.dfes.gov. uk) (see Anning in this volume) and No Child Left Behind in the United States that schools, in the future, will take on a much more extended role. This may well include the education of a broader range of the local population than those included in the current statutory school age range. It is also likely that schools will adopt a much broader range of educational imperatives than those dictated by a standards agenda as in England at the present. If anything is to be done about slowing down climate change and achieving more sustainable futures then the extended learning institutions which are envisaged in the Every Child Matters strategy which adopt a whole institution approach like the one we have advocated in this chapter, will have a significant role to play in achieving effective education for sustainable development. However, for that to happen the three spheres of influence of sustainability need to be in harmony with each other, moving in the same direction. At the time of writing that does not seem to be the case.

References

Alderson, P. (2000) Citizenship in theory and practice: being or becoming citizens with rights, in D. Lawton, J. Cairns and R. Gardner (eds) *Education for Citizenship*. London: Continuum.

Argyris, C. and Schon, D.A. (1996) *Organizational Learning II, Theory, Method, and Practice*. Reading, MA: Addison-Wesley.

Aspin, D.N. (1995) The conception of democracy: a philosophy of democratic education, in J. Chapman, I. Froumin and D. Aspin (eds) *Creating and Managing the Democratic School*. London: Falmer Press.

Bandura, A. (1986) *Social Foundations of Thought and Action: A Social Cognitive Theory*. Englewood Cliffs, NJ: Prentice-Hall.

Beane, J.A. and Apple, M.W. (1999) The case for democratic schools, in M.W. Apple and J.A. Beane (eds) *Democratic Schools: Lessons from the Chalk Face*. Buckingham: Open University Press.

Brain, J. (2001) True learning, *Resurgence* 204.

Carson, R. (1991) [1962] *Silent Spring*. Harmondsworth: Penguin.

Clayton, A.M.H. and Radcliffe N.J. (1996) *Sustainability, A Systems Approach*. London: Earthscan, WWF and The Institute for Policy Analysis.

Clover D. (2002) Traversing the gap: conscientization, educative activism in environmental adult education, *Environmental Education Research* 8(3).

Council of Europe (1999) Everyone can make a difference. Council of Europe pilot project on participation in and through school, initial training seminar for teachers, report. Strasbourg: Council of Europe.

Department of the Environment, Transport and Regions (DETR) (1998) *The UK Sustainable Development Strategy: Opportunities for Change.* Norwich: Stationery Office.

Department for Education and Employment (DfEE) and Qualifications and Curriculum Authority (QCA) (1999) *Citizenship.* London: QCA.

Department for Education and Skills (DfES) (2003) *Sustainable Development Action Plan for Education and Skills.* London: DfES.

Des Jardins, J.R. (1993) *Environmental Ethics: An Introduction to Environmental Philosophy.* Belmont, CA: Wadsworth.

Elliot, J. (1999) Sustainable society and environmental education: future perspectives and demands for the education system, *Cambridge Journal of Education* 29(3): 325–334.

Farrer, F. with Hawkes, N. (2000) *A Quiet Revolution: Encouraging Positive Values in Our Children.* London: Rider.

Foster, J. (2001) Education as sustainability, *Environmental Education Research* 7(2): 153–165.

Freeman, C. (1999) Children's participation in environmental decision making, in S. Buckingham-Hatfield and S. Percy (eds) *Constructing Local Environmental Agendas: People, Places and Participation.* London: Routledge, 68–80.

Giddens, A. (1979) *Central Problems in Social Theory Action, Structure and Contradiction in Social Analysis.* London: Macmillan.

Huckle, J. and Sterling, S. (1996) *Education for Sustainability.* London: WWF and Earthscan.

Jensen, B.B. (2002) Knowledge, action and pro-environmental behaviour, *Environmental Education Research* 8(3): 325–334.

John, M. (ed.) (1996) *Children in Charge: One Child's Right to a Fair Hearing.* London: Jessica Kingsley.

Lave, J. and Wenger, E. (1991) *Situated Learning: Legitimate Peripheral Participation.* Cambridge: Cambridge University Press.

Monbiot, G. (2005) It would seem that I was wrong about big business, *Guardian* 29 September. http://business.guardian.co.uk/story/0,,1574092,00.html#article_continue (accessed 29 Jan. 2006).

Orr, D.W. (1994) *Earth in Mind: On Education, Environment, and the Human Prospect.* Washington, DC: Island Press.

Porritt, J. (2006) *Capitalism as if the World Matters.* London: Earthscan.

Posch, P. (1993) Approaches to values in environmental education, in OECD/ENSI *Values in Environmental Education Conference Report.* Dundee: Scottish Consultative Council on the Curriculum.

Posch, P. (1999) The ecologisation of schools and its implications for educational policy, *Cambridge Journal of Education* 29(3): 340–348.

Quarrie, J. (ed.) (1992) *Earth Summit '92: The United Nations Conference on Environment and Development*. London: Regency Press Corporation.

Ridley, M. (1996) *The Origins of Virtue*. London: Viking.

Schnack, K. (1998) Why focus on conflicting interests in environmental education?, in M. Åhlberg and W. Leal Filho (eds) *Environmental Education for Sustainability: Good Environment, Good Life*. Frankfurt am Main: Peter Lang.

Shallcross, T. (2003) Education as second nature: deep ecology and school development through whole institution approaches to sustainability education. Unpublished PhD thesis, Manchester Metropolitan University.

Shallcross, T. (ed.) (2004) *School Development Through Whole School Approaches to Sustainability Education: The SEEPS Project*. Manchester: Manchester Metropolitan University.

Sterling, S. (2001) *Sustainable Education: Revisioning Learning and Change*. Dartington: Green Books.

UNESCO (1978) *Intergovernmental Conference on Environmental Education*. Tbilisi, Georgia: UNESCO.

UNESCO (1997) *Educating for a Sustainable Future: A Transdisciplinary Vision for Concerted Action*. Paris: UNESCO.

UNESCO (2004) *United Nations Decade of Education for Sustainable Development 2005–2014: Draft International Implementation Scheme*. Paris: UNESCO.

Uzzell, D., Davallon, J., Fontes, P.J., Gottesdiener, H., Jensen, B.B., Kofoed, J., Uhrenhodt, G. and Vognsen, C. (1994) *Children as Catalysts of Environmental Change*, Brussels, European Commission Directorate General for Science Research and Development.

van Matre, S. (1990) *Earth Education ... A New Beginning*. Cedar Cove, WV: Institute of Earth Education.

Vognsen, C. (1995) The QUARK programme, a collaboration on the development of environmental education and ecological technologies in local communities, in B.B. Jensen (ed.) *Research in Environmental and Health Education*. Copenhagen: Royal Danish School of Educational Studies.

Wals, A. and Jickling, B. (2002) 'Sustainability' in higher education: from doublethink and newspeak to critical thinking and meaningful learning. *International Journal of Sustainability in Higher Education*, 3(3), 221–233.

Wenger, E. (1999) *Communities of Practice: Learning, Meaning and Identity*. Cambridge: Cambridge University Press.

Wilson, E.O. (2002) *The Future of Life*. London: Little, Brown.

Worldwide Fund for Nature (WWF) (2005) *Linking Thinking: New perspectives on thinking and learning for sustainability*. Aberfeldy: WWF Scotland.

Index

academic approach to HE access, 130
academic mentoring, 26, 104
academies, 80, 81
accelerated learning, 46
action perspectives (ESD), 242–5
active citizenship, 239–40
activist habitus, 176–7
    women's role in state school development,
        177–84
Adams, Mary Bridges, 178
Alibhai-Brown, J., 142, 143, 144
Annan, Kofi, 235
Anning, A., 14
    and Edwards, A., 7
    et al., 10, 13
Apple, M., 111, 112, 114, 115, 116, 117,
        118, 119, 130
    and Beane, J.A., 120
    and Buras, K.L., 112, 115–16
Aspin, D.N., 58–9
Association of University Tutors (AUT),
        129
asylum-seekers *see* refugee children
attribution theory, 22
authoritarian populists, 112

Bentwich, Helen, 180–1, 183, 184
Besant, Annie, 178
Birth to Three Matters, 13
Blair, M. and Gillborn, D., 142
Blair, Tony, 77, 201–2, 245–6
Blunkett, David, 32, 66, 77, 185
Boaler, J., 52–3
Bolloten, B. and Spafford, T., 156, 157
Boruch, R.F., 102
Bourdieu, P., 117, 124, 125, 176
    and Passeron, J., 78
    and Wacquant, L., 124
brain functioning, 49–51
brain gym, 50

Bright, M., 83
Bronfenbrenner, U., 6, 156
Brown, M. *et al.*, 37, 38
Bullock Report, 35, 40
bullying victims, 167
Burns, C. and Myhill, D., 39

calculators, in mathematics teaching, 37–8
Callender, C. and Wilkinson, D., 128
Campbell, D.T. and Stanley, J.C., 27
capital
    cultural, 124–5, 176
    human capital theory, 205–6
    types of, 176
capitalism, 202–3
    see also globalisation; neo-conservatism;
        neo-liberalism
Capitalist Plan in Education, 82–3
Cathcart, B., 142, 143
charter schools, 119
child development models, 7
childcare, 5, 8–9
Children Act
    1989, 162, 171
    2004, 5–6, 14, 171
Children Leaving Care Act (2001), 171
choice
    parental, 90, 91–6
    pupil, at Summerhill, 57–8, 60, 62, 64–5,
        68
Christian schools *see* faith schools; home
        learning
citizenship education, 141, 144, 146, 239–41
city technology colleges, 91
class size reduction, 20, 24–5
Cockcroft Report, 37
cognitive dissonance theory, 24
cognitive styles *see* learning styles
community schools, for refugee children, 159
comprehensive schools, 90–1

Conservative government policies, 88, 90–2, 93, 139–40
'conservative modernisation', 111–12
cost-benefit analysis, of evidence-based education, 21
cross-age tutoring, 21–7
cultural capital, 124–5, 176
Curle, A., 213
curriculum
   early years education, 5, 13–14, 74
   national, 77, 78
Curriculum, Evaluation and Management (CEM) Centre, 20
Curry, L., 47

daily mathematics lesson (DML), 33
Darder, A., 208
Darling, Alistair, 186
Dawson, Agnes, 181
de-individuation, 23
democratic schooling, at Summerhill, 57, 58–9, 65, 67–8
Discretionary Leave to remain in UK (asylum-seekers), 150–1
diversity in education provision, 79–81, 90–5
Drake, Barbara, 182

Early Excellence Centres, 10–11, 12–13
early years education
   characteristics of effective, 8, 9
   childcare and, 5, 8–9
   conceptual and theoretical models, 7
   curriculum, 5, 13–14, 74
   family support and, 8–9
   integrated services, 10–13
   New Labour reforms, 5–6, 74–5
ecological model of human development, 6, 156
economic policy, 89–90
Education Acts (early), 174–5, 177
Education Reform Act (1988), 91, 140, 177
educational psychology theories, 22–3
Edwards, T. and Whitty, G., 91, 92
Eisenstadt, N., 8
Elbedour, S. et al., 156
emotional intelligence, 50–1
emotional learning, 57–8
employment
   effects on HE studying, 128
   older women, 188–92

English school system:, 21st century, 87–98
Eraut, M., 11–12
Eth, S. and Pynoos, R., 154
European Union (EU), 226–9
Every Child Matters, 5, 164, 169, 170, 246
evidence-based education
   cost-benefit analysis, 21
   Effect Size, 19, 20, 24–6
   intentions and outcomes, 18–20
   practice and research, 44–5
   quantitative, 24–7
   randomised controlled trials (RCTs), 18, 19–20, 26, 27
   using theories to design project, 21–4
expenditure see financial issues; funding
extended pre-school hours, 8–9

faith schools, 94
   see also mosque schools
family support, 8–9
field dependent (FD) and field independent (FI) learning styles, 47
Figueroa, P.M.E., 141
financial issues
   cost-benefit analysis, of evidence-based education, 21
   Pakistan education system, 215
   teachers' pay, 79
   see also funding
Fischman, G. and McLaren, P., 207, 208
Fitz-Gibbon, C.T., 20, 21, 23
forced compliance studies, 22
forced migrants see refugee children
formative assessment, 103
foster care, 162, 164
Foundation Stage curriculum (QCA), 5, 14
funding
   higher education for older people, 190–1
   for religiously motivated home schoolers, 118–19
   and spending, New Labour policy, 75–6, 76–7, 79, 82–3

Gardner, H., 51
Garrett, Elizabeth, 178
Giddens, A., 87, 89, 244
Gill, S., 221, 222, 224
Gillborn, D., 140, 141
   Blair, M. and, 142
Glasier, Katherine Bruce, 177

globalisation, 202–3, 221, 222, 223
grammar schools, 91–2
grant maintained schools, 91, 93
Guardian, 142, 185, 201, 202, 204

habitus, 176–7
Harker, J., 146
Harker, R. *et al*., 167, 170, 171
Hatcher, R., 205, 206
Hay McBer (UK management consultants),
    105
Hewitt, R., 143, 144
higher education
    as cultural capital, 124–5
    New Labour policy, 75, 77
    for older people, 189–91
    retention issues, 122–3, *124*, 129
    student needs, 123
higher education research study
    background, 125–6
    changes in provision, 129–30
    choice of study, 126
    employment effects whilst studying, 128
    entry qualifications, 128–9
    first generation students, 127
    initial findings, 127
    internal levels of support, 129
    locality of students, 127
    student characteristics, *127*
Hill, Rosamond Davenport, 179
home learning
    anti-State perspective, 114–17
    characteristics of movement, 112–14
    education and 'conservative
        modernisation', 111–12
    politics of redistribution and recognition,
        117–19
Horsbrugh, Florence, 182
human capital theory, 205–6
Humanitarian Protection, 150–1

Immigration and Asylum Act (1999), 152–3
Immigration and Nationality Directorate
    (IND), Home Office, 149–50
independent trust schools, 80–1, 83
integrated services, 10–13
inter-professional working
    early years education, 10–13
    looked after children, 170–1
internet, 44

Jackson, S., 168
    and Sachdev, D., 165, 166, 167, 168, 171
Jayasuriya, K., 224–5
Jinnah, Muhammad Ali, 213
Jones, R., 140–1, 145
    and Thomas, L., 130
    Wyse, D. and, 33, 39

Kanu, Y., 218
Kelly, Ruth, 182–3
Key Stage, 2 Strategy, 32, 33, 40
Key Stage, 3 Strategy, 33, 40
Klein, G., 138
knowledge, 'C' (codified) and 'P' (personal),
    11–12

Labour Party
    state school development, 177–8, 180,
        181–2
    see also New Labour; New Labour
        education policy
Lawrence, Stephen, 142–3
    Macpherson Report (Lawrence Inquiry),
        141, 142–3, 145
learning styles, 46–8
    school improvement and effectiveness,
        103–4
    visual, auditory and kinaesthetic (VAK),
        46–7
lifelong learning, 185, 186, 187, 193–4
literacy *see* National Literacy Strategy (NLS)
literacy hour (LH), 33, 35
Literacy Task Force, 33
Lodge, C., 100
London School Board (LSB), 177–8
looked-after children (in care)
    bullying victims, 167
    change of placements, 164–5
    educational experience, 164–8
    educational support, 165–6
    entering care, 162–3
    indicators of educational achievement,
        163–4
    inter-professional working, 170–1
    life chances, 164
    Personal Education Plan (PEP), 165
    policies and targets, 168–71
    special educational needs, 166–7
    teacher expectations, 168
Lowe, Eveline, 180, 181, 183

McNamara, O. and Corbin, B., 38
Macpherson Report (Lawrence Inquiry),
    141, 142–3, 145
Maguire, Meg, 188
managerialism, 78–9
Martinez, E. and Garcia, A., 203–4
Marx, K. and Engels, F., 202–3
Marxism, 205–6, 207
mathematics see National Numeracy
    Strategy (NNS)
media influences, 44
mentoring, 26, 104
metacognition, 48–9
Miller, Florence Fenwick, 178, 179
mind mapping, 50
Morris, Estelle, 182, 183
Morris, J., 165, 167, 168
Morrison, Herbert, 177, 180
mosque schools, 217
    see also faith schools
Moxley, D. et al., 123, 127, 129
Muller, Henrietta, 179
multi-agency teamwork see integrated
    services
multiple intelligences, 51
Munroe-Blum, H. et al., 155

Naidoo, R., 124–5
Nash, R., 124, 125
National Advisory Group for Continuing
    Education and Lifelong Learning
    (NAGGELL), 185
National Asylum Support Service (NASS),
    152–3
National Childcare Strategy (DfEE), 5
National Curriculum, 77, 78
    see also curriculum
National Literacy Strategy (NLS)
    politics of, 32–3, 35–40, 78
    research basis, 33–5
National Numeracy Strategy (NNS), 32
    key issues, 37–8
    politics of, 32–3, 39–40
    research basis, 37
National Union of Teachers (NUT), 138–9
Neill, A.S., 56, 57–8, 60, 63
neo-conservatism, 112
    New Labour policy, 77–8
neo-liberalism, 111–12, 203–5
    disciplinary and constitutional, 223–5

and education in Britain, 205–6
    New Labour education policy, 78–82
networking, 12–13
New Labour
    Capitalist Plan in Education, 82–3
    early years education, 5–6, 74–5
    globalisation/modernisation, 201–2
    lifelong learning, 185
    looked-after children (in care), 168–71
    New Right policies, 88–90, 92–3
    racial equality agenda, 141–2
    women MPs, 182–3
    see also poverty, New Labour policies
New Labour education policy, 74–82
    analysis, 73–4
    impacts and ideologies, 82–4
    themes, 76–82
    see also National Literacy Strategy (NLS);
        National Numeracy Strategy (NNS)
New Right see neo-conservatism; neo-
    liberalism
Numeracy Task Force, 37
nursery education see early years education

Ofsted (Office for Standards in Education),
    5, 6, 33–4
    Summerhill inspection, 59–62, 63–5
older people
    higher education for, 189–91
    lifelong learning, 185, 186, 187, 193–4
    women see working class (older) women
Open Method of Coordination (OMC), 227
Osler, A. and Starkey, H., 144, 146
O'Sullivan, E., 144, 145

Pagels, E., 112
Pakistan education system
    brief profile and history, 212–13
    present, 213–14
    reforms, 215–18
    successful innovations and field
        conditions, 214–15
parent-professionals partnership, 13
parental choice, 90, 91–6
parenting, 9
'parentocracy', 95–6
peer tutoring, 103
performance monitoring and feedback, 103
Personal Education Plan (PEP), 165
personalised learning, 43, 52–3

Peters, R.S., 63
Posch, P., 241
post-traumatic stress disorder (PTSD), 154,
    155, 156
poverty
    New Labour policies, 75
        National Asylum Support Service
            (NASS), 153
        social inclusion, 186–8
        Sure Start programme, 6–7, 8, 9,
            13–14, 15
    Pakistan, 215
    social justice function of education, 62–3
power issues, 125, 130
    geographic see rescaling, politics of
    and racism, 143–4
    and women, 175–6
privatisation, 81–2
psychiatric disorders, in refugee children,
    154–5
psychological theories
    and brain functioning, 49–51
    child development, 7
    ecological model of human development,
        6, 156
    metacognition, 48–9
    multiple intelligences, 51
    and pedagogical developments, 45–6
    personalised learning, 52–3
    use in design projects, 21–4
    see also learning styles
Public-Private partnership (PPP), 225–6

Qualified Teacher Status (QTS), 126
    see also higher education research study
Quarrie, J., 234–5

race/racism
    and asylum-seekers, 153, 159
    educational context of, 139–42
    Macpherson Report (Lawrence Inquiry),
        141, 142–3, 145
    and power relations, 143–4
    and teacher education, 138–9, 140–1, 144–
        6
randomised controlled trials (RCTs), 18,
    19–20, 26, 27
    see also evidence-based education
reading, National Literacy Strategy (NLS),
    34–5, 40

Reay, D., 176, 188–9
redistribution and recognition, politics of,
    117–19
refugee children, 149–51, 154–6
    asylum legislation, 152–4
    community schools, 159
    present provision - schools, 158
    psychiatric disorders, 154–5
    resilience and vulnerability, 156–7
    resilience-based framework of support,
        157–8
    teachers, 157–8
    way forward, 158–60
rescaling, politics of, 222–3
    contradictions, 229–31
    European educational space, 226–9
    see also neo-liberalism
resistance of teachers, 206
retention issues, in higher education, 122–3,
    124, 129
Rikowski, G., 203
Rousseau, C. and Drapeau, A., 155
Ruthven, K., 37–8
Rutter, M., 155, 156, 157, 158

school effectiveness, 92
    early years education, 8, 9
    research implications, 106–7
    research limitations, 104–6
school exclusion, 167
school improvement
    research implications, 103–4, 106–7
    research limitations, 99–102
school types, 80–1
Sherwood, M., 141
Siraj-Blatchford, I., 139
Smith, D.G., 207–8
social democracy see New Labour education
    policy
Social Exclusion Unit (SEU), 162, 164, 189
social inclusion/exclusion, 76–7, 92–3, 153,
    186–8
social influence of teachers, 23
social justice function of education, 62–3
social psychology theories, 21–2, 23–4
social workers, 170–1
socio-economic classes, 92, 93–4, 95
    authoritarian populists, 112
    see also working class (older) women
special educational needs, 166–7

specialist schools, 80, 94
staff *see* teacher education; teachers; tutors/
    tutoring
Sternberg, R., 51
Stronach, I., 57, 60, 61, 62, 63, 67
Summerhill, 57–8
    democratic schooling, 57, 58–9, 65, 67–8
    nature of evidence, 63–5
    Ofsted inspection and court processes,
        59–62, 63–5, 66–7
    pupil choice, 57–8, 60, 62, 64–5, 68
    values and learning, 65
    values and measurement, 62–3
support staff, New Labour policy, 75
Sure Start programme, 6–7, 8, 9, 13–14, 15
sustainable development, education for
        (ESD)
    action perspectives, 242–5
    critique, 245–6
    necessity for, 234–9
    whole institution approaches, 239–42
Swann Report, 138, 139–40
Sylva, K. *et al.* (EPPE study), 8, 9, 12
synthetic phonetics approach to reading, 34

teacher education
    and neo-liberalism, 207–8
    Pakistan, 214
    and racism, 138–9, 140–1, 144–6
teachers
    characteristics of 'effective', 104–5
    expectations of looked after children, 168
    NLS, 35–6
    NNS, 37
    Pakistan, 218–19
    pay and conditions, 79
    professional development, 44–5
    refugee support, 157–8
    resistance, 206
    and support staff, 75
    see also inter-professional working
Ten Year Strategy for Childcare (DfES), 5,
        8–9
Thatcher, Margaret, 139–40, 182
Third Generation Environmentalism
        (3GE), 233, 245–6
Times Educational Supplement, 168, 169
Tinto, V., 123, 124, 126, 127, 128
trainee teachers, and NLS, 36

transformative approach to HE access, 130
tutors/tutoring
    cross-age, 21–7
    peer, 103
Twisleton, S., 36

UN Convention Relating to the Status of
        Refugees, 149
UNESCO/UNDESD, 235–7, 240
Unger, R.M., 223–4
utilitarian approach to HE access, 130
Uzzell, D. *et al.*, 239–40, 242, 243, 244

values issues
    English school system, 88–90
    Summerhill, 62–3, 65
visual, auditory and kinaesthetic (VAK)
        learning style, 46–7
Vygotsky, L., 52

Walker, A. and Walker, C., 189
Walker, Anthony, 137, 146
Walker, J., 193
Warwick, D.P., 216, 217, 218
Weston, P., 52
Whitty, G., 91, 94
    Edwards, T. and, 91, 92
    et al., 112, 118
whole class interactive teaching, 38–9
whole institution approaches (ESD), 239–42
Wilkinson, Ellen, 177, 181–2, 183
Witkin, H.A., 47
women
    and educational policy, 174–5
    role in state school development, 177–84
    work and public life, 175–7
working class (older) women
    educational experiences, 192–3
    social inclusion policies, 186–8
    in the workforce, 188–92
World Trade Organization (WTO), 204–5,
        206, 224, 226
wrap-around care, 8–9
Wyse, D., 33, 34, 35, 40, 44
    and Jones, R., 33, 39

Young, H., 182

'zone of proximal development', 52

REFUGEE CHILDREN IN THE UK

Jill Rutter

Asylum migration causes intense media and political debate. However, little attention has been paid to how forced migrants can rebuild their lives in the UK or elsewhere. This timely book analyzes the social policies that impact on refugee children's education, and:

- Provides the background to the migration of refugees
- Explores how dominant discourses about trauma homogenise and label a very diverse group of children
- Examines how policy towards refugees is made, and how it relates to practice
- Offers alternative visions for refugee settlement

Drawing on case studies of the experiences of refugee children, *Refugee Children in the UK* brings a much-needed insight into the needs of refugee children. It is valuable reading for academics, policy makers, students of education, sociology and social policy as well as education, health and social work professionals.

Contents: *Series preface – Editor's preface Acknowledgements Glossary –* ***PART ONE: SETTING THE SCENE*** *– An Introduction – Who are refugee children? – Theoretical and research perspectives on refugee children –* ***PART TWO: UK RESPONSES TO REFUGEE CHILDREN*** *– Learning from history: responses to refugees 1900-89 – Modern asylum policy and its impact on children – How UK children view the refugee in their midst – National educational policy and the role of local authorities – School practices –* ***PART THREE: COMMUNITY CASE STUDIES*** *– The elusiveness of intergration: the educational experiences of Congolese refugee children – The Somalis: cultures of survival – Sucess stories: the southern Sudanese –* ***PART FOUR: NEW VISIONS FOR REFUGEE CHILDREN*** *– New visions for refugee children Bibliography Index.*

248pp   0 335 21373 1 Paperback   0 335 21374 X Hardback